The Trial of Jesus from a Lawyer's Stand

Vol. 2

Walter M. Chandler

Alpha Editions

This edition published in 2024

ISBN : 9789362097033

Design and Setting By
Alpha Editions
www.alphaedis.com
Email - info@alphaedis.com

As per information held with us this book is in Public Domain.
This book is a reproduction of an important historical work. Alpha Editions uses the best technology to reproduce historical work in the same manner it was first published to preserve its original nature. Any marks or number seen are left intentionally to preserve its true form.

VOLUME II

PREFACE TO VOLUME TWO

SUFFICIENT was said concerning the entire work in the preface to volume one to warrant a very brief preface to volume two.

The reader will notice that the plan of treatment of the Roman trial of Jesus is radically different from that employed in the Hebrew trial. There is no Record of Fact in the second volume, for the reason that the Record of Fact dealt with in the first volume is common to the two trials. Again, there is no Brief of the Roman trial and no systematic and exhaustive treatment of Roman criminal law in the second volume, corresponding with such a treatment of the Hebrew trial, under Hebrew criminal law, in the first volume. This is explained by the fact that the Sanhedrin found Jesus guilty, while both Pilate and Herod found Him not guilty. A proper consideration then of the Hebrew trial became a matter of review on appeal, requiring a Brief, containing a complete statement of facts, an ample exposition of law, and sufficient argument to show the existence of error in the judgment. The nature of the verdicts pronounced by Pilate and by Herod rendered these things unnecessary in dealing with the Roman trial.

In Part II of this volume, Græco-Roman Paganism at the time of Christ has been treated. It is evident that this part of the treatise has no legal connection with the trial of Jesus. It was added simply to give coloring and atmosphere to the painting of the great tragedy. It will serve the further purpose, it is believed, of furnishing a key to the motives of the leading actors in the drama, by describing their social, religious, and political environments. The strictly legal features of a great criminal trial are rarely ever altogether sufficient for a proper understanding of even the judicial aspects of the case. The religious faith of Pilate, the judge, is quite as important a factor in determining the merits of the Roman trial, as is the religious belief of Jesus, the prisoner. This contention will be fully appreciated after a careful perusal of Chapter VI of this volume.

Short biographical sketches of about forty members of the Great Sanhedrin who tried Jesus have been given under Appendix I at the end of this work. They were originally written by MM. Lémann, two of the greatest Hebrew scholars of France, and are doubtless authoritative and correct. These sketches will familiarize the reader with the names and characters of a majority of the Hebrew judges of Jesus. And it may be added that they are a very valuable addition to the general work, since the character of the tribunal is an important consideration in the trial of any case, civil or criminal.

The apocryphal Acts of Pilate have been given under Appendix II. But the author does not thereby xivouch for their authenticity. They have been added because of their very intimate connection with the trial of Jesus; and for the further reason that, whether authentic or not, quotations from them are to be found everywhere in literature, sacred and secular, dealing with this subject. The mystery of their origin, the question of their genuineness, and the final disposition that will be made of them, render the Acts of Pilate a subject of surpassing interest to the student of ancient documents.

WALTER M. CHANDLER.

NEW YORK CITY, July 1, 1908.

PART I
THE ROMAN TRIAL

Christus, Tiberio imperitante, per procuratorem Pontium Pilatum supplicio affectus est.—TACITUS.

CHAPTER I

A TWOFOLD JURISDICTION

THE Hebrew trial of Jesus having ended, the Roman trial began. The twofold character of the proceedings against the Christ invested them with a solemn majesty, an awful grandeur. The two mightiest jurisdictions of the earth assumed cognizance of charges against the Man of Galilee, the central figure of all history. "His tomb," says Lamartine, "was the grave of the Old World and the cradle of the New," and now upon His life before He descended into the tomb, Rome, the mother of laws, and Jerusalem, the destroyer of prophets, sat in judgment.

The Sanhedrin, or Grand Council, which conducted the Hebrew trial of Jesus was the high court of justice and the supreme tribunal of the Jews. It numbered seventy-one members. Its powers were legislative, executive, and judicial. It exercised all the functions of education, of government, and of religion. It was the national parliament of the Hebrew Theocracy, the human administrator of the divine will. It was the most august tribunal that ever interpreted or administered religion to man. Its judges applied the laws of the most peculiar and venerable system of jurisprudence known to civilized mankind, and condemned upon the charge of blasphemy against Jehovah, the most precious and illustrious of the human race. Standing alone, the Hebrew trial of Christ would have been the most thrilling and impressive judicial proceeding in all history. The Mosaic Code, whose provisions form the basis of this trial, is the foundation of the Bible, the most potent juridical as well as spiritual agency in the universe. In all the courts of Christendom it binds the consciences, if it does not mold the convictions, of judge and jury in passing judgment upon the rights of life, liberty, and property. The Bible is everywhere to be found. It is read in the jungles of Africa, while crossing burning deserts, and amidst Arctic snows. No ship ever puts to sea without this sacred treasure. It is found in the cave of the hermit, in the hut of the peasant, in the palace of the king, and in the Vatican of the pope. It adorns the altar where bride and bridegroom meet to pledge eternal love. It sheds its hallowing influence upon the baptismal font where infancy is christened into religious life. Its divine precepts furnish elements of morals and manliness in formative life to jubilant youth; cast a radiant charm about the strength of lusty manhood; and when life's pilgrimage is ended, offer to the dying patriarch, who clasps it to his bosom, a sublime solace as he crosses the great divide and passes into the twilight's purple gloom. This noble book has furnished not only the most enduring laws and the sublimest religious truths, but inspiration as well to the grandest intellectual triumphs. It is literally woven into the literature of the world, and few books of modern times are worth reading that do not reflect the sentiments of its sacred pages.

And it was the Mosaic Code, the basis of this book, that furnished the legal guide to the Sanhedrin in the trial of the Christ. Truly it may be said that no other trial mentioned in history would have been comparable to this, if the proceedings had ended here. But to the Hebrew was added Roman cognizance, and the result was a judicial transaction at once unique and sublime. If the sacred spirit of the Hebrew law has illuminated the conscience of the world in every age, it must not be forgotten that "the written reason of the Roman law has been silently and studiously transfused" into all our modern legal and political life. The Roman judicial system is incomparable in the history of jurisprudence. Judea gave religion, Greece gave letters, and Rome gave laws to mankind. Thus runs the judgment of the world. A fine sense of justice was native to the Roman mind. A spirit of domination was the mental accompaniment of this trait. The mighty abstraction called Rome may be easily resolved into two cardinal concrete elements: the Legion and the Law. The legion was the unit of the military system through which Rome conquered the world. The law was the cementing bond between the conquered states and the sovereign city on the hills. The legion was the guardian and protector of the physical boundaries of the Empire, and Roman citizens felt contented and secure, as long as the legionaries were loyal to the standards and the eagles. The presence of barbarians at the gate created not so much consternation and despair among the citizens of Rome, as did the news of the mutiny of the soldiers of Germanicus on the Rhine. What the legion was to the body, the law was to the soul of Rome—the highest expression of its sanctity and majesty. And when her physical body that once extended from Scotland to Judea, and from Dacia to Abyssinia was dead, in the year 476 A.D., her soul rose triumphant in her laws and established a second Roman Empire over the minds and consciences of men. The Corpus Juris Civilis of Justinian is a text-book in the greatest universities of the world, and Roman law is to-day the basis of the jurisprudence of nearly every state of continental Europe. The Germans never submitted to Cæsar and his legions. They were the first to resist successfully, then to attack vigorously, and to overthrow finally the Roman Empire. And yet, until a few years ago, Germans obeyed implicitly the edicts and decrees of Roman prætors and tribunes. Is it any wonder, then, that the lawyers of all modern centuries have looked back with filial love and veneration to the mighty jurisconsults of the imperial republic? Is it any wonder that the tragedy of the Prætorium and Golgotha, aside from its sacred aspects, is the most notable event in history? Jesus was arraigned in one day, in one city, before the sovereign courts of the universe; before the Sanhedrin, the supreme tribunal of a divinely commissioned race; before the court of the Roman Empire that determined the legal and political rights of men throughout the known world. The Nazarene stood charged with blasphemy and with treason against the enthroned monarchs represented by these courts; blasphemy against Jehovah who, from the lightning-lit summit of Sinai, proclaimed His laws to mankind; treason against Cæsar, enthroned and uttering his will to the world amidst the pomp and splendor of Rome. History records no other instance of a trial conducted before the courts of both Heaven and earth; the court of God and the court of man; under the law of Israel and the law of Rome; before Caiaphas and Pilate, as the representatives of these courts and administrators of these laws.

Approaching more closely the consideration of the nature and character of the Roman trial, we are confronted at once by several pertinent and interesting questions.

In the first place, were there two distinct trials of Jesus? If so, why were there two trials instead of one? Were the two trials separate and independent? If not, was the second trial a mere review of the first, or was the first a mere preliminary to the second?

Again, what charges were brought against Jesus at the hearing before Pilate? Were these charges the same as those preferred against Him at the trial before the Sanhedrin? Upon what charge was He finally condemned and crucified?

Again, what Roman law was applicable to the charges made against Jesus to Pilate? Did Pilate apply these laws either in letter or in spirit?

Was there an attempt by Pilate to attain substantial justice, either with or without the due observance of forms of law?

Did Pilate apply Hebrew or Roman law to the charges presented to him against the Christ?

What forms of criminal procedure, if any, were employed by Pilate in conducting the Roman trial of Jesus? If not legally, was Pilate politically justified in delivering Jesus to be crucified?

A satisfactory answer to several of these questions, in the introductory chapters of this volume, is deemed absolutely essential to a thorough understanding of the discussion of the trial proper which will follow. The plan proposed is to describe first the powers and duties of Pilate as presiding judge at the trial of Christ. And for this purpose, general principles of Roman provincial administration will be outlined and discussed; the legal and political status of the subject Jew in his relationship to the conquering Roman will be considered; and the exact requirements of criminal procedure in Roman capital trials, at the time of Christ, will, if possible, be determined. It is believed that in the present case it will be more logical and effective to state first what should have been done by Pilate in the trial of Jesus, and then follow with an account of what was actually done, than to reverse this order of procedure.

CHAPTER II

NUMBER OF REGULAR TRIALS

WERE there two regular trials of Jesus? In the first volume of this work this question was reviewed at length in the introduction to the Brief. The authorities were there cited and discussed. It was there seen that one class of writers deny the existence of the Great Sanhedrin at the time of Christ. These same writers declare that there could have been no Hebrew trial of Jesus, since there was no competent Hebrew court in existence to try Him. This class of critics assert that the so-called Sanhedrin that met in the palace of Caiaphas was an ecclesiastical body, acting without judicial authority; and that their proceedings were merely preparatory to charges to be presented to Pilate, who was alone competent to try capital cases. Those who make this contention seek to uphold it by saying that the errors were so numerous and the proceedings so flagrant, according to the Gospel account, that there could have been no trial at all before the Sanhedrin; that the party of priests who arrested and examined Jesus did not constitute a court, but rather a vigilance committee.

On the other hand, other writers contend that the only regular trial was that before the Sanhedrin; and that the appearance before Pilate was merely for the purpose of securing his confirmation of a regular judicial sentence which had already been pronounced. Renan, the ablest exponent of this class, says: "The course which the priests had resolved to pursue in regard to Jesus was quite in conformity with the established law. The plan of the enemies of Jesus was to convict Him, by the testimony of witnesses and by His own avowals, of blasphemy and of outrage against the Mosaic religion, to condemn Him to death according to law, and then to get the condemnation sanctioned by Pilate."

Still another class of writers contend that there were two distinct trials. Innes thus tersely and forcibly states the proposition: "Whether it was legitimate or not for the Jews to condemn for a capital crime, on this occasion they did so. Whether it was legitimate or not for Pilate to try over again an accused whom they had condemned, on this occasion he did so. There were certainly two trials. And the dialogue already narrated expresses with a most admirable terseness the struggle which we should have expected between the effort of the Jews to get a mere countersign of their sentence, and the determination of Pilate to assume the full judicial responsibility, whether of first instance or of révision." This contention, it is believed, is right, and has been acted upon in dividing the general treatise into two volumes, and in devoting each to a separate trial of the case.

Why were there two trials of Jesus? When the Sanhedrists had condemned Christ to death upon the charge of blasphemy, why did they not lead Him away to execution, and stone Him to death, as their law required? Why did they seek the aid of Pilate and invoke the sanction of Roman authority? The answer to these questions is to be found in the historic relationship that existed, at the time of the crucifixion, between the sovereign Roman Empire and the dependent province of Judea. The student of history will remember that the legions of Pompey overran Palestine in the year 63 B.C., and that the land of the Jews then became a subject state. After the deposition of Archelaus, A.D. 6, Judea became a Roman province, and was governed by procurators who were sent out from Rome. The historian Rawlinson has described the political situation of Judea, at the time of Christ, as "complicated and anomalous, undergoing frequent changes, but retaining through them all certain peculiarities which made that country unique among the dependencies of Rome. Having passed under Roman rule with the consent and by the assistance of a large party of its inhabitants, it was allowed to maintain for a while a sort of semi-independence. A mixture of Roman with native power resulted from this cause and a complication in a political status difficult to be thoroughly understood by one not native and contemporary."

The difficulty in determining the exact political status of the Jews at the time of Christ has given birth to the radically different views concerning the number and nature of the trials of Jesus. The most learned critics are in direct antagonism on the point. More than forty years ago Salvador and Dupin debated the question in France. The former contended that the Sanhedrin retained complete authority after the Roman conquest to try even capital crimes, and that sentence of death pronounced by the supreme tribunal of the Jews required only the countersign or approval of the Roman procurator. On the other hand, it was argued by Dupin that the Sanhedrin had no right whatever to try cases of a capital nature; that their whole procedure was a usurpation; and that the only competent and legitimate trial of Christ was the one conducted by Pilate. How difficult the problem is of solution will be apparent when we reflect that both these disputants were able, learned, conscientious men who, with the facts of history in front of them, arrived at entirely different conclusions. Amidst the general confusion and uncertainty, the reader must rely upon himself, and appeal to the facts and philosophy of history for light and guidance.

In seeking to ascertain the political relationship between Rome and Judea at the time of Christ, two important considerations should be kept in mind: (1) That there was no treaty or concordat, defining mutual rights and obligations, existing between the two powers; Romans were the conquerors and Jews were the conquered; the subject Jews enjoyed just so much religious and political freedom as the conquering Romans saw fit to grant them; (2) that it was the policy of the Roman government to grant to subject states the greatest amount of freedom in local self-government that was consistent with the interests and sovereignty of the Roman people. These two considerations are fundamental and indispensable in forming a correct notion of the general relations between the two powers.

The peculiar character of Judea as a fragment of the mighty Roman Empire should also be kept clearly in mind. Roman conquest, from first to last, resulted in three distinct types of political communities more or less strongly bound by ties of interest to Rome. These classes were: (1) Free states; (2) allied states; and (3) subject states. The communities of Italy were in the main, free and allied, and were members of a great military confederacy. The provinces beyond Italy were, in the main, subject states and dependent upon the good will and mercy of Rome. The free states received from Rome a charter of privileges (*lex data*) which, however, the Roman senate might at any time revoke. The allied cities were bound by a sworn treaty (*fœdus*), a breach of which was a cause of war. In either case, whether of charter or treaty, the grant of privileges raised the state or people on whom it was conferred to the level of the Italian communes and secured to its inhabitants absolute control of their own finances, free and full possession of their land, which exempted them from the payment of tribute, and, above all, allowed them entire freedom in the administration of their local laws. The subject states were ruled by Roman governors who administered the so-called law of the province (*lex provinciæ*). This law was peculiar to each province and was framed to meet all the exigencies of provincial life. It was sometimes the work of a conquering general, assisted by a commission of ten men appointed by the senate. At other times, its character was determined by the decrees of the emperor and the senate, as well as by the edicts of the prætor and procurator. In any case, the law of the province (*lex provinciæ*) was the sum total of the local provincial law which Rome saw fit to allow the people of the conquered state to retain, with Roman decrees and regulations superadded. These added decrees and regulations were always determined by local provincial conditions. The Romans were no sticklers for consistency and uniformity in provincial administration. Adaptability and expediency were the main traits of the lawgiving and government-imposing genius of Rome. The payment of taxes and the furnishing of auxiliary troops were the chief exactions imposed upon conquered states. An enlightened public policy prompted the Romans to grant to subject communities the greatest amount of freedom consistent with Roman sovereignty. Two main reasons formed the basis of this policy. One was the economy of time and labor, for the Roman official staff was not large enough to successfully perform those official duties which were usually incumbent upon the local courts. Racial and religious differences alone would have impeded and prevented a successful administration of local government by Roman diplomats and officers. Another reason for Roman noninterference in local provincial affairs was that loyalty was created and peace promoted among the provincials by the enjoyment of their own laws and religions. To such an extent was this policy carried by the Romans that it is asserted by the best historians that there was little real difference in practice between the rights exercised by free and those enjoyed by subject states. On this point, Mommsen says: "In regard to the extent of application, the jurisdiction of the native courts and judicatories among subject communities can scarcely have been much more restricted than among the federated communities; while in administration and in civil jurisdiction we find the same principles operative as in legal procedure and criminal laws."[1] The difference between the rights enjoyed by subject and those exercised by free states was that the former were subject to the whims and caprices of Rome, while the latter were protected by a written charter. A second difference was that Roman citizens residing within the boundaries of subject states had their own law and their own judicatories. The general result was that the citizens of subject states were left free to govern themselves subject to the two great obligations of taxation and military service. The Roman authorities, however, could and did interfere in legislation and in administration whenever Roman interests required.

Now, in the light of the facts and principles just stated, what was the exact political status of the Jews at the time of Christ? Judea was a subject state. Did the general laws of Roman provincial administration apply to this province? Or were peculiar rights and privileges granted to the strange people who inhabited it? A great German writer answers in the affirmative. Geib says: "Only one province ... namely Judea, at least in the earlier days of the empire, formed an exception to all the arrangements hitherto described. Whereas in the other provinces the whole criminal jurisdiction was in the hands of the governor, and only in the most important cases had the supreme imperial courts to decide—just as in the least important matters the municipal courts did—the principle that applied in Judea was that at least in regard to questions of religious offenses the high priest with the Sanhedrin could pronounce even death sentences, for the carrying out of which, however, the confirmation of the procurator was required."

That Roman conquest did not blot out Jewish local self-government; and that the Great Sanhedrin still retained judicial and administrative power, subject to Roman authority in all matters pertaining to the local affairs of the Jews, is thus clearly and pointedly stated by Schürer: "As regards the area over which the jurisdiction of the supreme Sanhedrin extended, it has been already remarked above that its *civil* authority was restricted, in the time of Christ, to the eleven toparchies of Judea proper. And accordingly, for this reason, it had no judicial authority over Jesus Christ so long as He remained in Galilee. It was only as soon as He entered Judea that He came directly under its jurisdiction. In a certain sense, no doubt, the Sanhedrin exercised such jurisdiction over *every* Jewish community in the world, and in that sense over Galilee as well. Its orders were regarded as binding throughout the entire domain of orthodox Judaism. It had power, for example, to issue warrants to the congregations (synagogues) in Damascus for the apprehension of the Christians in that quarter (Acts ix. 2; xxii. 5; xxvi. 12). At the same time, however, the extent to which the Jewish communities were willing to yield obedience to the orders of the Sanhedrin always depended on how far they were favorably disposed toward it. It was only within the limits of Judea proper that it exercised any direct authority. There could not possibly be a more erroneous way of defining the extent of its jurisdiction as regards the kind of causes with which it was competent to deal than to say that it was the *spiritual or theological* tribunal in contradistinction to the civil judicatories of the Romans. On the contrary, it would be more correct to say that it formed, in contrast to the foreign authority of Rome, that *supreme native* court which here, as almost everywhere else, the Romans had allowed to continue as before, only imposing certain restrictions with regard to competency. To this tribunal then belonged all those judicial matters and all those measures of an administrative character which either could not be competently dealt with by the inferior or local courts or which the Roman procurator had not specially reserved for himself."[2]

The closing words of the last quotation suggest an important fact which furnishes the answer to the question asked at the beginning of this chapter, Why were there two trials of Jesus? Schürer declares that the Sanhedrin retained judicial and administrative power in all local matters which the "procurator had not specially reserved for himself." Now, it should be borne in mind that there is not now in existence and that there probably never existed any law, treaty or decree declaring what judicial acts the Sanhedrin was competent to perform and what acts were reserved to the authority of the Roman governor. It is probable that in all ordinary crimes the Jews were allowed a free hand and final decision by the Romans. No interference took place unless Roman interests were involved or Roman sovereignty threatened. But one fact is well established by the great weight of authority: that the question of sovereignty was raised whenever the question of life and death arose; and that Rome reserved to herself, in such a case, the prerogative of final judicial determination. Even this contention, however, has been opposed by both ancient and modern writers of repute; and, for this reason, it has been thought necessary to cite authorities and offer arguments in favor of the proposition that the right of life or death, *jus vitæ aut necis*, had passed from Jewish into Roman hands at the time of Christ. Both sacred and profane history support the affirmative of this proposition.

Regarding this matter, Schürer says: "There is a special interest attaching to the question as to how far the jurisdiction of the Sanhedrin was limited by the authority of the Roman procurator. We accordingly proceed to observe that, inasmuch as the Roman system of provincial government was not strictly carried out in the case of Judea, as the simple fact of its being administered by means of a procurator plainly shows, the Sanhedrin was still left in the enjoyment of a comparatively high degree of independence. Not only did it exercise civil jurisdiction, and that according to Jewish law (which was only a matter of course, as otherwise a Jewish court of justice would have been simply inconceivable), but it also enjoyed a considerable amount of criminal jurisdiction as well. It had an independent authority in regard to political affairs, and consequently possessed the right of ordering arrests to be made by its own officers (Matt. xxvi. 47; Mark xiv. 43; Acts iv. 3; v. 17, 18). It had also the power of finally disposing, on its own authority, of such cases as did not involve sentence of death (Acts iv. 5-23; v. 21-40). It was only in cases in which such sentence of death was pronounced that the judgment required to be ratified by the authority of the procurator."[3]

The Jews contend, and, indeed, the Talmud states that "forty years before the destruction of the temple the judgment of capital cases was taken away from Israel."

Again, we learn from Josephus that the Jews had lost the power to inflict capital punishment from the day of the deposition of Archelaus, A.D. 6, when Judea became a Roman province and was placed under the control of Roman procurators. The great Jewish historian says: "And now Archelaus's part of Judea was reduced into a province, and Coponius, one of the equestrian order among the Romans, was sent as procurator, having the power of life and death put into his hands by Cæsar."[4]

Again, we are informed that Annas was deposed from the high priesthood by the procurator Valerius Gratus, A.D. 14, for imposing and executing capital sentences. One of his sons, we learn from Josephus, was also deposed by King Agrippa for condemning James, the brother of Jesus, and several others, to death by stoning. At the same time, Agrippa reminded the high priest that the Sanhedrin could not lawfully assemble without the consent of the procurator.[5]

That the Jews had lost and that the Roman procurators possessed the power over life and death is also clearly indicated by the New Testament account of the trial of Jesus. One passage explicitly states that Pilate claimed the right to impose and carry out capital sentences. Addressing Jesus, Pilate said: "Knowest thou not that I have power to crucify thee and have power to release thee?"[6]

In another passage, the Jews admitted that the power of life and death had passed away from them. Answering a question of Pilate, at the time of the trial, they answered: "It is not lawful for us to put any man to death."[7]

If we keep in mind the fact stated by Geib that "the principle that applied in Judea was that at least in regard to questions of religious offense the high priest with the Sanhedrin could pronounce even death sentences, for the carrying out of which, however, the confirmation of the procurator was required," we are then in a position to answer finally and definitely the question, Why were there two trials of Jesus?

In the light of all the authorities cited and discussed in this chapter, we feel justified in asserting that the Sanhedrin was competent to take the initiative in the arrest and trial of Jesus on the charge of blasphemy, this being a religious offense of the most awful gravity; that this court was competent not only to try but to pass sentence of death upon the Christ; but that its proceedings had to be retried or at least reviewed before the sentence could be executed. Thus two trials were necessary. The Hebrew trial was necessary, because a religious offense was involved with which Rome refused to meddle, and of which she refused to take cognizance in the first instance. The Roman trial was necessary, because, instead of an acquittal which would have rendered Roman interference unnecessary, a conviction involving the death sentence had to be reviewed in the name of Roman sovereignty.

Having decided that there were two trials, we are now ready to consider the questions: Were the two trials separate and independent? If not, was the second trial a mere review of the first, or was the first a mere preliminary to the second? No more difficult questions are suggested by the trial of Jesus. It is, in fact, impossible to answer them with certainty and satisfaction.

A possible solution is to be found in the nature of the charge preferred against Jesus. It is reasonable to suppose that in the conflict of jurisdiction between Jewish and Roman authority the character of the crime would be a determining factor. In the case of ordinary offenses it is probable that neither Jews nor Romans were particular about the question of jurisdiction. It is more than probable that the Roman governor would assert his right to try the case *de novo*, where the offense charged either directly or remotely involved the safety and sovereignty of the Roman state. It is entirely reasonable to suppose that the Jews would insist on a final determination by themselves of the merits of all offenses of a religious nature; and that they would insist that the Roman governor should limit his action to a mere countersign of their decree. It is believed that ordinarily these principles would apply. But the trial of Jesus presents a peculiar feature which makes the case entirely exceptional. And this peculiarity, it is felt, contains a correct answer to the questions asked above. Jesus was tried before the Sanhedrin on the charge of blasphemy. This was a religious offense of the most serious nature. But when the Christ was led before Pilate, this charge was abandoned and that of high treason against Rome was substituted. Now, it is certain that a Roman governor would not have allowed a Jewish tribunal to try an offense involving high treason against Cæsar. This was a matter exclusively under his control. It is thus certain that Pilate did not merely review a sentence which had been passed by the Sanhedrin after a regular trial, but that he tried *ab initio* a charge that had not been presented before the Jewish tribunal at the night session in the palace of Caiaphas.

It will thus be seen that there were two trials of Jesus; that these trials were separate and independent as far as the charges, judges, and jurisdictions were concerned; and that the only common elements were the persons of the accusers and the accused.

CHAPTER III

POWERS AND DUTIES OF PILATE

WHAT were the powers and duties of Pilate as procurator of Judea? What forms of criminal procedure, if any, were employed by him in conducting the Roman trial of Jesus? This chapter will be devoted to answering these questions.

The New Testament Gospels denominate Pilate the "governor" of Judea. A more exact designation is contained in the Latin phrase, *procurator Cæsaris*; the procurator of Cæsar. By this is meant that Pilate was the deputy, attorney, or personal representative of Tiberius Cæsar in the province of Judea. The powers and duties of his office were by no means limited to the financial functions of a Roman quæstor, a *procurator fiscalis*. "He was a procurator *cum potestate*; a governor with civil, criminal, and military jurisdiction; subordinated no doubt in rank to the adjacent governor of Syria, but directly responsible to his great master at Rome."

A clear conception of the official character of Pilate is impossible unless we first thoroughly understand the official character of the man whose political substitute he was. A thorough understanding of the official character of Tiberius Cæsar is impossible unless we first fully comprehend the political changes wrought by the civil wars of Rome in which Julius Cæsar defeated Cneius Pompey at the battle of Pharsalia and made himself dictator and undisputed master of the Roman world. With the ascendency of Cæsar the ancient republic became extinct. But liberty was still cherished in the hearts of Romans, and the title of king was detestable. The hardy virtues and democratic simplicity of the early republic were still remembered; and patriots like Cicero had dreamed of the restoration of the ancient order of things. But Roman conquest was complete, Roman manners were corrupt, and Roman patriotism was paralyzed. The hand of a dictator guided by a single intelligence was the natural result of the progressive degradation of the Roman state. The logical and inevitable outcome of the death of Cæsar and the dissolution of the Triumvirate was the régime of Augustus, a monarchy veiled under republican forms. Recognizing Roman horror of absolutism, Roman love of liberty, and Roman detestation of kingly power, Augustus, while in fact an emperor, claimed to be only a plain Roman citizen intrusted with general powers of government. He affected to despise public honors, disclaimed every idea of personal superiority, and exhibited extreme simplicity of manners in public and private life. This was the strategy of a successful politician who sought to conceal offensive reality under the cloak of a pleasant deception. Great Cæsar fallen at the foot of Pompey's statue was a solemn reminder to Augustus that the dagger of the assassin was still ready to defend the memory of freedom, after liberty was, in reality, dead. And the refusal by the greatest of the Romans, at the feast of the Lupercal, to accept a kingly crown when it was thrice offered him by Antony, was a model of discreet behavior and political caution for the first and most illustrious of the emperors. In short, Augustus dared not destroy the laws or assault the constitution of the state. But he accomplished his object, nevertheless. "He gathered into his own hands the whole honors and privileges, which the state had for centuries distributed among its great magistrates and representatives. He became perpetual Princeps Senatus, or leader of the legislative house. He became perpetual Pontifex Maximus, or chief of the national religion. He became perpetual Tribune, or guardian of the people, with his person thereby made sacred and inviolable. He became perpetual Consul, or supreme magistrate over the whole Roman world, with the control of its revenues, the disposal of its armies, and the execution of its laws. And lastly he became perpetual Imperator, or military chief, to whom every legionary throughout the world took the *sacramentum*, and whose sword swept the globe from Gibraltar to the Indus and the Baltic. And yet in all he was a simple citizen—a mere magistrate of the Republic. Only in this one man was now visibly accumulated and concentrated all that for centuries had broadened and expanded under the magnificent abstraction of Rome." The boundless authority of Rome was thus centered in the hands of a single person. Consuls, tribunes, prætors, proconsuls, and procurators were merely the agents and representatives of this person.

Tiberius Cæsar, the political master of Pontius Pilate, was the successor of Augustus and the first inheritor of his constitution. Under this constitution, Augustus had divided the provinces into two classes. The centrally located and peacefully disposed were governed by proconsuls appointed by the senate. The more distant and turbulent were subjected by Augustus to his personal control, and were governed by procurators who acted as his deputies or personal representatives. Judea came in his second class, and the real governor of his province was the emperor himself. Tiberius Cæsar was thus the real procurator of Judea at the time of the crucifixion and Pilate was his political substitute who did his bidding and obeyed his will. Whatever Tiberius might have done, Pilate might have done. We are thus enabled to judge the extent of Pilate's powers; powers clothed with *imperium* and revocable only by the great procurator at Rome.

In the government of the purely subject states of a province, the procurator exercised the unlimited jurisdiction of the military *imperium*. No law abridged the single and sovereign exercise of his will. Custom, however, having in fact the force of law, prescribed that he should summon to his aid a council of advisers. This advisory body was composed of two elements: (1) Roman citizens resident in this particular locality where the governor was holding court; and (2) members of his personal staff known as the Prætorian Cohort. The governor, in his conduct of judicial proceedings, might solicit the opinions of the members of his council. He might require them to vote upon the question at issue; and might, if he pleased, abide by the decision of the majority. But no rule of law required him to do it; it was merely a concession and a courtesy; it was not a legal duty.

Again, when it is said that the procurator exercised the "unlimited jurisdiction of the military *imperium*," we must interpret this, paradoxical though it may seem, in a restricted sense; that is, we must recognize the existence of exceptions to the rule. It is unreasonable to suppose that Rome, the mother of laws, ever contemplated the rule of despotism and caprice in the administration of justice in any part of the empire. It is true that the effect of the *imperium*, "as applied to provincial governorship, was to make each *imperator* a king in his own domain"; but kings themselves have nearly always been subject to restrictions; and the authorities are agreed that the *imperium* of the Roman procurator of the time of Christ was hemmed in by many limitations. A few of these may be named.

In the first place, the rights guaranteed to subject states within the provincial area by the law of the province (*lex provinciæ*) were the first limitations upon his power.

Again, it is a well-known fact that Roman citizens could appeal from the decision of the governor, in certain cases, to the emperor at Rome. Paul exercised this right, because he was a Roman citizen.[8] Jesus could not appeal from the judgment of Pilate, because He was not a Roman citizen.

Again, fear of an aroused and indignant public sentiment which might result in his removal by the emperor, exercised a salutary restraint upon the conduct, if it did not abridge the powers of the governor.

These various considerations bring us now to the second question asked in the beginning of this chapter: What forms of criminal procedure, if any, were employed by Pilate in conducting the Roman trial of Jesus?

It is historically true that Pilate exercised, as procurator of Judea, the unlimited jurisdiction of the military *imperium*; and that this *imperium* made him virtually an "*imperator*, a king in his own domain." It is also historically true that the inhabitants of the purely subject states of a province, who were not themselves Roman citizens, when accused of crime, stood before a Roman governor with no protection except the plea of justice against the summary exercise of absolute power. In other words, in the employment of the unlimited jurisdiction of the military *imperium*, a Roman governor, in the exercise of his discretion, might, in the case of non-Roman citizens of a subject state, throw all rules and forms of law to the wind, and decide the matter arbitrarily and despotically. It may be that Pilate did this in this case. But the best writers are agreed that this was not the policy of the Roman governors in the administration of justice in the provinces at the time of Christ. The lawgiving genius of Rome had then reached maturity and approximate perfection in the organization of its criminal tribunals. It is not probable, as before suggested, that despotism and caprice would be systematically tolerated anywhere in the Roman world. If the emperors at Rome were forced, out of regard for public sentiment, to respect the constitution and the laws, it is reasonable to infer that their personal representatives in the provinces were under the same restraint. We feel justified then in asserting that Pilate, in the trial of Jesus, should have applied certain laws and been governed by certain definite rules of criminal procedure. What were these rules? A few preliminary considerations will greatly aid the reader in arriving at an answer to this question. It should be understood:

(1) That Pilate was empowered to apply either Roman law or the local law in the trial of any case where the crime was an offense against both the province and the empire, as in the crime of murder; but that in the case of treason with which Jesus was charged he would apply the law of Rome under forms of Roman procedure. It has been denied that Pilate had a right to apply Jewish law in the government of his province; but this denial is contrary to authority. Innes says: "The Roman governor sanctioned, or even himself administered, the old law of the region."[9] Schürer says: "It may be assumed that the administration of the civil law was wholly in the hands of the Sanhedrin and native or local magistrates: Jewish courts decided according to Jewish law. But even in the criminal law this was almost invariably the case, only with this exception, that death sentences required to be confirmed by the Roman procurator. In such cases, the procurator decided, if he pleased, according to Jewish law."[10] Greenidge says: "Even the first clause of the Sicilian *lex*, if it contained no reference to jurisdiction by the local magistrate, left the interpretation of the *native law* wholly to Roman *proprætors*."[11] It is thus clearly evident that Roman procurators might apply either Roman or local laws in ordinary cases.

(2) That Roman governors were empowered to apply the adjective law of Rome to the substantive law of the province. In support of this contention, Greenidge says: "The edict of the *proprætor* or pro-consul, ... clearly could not express the native law of each particular state under its jurisdiction; but its generality and its expansiveness admitted, as we shall see, of an application of Roman forms to the substantive law of any particular city."[12]

(3) That the criminal procedure employed by Pilate in the trial of Jesus should have been the criminal procedure of a capital case tried at Rome, during the reign of Tiberius Cæsar. This fact is very evident from the

authorities. The trial of capital cases at Rome furnished models for similar trials in the provinces. In the exercise of the unlimited jurisdiction of the military *imperium*, Roman governors might disregard these models. But, ordinarily, custom compelled them to follow the criminal precedents of the Capital of the empire. The following authorities support this contention.

Rosadi says: "It is also certain that in the provinces the same order was observed in criminal cases as was observed in cases tried at Rome."[13] This eminent Italian writer cites, in proof of this statement, Pothier, Pandect. XLVIII. 2, n. 28.

Greenidge says: "Yet, in spite of this absence of legal checks, the criminal procedure of the provinces was, in the protection of the citizen as in other respects, closely modelled on that of Rome."[14]

To the same effect, but more clearly and pointedly expressed, is Geib, who says: "It is nevertheless true that the knowledge which we have, imperfect though it may be, leaves no doubt that the courts of the Italian municipalities and provinces had, in all essential elements, the permanent tribunals (*quæstiones perpetuæ*) as models; so that, in fact, a description of the proceedings in the permanent tribunals is, at the same time, to be regarded as a description of the proceedings in the provincial courts."[15]

These permanent tribunals (*quæstiones perpetuæ*) were courts of criminal jurisdiction established at Rome, and were in existence at the time of the crucifixion. Proceedings in these courts in capital cases, were models of criminal procedure in the provinces at the time of Christ. It logically follows then that if we can ascertain the successive steps in the trial of a capital case at Rome before one of the permanent tribunals, we have accurate information of the exact form of criminal procedure, not that Pilate did employ, but which he should have employed in the trial of Jesus.

Fortunately for the purposes of this treatise, every step which Roman law required in the trial of capital cases at Rome is as well known as the provisions of any modern criminal code. From the celebrated Roman trials in which Cicero appeared as an advocate, may be gleaned with unerring accuracy the fullest information touching all the details of capital trials at Rome at the time of Cicero.

It should be observed, at this point, that the period of Roman jurisprudence just referred to was in the closing years of the republic; and that certain changes in the organization of the tribunals as well as in the forms of procedure were effected by the legislation of Augustus. But we have it upon the authority of Rosadi that these changes were not radical in the case of the criminal courts and that the rules and regulations that governed procedure in them during the republic remained substantially unchanged under the empire. The same writer tells us that the permanent tribunals for the trial of capital cases did not go out of existence until the third century of the Christian era.[16]

The following chapter will be devoted, in the main, to a description of the mode of trial of capital cases at Rome before the permanent tribunals at the time of Christ.

CHAPTER IV

MODE OF TRIAL IN ROMAN CAPITAL CASES

THE reader should keep clearly and constantly in mind the purpose of this chapter: to describe the mode of trial in capital cases at Rome during the reign of Tiberius Cæsar; and thus to furnish a model of criminal procedure which Pilate should have imitated in the trial of Jesus at Jerusalem. In the last chapter, we saw that the proceedings of the permanent tribunals (*quæstiones perpetuæ*) at Rome furnished models for the trial of criminal cases in the provinces. It is now only necessary to determine what the procedure of the permanent tribunals at the time of Christ was, in order to understand what Pilate should have done in the trial of Jesus. But the character of the *quæstiones perpetuæ*, as well as the rules and regulations that governed their proceedings, cannot well be understood without reference to the criminal tribunals and modes of trial in criminal cases that preceded them. Roman history discloses two distinct periods of criminal procedure before the organization of the permanent tribunals about the beginning of the last century of the Republic: (1) The period of the kings and (2) the period of the early republic. Each of these will be here briefly considered.

The Regal Period.—The earliest glimpses of Roman political life reveal the existence of a sacred and military monarchy in which the king is generalissimo of the army, chief pontiff of the national religion, and supreme judge in civil and criminal matters over the lives and property of the citizens. These various powers and attributes are wrapped up in the *imperium*. By virtue of the *imperium*, the king issued commands to the army and also exercised the highest judicial functions over the lives and fortunes of his fellow-citizens. The kings were thus military commanders and judges in one person, as the consuls were after them. The monarch might sit alone and judge cases and impose sentences; but the trial was usually a personal investigation undertaken by him with the advice and aid of a chosen body of judges from the senate or the pontifical college. According to Dionysius, Romulus ordered that all crimes of a serious nature should be tried by the king, but that all lighter offenses should be judged by the senate.[17] Little confidence can be reposed in this statement, since the age and deeds of Romulus are exceedingly legendary and mythical. But it is historically true that in the regal period of Rome the kings were the supreme judges in all civil and criminal matters.

The Early Republican Period.—The abolition of the monarchy and the establishment of the republic witnessed the distribution of the powers of government formerly exercised by the king among a number of magistrates and public officers. Consuls, tribunes, prætors, ædiles, both curule and plebeian, exercised, under the republic, judicial functions in criminal matters.

The consuls were supreme criminal judges at the beginning of the republic, and were clothed with unlimited power in matters of life and death. This is shown by the condemnation and execution of the sons of Brutus and their fellow-conspirators.[18] Associated with the consuls were, at first, two annually appointed quæstors whom they nominated. The functions of the quæstors were as unlimited as those of their superiors, the consuls; but their jurisdiction was confined chiefly to criminal matters and finance.

The tribunes, sacred and inviolable in their persons as representatives of the *plebs* and as their protectors against patrician oppression, exercised at first merely a negative control over the regular magistracies of the community. But, finally, they became the chief public prosecutors of political criminals.

The prætors, whose chief jurisdiction was in civil matters, were potentially as fully criminal judges as the consuls, and there may have been a time when a portion of criminal jurisdiction was actually in their hands. In the later republic, they presided over the *quæstiones perpetuæ*, permanent criminal tribunals.

The ædiles are found in Roman history exercising functions of criminal jurisdiction, although their general powers were confined to the special duties of caring for the games, the market, and the archives.

But the criminal jurisdiction of the magistrates who replaced the king at the downfall of the monarchy was abridged and almost destroyed by the famous *lex Valeria* (*de provocatione*). This law was proposed 509 B.C. by Publius Valerius, one of the first consuls of Rome, and provided that no magistrate should have power to execute a sentence of death against a Roman citizen who had appealed to the judgment of the people in their public assembly. This *lex* was the *magna charta* of the Romans and was justly regarded by them as the great palladium of their civil liberty. And it was this law that inaugurated the popular jurisdiction of the *comitia*. The result was that for more than three hundred years the final determination of the question of life or death was in the hands of the people themselves. From the passage of the Valerian law the function of the magistrates was limited to the duty of convincing the people of the guilt of an alleged criminal against whom they themselves had already pronounced a preliminary sentence. The magistrates were, therefore, not so much judges as prosecutors; the people were the final judges in the case.

Mode of Trial in the Comitia, or Public Assembly.—On a certain day, the prosecuting magistrate, who had himself pronounced the preliminary sentence against an accused person who had appealed to the people in their public assembly, mounted the *rostra*, and called the people together by the voice of a herald. He then made a proclamation that on a certain day he would bring an accusation against a certain person upon a given charge. At the same time, he called upon this person to come forward and hear the charges against him. The defendant then presented himself, listened to the accusation, and immediately furnished bond for his appearance, or in default of bail, was thrown into prison. Upon the day announced at the opening of the trial, the prosecuting magistrate again mounted the *rostra*, and summoned the accused by a herald, if he was at large, or had him brought forth if he was in prison. The prosecutor then produced evidence, oral and documentary, against the prisoner. The indictment had to be in writing, and was published on three market days in the Forum. The prosecution came to an end on the third day, and the accused then began his defense by mounting the *rostra* with his patron and presenting evidence in his own behalf. The prosecutor then announced that on a certain day he would ask the people to render judgment by their votes. In the early years of the republic, the people voted by shouting their approval or disapproval of the charges made; but later a tablet bearing one of the two letters V. (*uti rogas*) or A. (*absolvo*) was used as a ballot.

The effect of popular jurisdiction in criminal processes at Rome was in the nature of a two-edged sword that cut both ways. It was beneficial in the limitations it imposed upon the conduct of single magistrates who were too often capricious and despotic. But this benefit was purchased at the price of a kind of popular despotism not less dangerous in its way. It has always been characteristic of popular assemblies that their decisions have been more the outcome of passion and prejudice than the result of calm wisdom and absolute justice. The trouble at Rome was that the people were both legislators and judges in their public assemblies; and it nearly always happened that the lawmakers rose above and trampled upon the very laws which they themselves had made. The natural offspring of this state of things is either anarchy or despotism; and it was only the marvelous vitality of the Roman Commonwealth that enabled it to survive.

The reports of the great criminal trials before the *comitia* reveal the inherent weakness of a system of popular jurisdiction in criminal matters. Personal and political considerations foreign to the merits of the case were allowed to take the place of competent evidence; and issues of right and expediency were too frequently mixed up. The accused, at times, trusted not so much in the righteousness of his cause as in the feelings of compassion and prejudice that moved the people as popular judges. And to excite these feelings the most ludicrous and undignified steps were sometimes taken. The defendant nearly always appeared at the trial in mourning garb, frequently let his hair and beard grow long, and often exhibited the scars and wounds received in battle whilst fighting for his country. He sometimes offered prayers to the immortal gods and wept bitterly; at other times he caused his children and other relatives to appear at the trial, wailing, and tearing their clothes. Not content with presenting all the pathetic features of his own life, he left nothing undone to expose his opponents to hatred and contempt. It thus happened that many of the great criminal causes of Rome were mere farcical proceedings. A few instances may be cited.

Horatius, though tried in the time of the third Roman king, was pardoned by the people for the murder of his sister because of his heroic deed in single combat with the three Curiatii, and because his father had lost three children in the service of the state.

In the year 98, Manlius Aquillius, the pacificator of Sicily, was tried for embezzlement. Marcus Antonius, his advocate, ended his argument for the defense by tearing the tunic of Aquillius to show the breast of the veteran warrior covered with scars. The people were moved to tears and Aquillius was acquitted, although the evidence was very clear against him.

In the trial of M. Manlius, 384 B.C., new tactics were employed. The accused refused to appear in mourning. There was no weeping in his behalf. On the other hand, Manlius relied upon his services to the state for acquittal. He brought forward four hundred citizens who by his generosity he had saved from bondage for debt; he exhibited the spoils taken from thirty slain enemies, also military decorations received for bravery in battle—among them two mural and eight civic crowns; he then produced many citizens rescued by him from the hands of the enemy; he then bared his breast and exhibited the scars received by him in war; and, lastly, turning toward the Capitol, he implored Jupiter to protect him, and to infuse, at this moment, into the Roman people, his judges, the same spirit of courage and patriotism that had given him strength to save the city of Rome and his whole country from the hands of the Gauls. He begged the people to keep their eyes fixed on the Capitol while they were pronouncing sentence against him to whom they owed life and liberty. It is said that his prosecutors despaired of convicting him amidst such surroundings, and adjourned the trial to another place, where the Capitol could not be seen; and that thereupon the conviction of Manlius was secured and his condemnation pronounced.

In the year 185 B.C., the tribune M. Nævius, at the instigation of Cato, accused Scipio Africanus before the tribes of having been bribed to secure a dishonorable peace. It was clearly evident that a charge of this kind could not well be sustained by evidence; but it was believed that a conviction could be secured by an appeal to the passion and prejudice of the multitude. But this advantage operated as greatly in favor of Scipio as it did in favor of his accusers. And he did not fail to use the advantage to the fullest extent. In seeming imitation of M. Manlius, two hundred years before, he appealed for acquittal to the people on account of his public services. He refused to appear in mourning, offered no evidence in his own behalf, nor did he exhibit the usual humility of an accused Roman before his countrymen. With proud disdain, he spurned the unworthy imputation of bribery, and pointed the people to the magnificent achievements of his brilliant public career. He reminded them that the day of the trial was itself the anniversary of his victory over the greatest enemy that Rome ever had, at Zama. It was degrading, he exclaimed, both to him and to the Roman nation, to bring such a charge on this day against the man to whom it was due that the Commonwealth of Rome still existed. He refused to lower himself, he said, by listening to the insolent charges of a vulgar brawler who had never done anything for the state. He declared that instead he would repair at once to the temple of Jupiter and render thanks for his victory over Hannibal to the protecting gods of his country. With these words, he left the Forum and went to the Capitol and from there to his house, accompanied by the great majority of the people, while the accusing tribune and his official staff were left alone in the market place.

The inevitable result of these cases of miscarriage of justice, in which patriotic bravado and rhetorical claptrap took the place of legal rules, was a desire and demand for the reform of criminal procedure. Besides, it had ever been found troublesome and inconvenient to summon the whole body of the Roman people to try ordinary offenses. It was only in cases of great gravity that the ponderous machinery of the *comitia centuriata* could be set in motion. This difficulty was increased with the growth of the republic, in which crimes also grew in number and magnitude. The necessity for the reform of the criminal law resulted in the institution of permanent tribunals (*quæstiones perpetuæ*). A series of legal enactments accomplished this result. The earliest law that created a permanent *quæstio* was the *lex Calpurnia* of 149 B.C. And it was the proceedings in these courts, which we shall now describe, that should have guided Pilate in the trial of Jesus.

Mode of Trial in the Permanent Tribunals.—We shall attempt to trace in the remaining pages of this chapter the successive steps in the trial of criminal cases before the permanent tribunals at Rome.

First Stage (postulatio).—A Roman criminal trial before a *quæstio perpetua* commenced with an application to the presiding magistrate, the prætor or the *iudex quæstionis*, for permission to bring a criminal charge against a certain person. The technical Latin expression for this request to prosecute is *postulatio*. It should be here noted that State's attorneys or public prosecutors, in a modern sense, were not known to the Romans at this time. Private citizens took upon themselves public prosecutions in behalf of the state. They were encouraged to do this from motives of personal profit as well as patriotic interest in the welfare of the community. As young men in modern times, just admitted to the bar, often accept criminal cases by assignment from the court in order to make a beginning in their professional careers, so young Roman nobles in ancient times sought to make reputations for themselves by accusing and prosecuting public delinquents. And not only professional reputation, but financial compensation as well could be gained in this way. The Roman laws of the time of Cicero provided that a successful prosecutor should receive one-fourth part of the property confiscated or the fine imposed. A Macedonian inscription offered a reward of 200 denarii to the prosecutor who should bring to justice the desecrators of a tomb.[19]

Second Stage (divinatio).—It often happened that more than one accuser desired to prosecute a single offense; but more than one prosecutor was not permitted by Roman law unless there was more than one crime charged. Then, in case of a concurrence of would-be accusers, a preliminary trial was had to determine which one of these was best fitted to bring the accusation. This initial hearing was known in Roman law as the *divinatio*. It was indeed more than a mere hearing; it was a regular trial in which the question of the fitness of the different candidates for the position of *delator* was argued before the president and the jury. This jury was in many cases distinct from the one that finally tried the case on the merits. The purpose of the whole proceeding known as the *divinatio* was to secure a prosecutor who was at once both able and sincere; and both these qualities were generally very strenuously urged by all those who desired to assume the rôle of accuser. Indeed all personal qualifications involving the mental and moral attributes of the would-be prosecutors were pointedly urged. At the hearing, the different candidates frequently became animated and even bitter opponents of each other. Crimination and recrimination then followed as a natural consequence. An applicant might show that he was thoroughly familiar with the affairs of a province, as a special fitness in the prosecution of a public official for extortion in that province. An opponent, on the other hand, might show that said applicant had been associated with said official in the government of the province and had been, and was now, on the friendliest terms with him. After the meritorious qualifications of all the claimants had been presented, the president and jury rendered their decision. The details of the evidence affecting the merits of the charge were not considered at this preliminary trial. Only such facts were considered as affected the personal qualifications of the different candidates for the place of accuser. When these qualifications were about equally balanced in point of merit between two applicants, the abler speaker was generally chosen.

Third Stage (nominis delatio).—It frequently happened that the *postulatio*, the request to prosecute, was not followed by the *divinatio*, the preliminary hearing on the merits of different applicants, because there was only one would-be accuser; and his qualifications were beyond dispute. In such a case, when a request to bring a criminal charge against a certain person had been presented by a citizen to the prætor, there followed, after a certain interval of time, a private hearing before the president of the court for the purpose of gaining fuller and more definite information concerning the charge. This private proceeding was styled the *nominis* or *criminis delatio*, and took place before the president alone. Its main object was to secure a specification of the personality of the accused as well as of the charges brought against him. At this stage of the trial the presence of the accused person was necessary, unless he was absent under valid excuse. The *lex Memmia*, passed in the year 114 B.C., permitted a delinquent to plead that he was absent from Rome on public business, as an excuse for not appearing at the *nominis delatio*. In the year 58 B.C., the tribune L. Antistius impeached Julius Cæsar. But the colleagues of Antistius excused Cæsar from personal attendance because he was absent in the service of the state in Gaul. But, if the accused appeared at the *nominis delatio*, the prosecutor interrogated him at length concerning the facts of the crime. The purpose of this interrogation (*interrogatio*) was to satisfy the president that there was a prima facie case to carry before the regular tribunal in open trial. The proceedings of the *nominis delatio* were thus in the nature of a modern Grand Jury investigation, instituted to determine if a serious prosecution should be had.

Fourth Stage (inscriptio).—If the interrogation convinced the president that the prosecutor had a prima facie case to take before the permanent tribunal, he framed a form of indictment called the *inscriptio*. This indictment was signed by the chief prosecutor and also by a number of witnesses against the accused called *subscriptores*. The charge was now definitely fixed; and, from this moment, it was the only offense that could be prosecuted at the trial. The drawing up of this charge by the president was similar to the framing of an indictment by a modern Grand Jury.

Fifth Stage (nominis receptio).—After the indictment or inscription had been framed, it was formally received by the president. This act was styled the *nominis receptio* and corresponds, in a general way, with the presentment of an indictment by a modern Grand Jury. When the *nominis receptio* was complete, the case was said to be *in judicio*, and the accused was said to be *in reatu*. The president then fixed a day certain for the appearance of the accused and the beginning of the trial. The time fixed was usually ten days from the *nominis receptio*. However, a longer time was allowed if evidence had to be secured from beyond the sea. Thirty days were allowed the accusers in the prosecution of Scaurus. Cicero was given one hundred and ten days to secure evidence against Verres; but he actually employed only sixty. The time granted the prosecutor was also required by the law to be utilized by the defendant in preparing his case.

The preliminary steps in the prosecution were now complete, and the accused awaited the day of trial. In the meantime, he was allowed to go at large, even when charged with a grave offense like murder. Imprisonment to prevent escape had almost ceased at the time of which we write. If the evidence against the accused was weak, it was felt that he would certainly appear at the trial. If the evidence against him was very strong, it was thought that he would seek to escape a sentence of death in voluntary exile, a step which Romans always encouraged, as they were averse, at all times, to putting a Roman citizen to death.

Sixth Stage (citatio).—At the expiration of the time designated by the president for the beginning of the trial, the proceedings before the judges began. All the necessary parties, including the judges or jurors, were summoned by a herald to appear. This procedure was termed the *citatio*. Strange to say, if the accused failed to appear the case could proceed without him. The reason for the requirement of his presence at the *nominis delatio*, but not at the trial is not clear; especially when viewed in the light of a modern trial in which the defendant must be present at every important step in the proceedings. Under Roman procedure, the presence of the defendant was not necessary, whether he was in voluntary exile, or was obstinately absent. In 52 B.C., Milo was condemned in his absence; and we read in Plutarch that the assassins of Cæsar were tried in their absence, 43 B.C.

Excusable absence necessitated an adjournment of the case. The chief grounds for an adjournment were: (1) Absence from the city in the public service; (2) that the accused was compelled to appear in another court on the same day; (3) illness.

The absence of the accused did not prevent the prosecution of the case, but the nonappearance of the prosecutor on the day fixed for the beginning of the trial usually terminated the proceedings at once. The fact that the case had to be dismissed if the accuser failed to appear only serves to illustrate how dependent the state was on the sincerity of the citizen who undertook the prosecution. The obligations of the prosecutor honestly and vigorously to follow up a suit which he had set in motion were felt to be so serious a matter by the Romans that special laws were passed to hold him in the line of duty. The *lex Remmia* provided that if any citizen knowingly accused another citizen falsely of a crime, the accuser should be prosecuted for calumny (*calumnia*). It further provided that, in case of conviction, the letter K should be branded on the forehead of the condemned. Such laws were found necessary to protect the good name of Roman citizens against bad men who desired to use the legal machinery of the state to gratify private malevolence against their enemies. It may thus be seen that the system which permitted public prosecutions on the motion of private citizens was attended by both good and bad results. Cicero regarded such a system as a positive benefit to the state.[20] Its undoubted effect was to place a check upon corruption in public office by subjecting the acts of public officials to the scrutiny and, if need be, to the censure of every man in the nation. On the other hand, accusers in public prosecutions came finally to be identified, in the public mind, with coarse and vulgar informers whose only motive in making public accusations was to create private gain. So thoroughly were they despised that one of the parasites of Plautus scornfully exclaims that he would not exchange his vocation, though low and groveling, with that of the man who makes a legal proceeding "his net wherein to catch another man's goods."[21]

Seventh Stage (impaneling the judges).—But if the prosecutor appeared in due time, the trial formally began by the impaneling of the judges. This was usually done by the prætor or *iudex quæstionis* who, at the beginning of the trial, placed the names of the complete panel of jurors, inscribed on white tablets, into an urn, and then drew out a certain number. Both prosecutor and accused had the right to challenge a limited number, as the names were being drawn. The number of challenges allowed varied from time to time.

Eighth Stage (beginning of the trial).—When the judges had been impaneled, the regular proceedings began. The place of trial was the Forum. The curule chair of the prætor and the benches of the judges, constituting the tribunal, were here placed. On the ground in front of the raised platform upon which the prætor and judges sat, were arranged the benches of the parties, their advocates and witnesses. Like the ancient Hebrew law, Roman law required that criminal cases should be tried only by daylight, that is, between daybreak and one hour before sunset. At the opening of the trial, the prosecutor, backed by the *subscriptores*, and the accused, supported by his patrons and advocates, appeared before the tribunal.

In a modern criminal trial the case is opened by the introduction of testimony which is followed by regular speeches of counsel for the people and the defendant. In those jurisdictions where opening addresses are required before the examination of the witnesses, the purpose is to inform the jury of the facts which it is proposed to prove. Argument and characterization are not permitted in these opening speeches. The real speeches in which argument and illustration are permitted come after the evidence has been introduced. The purpose of these closing speeches is to assist the jury in determining matters of fact from conflicting testimony.

Under the Roman system of trial in criminal cases, the order was reversed. The regular speeches containing argument, characterization, and illustration, as well as a statement of the facts proposed to be proved, were made in the very beginning. Evidence was then introduced to show that the orators had told the truth in their speeches.

It is not practicable in this place to discuss the kinds and relevancy of evidence under Roman criminal procedure. Suffice it to say that slaves were always examined under torture.

The close of the evidence was followed by the judgment of the tribunal.

Ninth Stage (voting of the judges).—The judges voted by ballot, and a majority of votes decided the verdict. The balloting was done with tablets containing the letters A. (*absolvo*), C. (*condemno*) and N. L. (*non liquet*). When the votes had been cast, the tablets were then counted by the president of the tribunal. If the result indicated a condemnation, he pronounced the word *fecisse*; if an acquittal, the phrase, *non fecisse videtur*; if a doubtful verdict (*non liquet*), the words *amplius esse cognoscendum*. The result of a doubtful (*non liquet*) verdict was a retrial of the case at some future time.

Such were the main features of the trial of a capital case at Rome at the date of the crucifixion. Such was the model which, according to the best authorities, Pilate was bound to follow in the trial of Jesus. Did he imitate this model? Did he observe these rules and regulations? We shall see.

CHAPTER V

ROMAN FORMS OF PUNISHMENT

ACCORDING to Gibbon, the laws of the Twelve Tables, like the statutes of Draco, were written in blood. These famous decrees sanctioned the frightful principle of the *lex talionis*; and prescribed for numerous crimes many horrible forms of punishment. The hurling from the Tarpeian Rock was mild in comparison with other modes of execution. The traitor to his country had his hands tied behind his back, his head shrouded in a veil, was then scourged by a lictor, and was afterwards crucified, in the midst of the Forum by being nailed to the *arbor infelix*. A malicious incendiary, on a principle of retaliation, was delivered to the flames. He was burned to death by being wrapped in a garment covered with pitch which was then set on fire.[22] A parricide was cast into the Tiber or the sea, inclosed in a sack, to which a cock, a viper, a dog, and a monkey had been successively added as fit companions in death.[23]

But the development of Roman jurisprudence and the growth of Roman civilization witnessed a gradual diminution in the severity of penal sanctions, in the case of free citizens, until voluntary exile was the worst punishment to which a wearer of the toga was compelled to submit. The Porcian and Valerian laws prohibited the magistrates from putting any Roman citizen to death. The principle underlying these laws was the offspring of a proud and patriotic sentiment which exempted the masters of the world from the extreme penalties reserved for barbarians and slaves. Greenidge, interpreting Cicero, very elegantly expresses this sentiment: "It is a *facinus* to put a Roman citizen in bonds, a *scelus* to scourge him, *prope parricidium* to put him to death."

The subject of this volume limits the discussion in this chapter to a single Roman punishment: Crucifixion. Around this word gather the most frightful memories and, at the same time, the sweetest and sublimest hopes of the human race. A thorough appreciation of the trial of Jesus, it is felt, renders necessary a comparatively exhaustive treatment of the punishment in which all the horrors and illegalities of the proceedings against Him culminated.

History.—Tradition attributes the origin of crucifixion, the most frightful and inhuman form of punishment ever known, to a woman, Semiramis, Queen of Assyria. We are reminded by this that quartering, drawing at a horse's tail, breaking on the wheel, burning and torture with pincers, were provisions in a codex bearing the name of a woman: Maria Theresa.[24]

Crucifixion was practiced by the ancient Egyptians, Carthaginians, Persians, Germans, Assyrians, Greeks, and Romans. The Romans employed this form of punishment on a colossal scale. The Roman general Varus crucified 2,000

Jews in one day at the gates of Jerusalem. The close of the war with Spartacus, the gladiator, witnessed the crucifixion of 10,000 slaves between Capua and Rome.

Crucifixion, as a form of punishment, was unknown to the ancient Hebrews. The penalty of death was enforced among them by burning, strangling, decapitation, and stoning. The "hanging" of criminals "on a tree," mentioned in Deut. xxi. 22, was a posthumous indignity offered the body of the criminal after death by stoning, and struck horror to the soul of every pious Israelite who beheld it. Among the Romans also degradation was a part of the infliction, since crucifixion was peculiarly a *supplicium servile*. Only the vilest criminals, among free men, such as were guilty of robbery, piracy, assassination, perjury, sedition, treason, and desertion from the army, met death in this way. The *jus civitatis* protected Roman citizens against this punishment.

Mode of Crucifixion.—A sentence of death having been pronounced by a Roman magistrate or tribunal, scourging became a preliminary to execution. This was done with the terrible *flagellum* into which the soldiers frequently stuck nails, pieces of bone, and other hard substances to heighten the pain which was often so intense as to produce death. The victim was generally bound to a column to be scourged. It was claimed by Jerome, Prudentius, Gregory of Tours, and others that they had seen the one to which Jesus was bound before His scourging began. After the flagellation, the prisoner was conducted to the place of execution. This was outside the city, often in some public road, or other conspicuous place like the Campus Martius at Rome. The criminal was compelled to carry his own cross; and when he had arrived at the place of crucifixion, he was compelled to watch the preparations for his torture. Before his eyes and in his presence, the cross was driven into the ground; and, after having been stripped naked, he was lifted upon and nailed to it. It sometimes happened that he was stretched upon it first and then lifted with it from the ground. The former method was the more common, however, as it was desired to strike terror into the victim by the sight of the erection of the cross. The body was fastened to the cross by nails driven into the hands and sometimes into the feet; more frequently, however, the feet were merely bound by cords.

The pictures of crosses in works of art are misrepresentations, in that they are too large and too high. The real cross of antiquity was very little longer than the victim, whose head was near the top, and whose feet often hung only twelve or fifteen inches from the ground. Pictorial art is also false because it fails to show the projecting beam from near the center of the cross upon which the criminal sat. That there was such a beam is attested by the almost unanimous voice of antiquity.

Crucifixion was conducted, under Roman auspices, by a *carnifex*, or hangman, assisted by a band of soldiers. At Rome, execution was done under the supervision of the *Triumviri Capitales*. The duty of the soldiers was not only to erect the cross and nail the victim to it, but also to watch him until he was dead. This was a necessary precaution to prevent friends and relatives from taking the criminal down and from carrying him away, since he sometimes continued to live upon the cross during several days. If taken down in time, the suffering man might easily be resuscitated and restored to health. Josephus tells us that three victims were ordered to be taken down by Titus at his request, and that one of them recovered. "In the later persecutions of the Christians, the guards remained four or six days by the dead, in order to secure them to the wild beasts and to cut off all possibility of burial and resurrection; and in Lyons the Christians were not once able by offers of much gold to obtain the privilege of showing compassion upon the victims of the pagan popular fury. Sometimes, however, particularly on festival days, e.g., the birthdays of the emperors, the corpse was given up to the friends of the deceased, either for money or without money, although even Augustus could be cruel enough to turn a deaf ear to the entreaties of the condemned for sepulture."[25]

Roman records tell us that the soldiers frequently hastened death by breaking the legs of the criminal; at other times, fires were built about the cross beneath him; and, again, wild beasts were turned loose upon him.

It was the general custom to allow the body to remain and rot upon the cross, or to be devoured by wild beasts and birds of prey. "Distracted relatives and friends saw the birds of prey attack the very faces of those whom they loved; and piety often took pains to scare away the birds by day and the beasts by night, or to outwit the guards that watched the dead."[26]

Sepulture was generally forbidden by law, though there were exceptions to the rule. At the request of Joseph of Arimathea, Pilate consented that Jesus should be taken down and buried.[27] A national exception seems also to have been made in the case of the Jews on account of the requirements of Deut. xxi. 22, 23.

Pathology.—The following pathological phases of death by crucifixion are from a treatise by the celebrated physician, Richter (in John's "Bibl. Arch."), which have been reproduced in Strong and McClintock's "Cyclopedia":

"(1) The unnatural position and violent tension of the body, which cause a painful sensation from the least motion.

"(2) The nails, being driven through parts of the hands and feet which are full of nerves and tendons (and yet at a distance from the heart) create the most exquisite anguish.

"(3) The exposure of so many wounds and lacerations brings on inflammation, which tends to become gangrene, and every movement increases the poignancy of suffering.

"(4) In the distended parts of the body, more blood flows through the arteries than can be carried back into the veins: hence too much blood finds its way from the aorta into the head and stomach, and the blood vessels of the head become pressed and swollen. The general obstruction of circulation which ensues causes an intense excitement, exertion, and anxiety more intolerable than death itself.

"(5) The inexpressible misery of *gradually increasing* and lingering anguish.

"(6) Burning and raging thirst.

"Death by crucifixion (physically considered) is, therefore, to be attributed to the sympathetic fever which is excited by the wounds, and aggravated by exposure to the weather, privation of water, and the painfully constrained position of the body. Traumatic fever corresponds, in intensity and in character, to the local inflammation of the wound, is characterized by heat, swelling, and great pain, the fever is highly inflammatory, and the sufferer complains of heat, throbbing headache, intense thirst, restlessness, and anxiety. As soon as suppuration sets in, the fever somewhat abates, and partially ceases as suppuration diminishes and the stage of cicatrization approaches. But if the wound be prevented from healing and suppuration continues, the fever assumes a hectic character, and will sooner or later exhaust the powers of life. When, however, the inflammation of the wound is so intense as to produce mortification, nervous depression is the immediate consequence; and, if the cause of this excessive inflammation of the wound still continues, as is the case in crucifixion, the sufferer rapidly sinks. He is no longer sensible of pain, but his anxiety and sense of prostration are excessive; hiccough supervenes, his skin is moistened with a cold clammy sweat, and death ensues. It is in this manner that death on the cross must have taken place in an ordinarily healthy constitution."

The intense sufferings and prolonged agony of crucifixion can be best illustrated by an account of several cases of this form of punishment taken from history.

From the "Chrestomathia Arabica" of Kosegarten, published in 1828, is taken the following story of the execution of a Mameluke. The author of this work gleaned the story from an Arabic manuscript entitled "The Meadow of Flowers and the Fragrant Odour":

"It is said that he had killed his master for some cause or other, and he was crucified on the banks of the river Barada under the castle of Damascus, with his face turned toward the East. His hands, arms, and feet were nailed, and he remained so from midday on Friday to the same hour on Sunday, when he died. He was remarkable for his strength and prowess; he had been engaged with his master in sacred war at Askelon, where he slew great numbers of the Franks; and when very young he had killed a lion. Several extraordinary things occurred at his being nailed, as that he gave himself up without resistance to the cross, and without complaint stretched out his hands, which were nailed and after them his feet: he in the meantime looked on, and did not utter a groan, or change his countenance or move his limbs. I have heard this from one who witnessed it, and he thus remained till he died, patient and silent, without wailing, but looking around him to the right and the left upon the people. But he begged for water, and none was given him, and he gazed upon it and longed for one drop of it, and he complained of thirst all the first day, after which he was silent, for God gave him strength."

Describing the punishments used in Madagascar, Rev. Mr. Ellis says: "In a few cases of great enormity, a sort of crucifixion has been resorted to; and, in addition to this, burning or roasting at a slow fire, kept at some distance from the sufferer, has completed the horrors of this miserable death.... In the year 1825, a man was condemned to crucifixion, who had murdered a female for the sake of stealing her child. He carried the child for sale to the public market, where the infant was recognized, and the murderer detected. He bore his punishment in the most hardened manner, avenging himself by all the violence he was capable of exercising upon those who dragged him to the place of execution. Not a single groan escaped him during the period he was nailed to the wood, nor while the cross was fixed upright in the earth."[28]

More horrible still than punishment by crucifixion was that of impalement and suspension on a hook. The following description of the execution, in 1830, at Salonica, of Chaban, a captain of banditti, is given by Slade: "He was described by those who saw him as a very fine-looking man, about thirty-five. As a preparatory exercise, he was suspended by his arms for twelve hours. The following day a hook was thrust into his side, by which he was suspended to a tree, and there hung enduring the agony of thirst till the third evening, when death closed the scene; but before that about an hour the birds, already considering him their own, had alighted upon his brow to pick his eyes. During this frightful period he uttered no unmanly complaints, only repeated several times, 'Had I known that I was to suffer this infernal death, I would never have done what I have. From the moment I led the klephte's life I had death before my eyes, and was prepared to meet it, but I expected to die as my predecessors, by decapitation.'"[29]

The Cross.—The instrument of crucifixion, called the Cross, was variously formed. Lipsius and Gretser have employed a twofold classification: the *crux simplex*, and the *crux composita* or *compacta*. A single upright stake was distinguished as a *crux simplex*. The *crux composita*, the compound or actual cross, was subject to the following modifications of form: *Crux immissa*, formed as in the Figure †; *crux commissa* thus formed **T**; and the *crux decussata*, the cruciform figure, set diagonally after the manner of the Roman letter X. It is generally thought that Jesus was crucified upon the *crux immissa*, the "Latin cross."

According to the well-known legend of the "Invention of the Cross," the actual cross on which Jesus was crucified was discovered in the year 326 A.D. by the Empress Helena, the mother of Constantine the Great. As the story goes, while visiting Jerusalem and the scenes of the passion, she was guided to the summit of Calvary by an aged Jew. Here an excavation was made, and, at a considerable depth, three crosses were found; and, with them, but lying aside by itself, was the inscription, in Hebrew, Latin, and Greek, placed above the head of Christ at the time of the crucifixion. To determine which of the three crosses was the one upon which Jesus suffered, it was decided, at the suggestion of Macarius, bishop of Jerusalem, to employ a miracle. The sick were brought and required to touch the three. According to the legend, the one upon which the Savior died immediately imparted miraculous healing. A church was at once built above the excavation and in it was deposited the greater part of the supposed real cross, and the remainder was sent to Byzantium, and from there to Rome, where it was placed in the church of Santa Croce in Gerusalemme, built especially to receive the precious relic. The genuineness of this relic was afterwards attested by a Bull of Pope Alexander III.

In connection with the legend of the discovery of the actual cross upon which Christ was crucified, goes a secondary story that the nails used at the crucifixion were also found at the same time and place. Later tradition declared that one of these was thrown by Helena into the Adriatic when swept by a terrific storm, and that this was followed by an instantaneous calm.

The popular impression among Christians that the cross is exclusively a Christian religious symbol, seems to be without historical foundation. It is quite certain, indeed, that it was a religious emblem among several ancient races before the beginning of the Christian era.

The ancient Egyptians adored the cross with the most holy veneration; and this sacred emblem was carved upon many of their monuments. Several of these monuments may be seen to-day in the British Museum.[30] A cross upon a Calvary may also be seen upon the breast of one of the Egyptian mummies in the Museum of the London University.[31] The ancient

Egyptians were accustomed to putting a cross on their sacred cakes, just as the Christians of to-day do, on Good Friday.[32]

The cross was also adored by the ancient Greeks and Romans, long before the crucifixion of Christ. Greek crosses of equal arms adorn the tomb of Midas, the ancient Phrygian king.[33] One of the early Christian Fathers, Minucius Felix, in a heated controversy with the pagan Romans, charged them with adoration of the cross. "As for adoration of the cross," said he to the Romans, "which you object against us, I must tell you that we neither adore crosses nor desire them. You it is, ye Pagans, who worship wooden gods, who are the most likely people to adore wooden crosses, as being part of the same substance with your deities. For what else are your ensigns, flags, and standards, but crosses, gilt and beautiful? Your victorious trophies *not only represent a cross, but a cross with a man upon it.*"[34]

It also seems that, at a time antedating the early Romans, Etruscans and Sabines, a primitive race inhabited the plains of Northern Italy, "to whom the cross was a religious symbol, the sign beneath which they laid their dead to rest; a people of whom history tells nothing, knowing not their name; but of whom antiquarian research has learned this, that they lived in ignorance of the arts of civilization, that they dwelt in villages built on platforms over lakes, and that they trusted to the cross to guard, and maybe to revive, their loved ones whom they committed to the dust."

The cross was also a sacred symbol among the ancient Scandinavians. "It occurs," says Mr. R. P. Knight, "on many Runic monuments found in Sweden and Denmark, which are of an age long anterior to the approach of Christianity to those countries, and, probably, to its appearance in the world."[35]

When the Spanish missionaries first set foot on the soil of Mexico, they were amazed to find that the Aztecs worshiped the cross as an object of supreme veneration. They found it suspended as a sacred symbol and an august emblem from the walls of all the Aztec temples.[36] When they penetrated farther south and entered Peru, they found that the Incas adored a cross made out of a single piece of jasper.[37] "It appears," says "Chambers's Encyclopedia," "that the sign of the cross was in use as an emblem having certain religious and mystic meanings attached to it, long before the Christian era; and the Spanish conquerors were astonished to find it an object of religious veneration among the nations of Central and South America."[38]

That the ancient Mexicans should have worshiped the cross and also a crucified Savior, called Quetzalcoatle,[39] is one of the strangest phenomena of sacred history. It is a puzzle which the most eminent theologians have found it impossible to solve. They have generally contented themselves with declaring the whole thing a myth built upon primitive superstition and ignorance. This worship of the cross and Quetzalcoatle was going on before Columbus discovered America, and it seems impossible to establish any historical or geographical connection between it and the Christian worship of the cross and the crucified Jesus.

Several writers of eminence have contended that the widespread adoration of the cross, as a sacred symbol, among so many races of mankind, ancient and modern, proves a universal spiritual impulse, culminating in the crucifixion of Jesus as the common Savior of the world. "It is more than a coincidence," says the Rev. S. Baring-Gould, "that Osiris by the cross should give life eternal to the spirits of the just; that with the cross Thor should smite the head of the great Serpent, and bring to life those who were slain; that beneath the cross the Muysca mothers should lay their babes, trusting to that sign to secure them from the power of evil spirits; that with that symbol to protect them, the ancient people of Northern Italy should lay them down in the dust."[40]

But it is not with the mythical crucifixions of mythical gods that we have to deal. The real, historical death of Jesus upon the cross with its accompanying incidents of outrageous illegality is the purpose of this treatise; and to the accomplishment of that design we now return.

CHAPTER VI

ROMAN LAW APPLICABLE TO THE TRIAL OF JESUS

WHAT *was the law of Rome in relation to the trial of Jesus?* The answer to this question is referable to the main charge brought against the Master before Pilate. A single verse in St. Luke contains the indictment: "And they began to accuse him, saying, We found this fellow perverting the nation, and forbidding to give tribute to Cæsar, saying that he himself is Christ a King." Three distinct elements are wrapped up in this general accusation; but they are all interwoven with and culminate in the great charge that Jesus claimed to be "Christ a King." Of this accusation alone, Pilate took cognizance. And there is no mistake as to its nature and meaning. It was High Treason against Cæsar—the most awful crime known to Roman law. This was the charge brought by the priests of the Sanhedrin against the Nazarene. What then was the law of Rome in relation to the crime of high treason? The older Roman law, *crimen perduellionis*, applied chiefly to offenses committed in the military service. Deserters from the army were regarded as traitors and punished as public enemies either by death or interdiction of fire and water. Later Roman law broadened the definition of treason until it comprehended any offense against the Roman Commonwealth that affected the dignity and security of the Roman people. Ulpian, defining treason, says: "*Majestatis crimen illud est quod adversus populum Romanum vel adversus securitatem ejus committitur.*"[41] Cicero very admirably describes the same crime as: "*Majestatem minuere est de dignitate aut amplitudine aut potestate populi aut eorum quibus populus potestatem dedit aliquid derogare.*"[42] The substance of both these definitions is this: Treason is an insult to the dignity or an attack upon the sovereignty and security of the Roman State. From time to time, various laws were passed to define this crime and to provide penalties for its commission. Chief among these were the *lex Julia Majestatis*, 48 B.C. Other laws of an earlier date were the *lex Cornelia*, 81 B.C.; *lex Varia*, 92 B.C.; and the *lex Appuleia*, 100 B.C. The *lex Julia* was in existence at the time of Christ, and was the basis of the Roman law of treason until the closing years of the empire. One of its provisions was that every accusation of treason against a Roman citizen should be made by a written libel. But it is not probable that provincials were entitled to the benefit of this provision; and it was not therefore an infraction of the law that the priests and Pilate failed to present a written charge against Jesus.

TIBERIUS CÆSAR (ANTIQUE SCULPTURE)

In studying the trial of Jesus and the charge brought against Him, the reader should constantly remind himself that the crucifixion took place during the reign of Tiberius Cæsar, a morbid and capricious tyrant, whose fretful and suspicious temper would kindle into fire at the slightest suggestion of treason in any quarter. Tacitus records fifty-two cases of prosecution for treason during his reign. The enormous development of the law of *majestas* at this time gave rise to a class of professional informers, *delatores*, whose infamous activity against private citizens helped to blacken the name of Tiberius. The most harmless acts were at times construed into an affront to the majesty or into an assault upon the safety of this miserable despot. Cotta Messalinus was prosecuted for treason because it was alleged "that he had given Caligula the nickname of Caia, as contaminated by incest"; and again on another charge that he had styled a banquet among the priests on the birthday of Augusta, a "funeral supper"; and again on another charge that, while complaining of the influence of Manius Lepidus and Lucius Arruntius, with whom he had had trouble in court, he had said that "they indeed will be supported by the senate, but I by my little Tiberius."[43]

Manercus Scaurus was prosecuted for treason because he wrote a tragedy in which were certain lines that might be made to apply in an uncomplimentary manner to Tiberius. We are told by Dio that this tragedy was founded on the story of Atreus; and that Tiberius, believing himself referred to, said, "Since he makes me another Atreus, I will make him an Ajax," meaning that he would compel him to destroy himself.[44]

"Nor," says Tacitus, "were even women exempt from danger. With designs to usurp the government they could not be charged; their tears are therefore made treason; and Vitia, mother to Fusius Geminus, once consul, was executed in her old age for bewailing the death of her son."[45]

An anecdote taken from Seneca but related in Tacitus, illustrates the pernicious activity of the political informers of this age. At a banquet in Rome, one of the guests wore the image of Tiberius on his ring. His slave, seeing his master intoxicated, took the ring off his finger. An informer noticed the act, and, later in the evening, insisted that the owner, to show his contempt of Tiberius, was sitting upon the figure of the emperor. Whereupon he began to draw up an accusation for high treason and was getting ready to have it attested by subscribing witnesses, when the slave took the ring from his own pocket, and thus demonstrated to the whole company that he had had it in his possession all the time. These instances fully serve to illustrate the political tone and temper of the age that witnessed the trial and crucifixion of Jesus. They also suggest the exceedingly delicate and painful position of Pilate when sitting in judgment upon the life of a subject of Tiberius who claimed to be a king.

It is deemed entirely appropriate, in this place, to discuss a peculiar phase of the law of treason in its relationship to the trial of Jesus. It is easily demonstrable that the teachings of Christ were treasonable under Roman public law. An essential and dominating principle of that law was that the imperial State had the right to regulate and control the private consciences of men in religious matters. It was held to be an attribute of the sovereignty of Rome that she had the right to create or destroy religions. And the theory of the Roman constitution was that the exercise of this right was not a religious but a governmental function. The modern doctrine of the separation of Church and State had no place in Roman politics at the time of Christ. Tiberius Cæsar, at the beginning of his reign, definitely adopted the principle of a state religion, and as Pontifex Maximus, was bound to protect the ancient Roman worship as a matter of official duty.

Roman treatment of foreign religions, from first to last, is a most interesting and fascinating study. Polytheistic above all other nations, the general policy of the Roman empire was one of toleration. Indeed she not only tolerated but adopted and absorbed foreign worships into her own. The Roman religion was a composite of nearly all the religions of the earth. It was thus natural that the imperial State should be indulgent in religious matters, since warfare upon foreign faiths would have been an assault upon integral parts of her own sacred system. It is historically true that attempts were made from time to time by patriotic Romans to preserve the old Latin faith in its original purity from foreign invasion. The introduction of Greek gods was at first vigorously opposed, but the exquisite beauty of Greek sculpture, the irresistible influence of Greek literature, and the overwhelming fascination of Greek myths, finally destroyed this opposition, and placed Apollo and Æsculapius in the Roman pantheon beside Jupiter and Minerva.

At another time the senate declared war on the Egyptian worship which was gradually making its way into Rome. It had the images of Isis and Serapis thrown down; but the people set them up again. It decreed that the temples to these deities should be destroyed, but not a single workman would lay hands upon them. Æmilius Paulus, the consul, was himself forced to seize an ax and break in the doors of the temple. In spite of this, the worship of Isis and Serapis was soon again practiced unrestrained at Rome.[46]

It is further true that Rome showed not only intolerance but mortal antagonism to Druidism, which was completely annihilated during the reign of the Emperor Claudius.

A decree of the Roman senate, during the reign of Tiberius, ordered four thousand freemen charged with Egyptian and Jewish superstitions out to Sardinia to fight against and be destroyed by the banditti there, unless they saw fit to renounce these superstitions within a given time.[47]

But it must be remembered that these are exceptional cases of intolerance revealed by Roman history. The general policy of the empire, on the other hand, was of extreme tolerance and liberality. The keynote of this policy was that all religions would be tolerated that consented to live side by side and in peace with all other religions. There was but one restriction upon and limitation of this principle, that foreign religions would be tolerated only in their local seats, or, at most, among the races in which such religions were native. The fact that the worship of Serapis was left undisturbed on the banks of the Nile, did not mean that the same worship would be tolerated on the banks of the Tiber. An express authorization by Rome was necessary for this purpose. Said authorization made said worship a *religio licita*. And the peregrini, or foreigners in Rome, were thus permitted to erect their own altars, and to assemble for the purpose of worshiping their own gods which they had brought with them. The reverse side of this general principle of religious tolerance shows that Roman citizens were not only permitted but required to carry the Roman faith with them throughout the world. Upon them, the Roman state religion was absolutely binding; and for all the balance of the world it was the dominant cult. "The provinces," says Renan, "were entirely free to adhere to their own rights, on the sole condition of not interfering with those of others." "Such toleration or indifference, however," says Döllinger, "found its own limits at once whenever the doctrine taught had a practical bearing on society, interfered with the worship of the state gods, or confronted their worship with one of its own; as well as when a strange god and *cultus* assumed a hostile attitude toward Roman gods, could be brought into no affinity or corporate relation with them, and would not bend to the supremacy of Jupiter Capitolinus."

Now, the principles declared by Renan and Döllinger are fundamental and pointed in the matter of the relationship between the teachings of Jesus and the theory of treason under Roman law. These principles were essential elements of Roman public law, and an attempt to destroy them was an act of treason under the definitions of both Ulpian and Cicero. The Roman constitution required that a foreign religion, as a condition of its very existence, should live in peace with its neighbors; that it should not make war upon or seek to destroy other religions; and that it should acknowledge the dominance and superior character of the imperial religion. All these things Jesus refused to do, as did his followers after Him. The Jews, it is true, had done the same thing, but their nationality and lack of aggressiveness saved them until the destruction of Jerusalem. But Christianity was essentially aggressive and proselytizing. It sought to supplant and destroy all other religions. No compromises were proposed, no treaties concluded. The followers of the Nazarene raised a black flag against paganism and every heathen god. Their strange faith not only defied all other religions, but mocked all earthly government not built upon it. Their propaganda was nothing less than a challenge to the Roman empire in the affairs of both law and religion. Here was a faith which claimed to be the only true religion; that proclaimed a monotheistic message which was death to polytheism; and that refused to be confined within local limits. Here was a religion that scorned an authorization from Rome to worship its god and prophet; a religion that demanded acceptance and obedience from all the world—from Roman and Greek, as well as Jew and Egyptian. This scorn and this demand were an affront to the dignity and a challenge to the laws of the Roman Commonwealth. Such conduct was treason against the constitution of the empire.

"The substance of what the Romans did," says Sir James Fitz-James Stephen, "was to treat Christianity by fits and starts as a crime."[48] But why a crime? Because the Roman religion, built upon polytheism, was an integral and inseparable part of the Roman State, and whatever menaced the life of the one, threatened the existence of the other. The Romans regarded their religion as "an engine of state which could not be shaken without the utmost danger to their civil government." Cicero further says: "The institutions of the fathers must be defended; it is the part of wisdom to hold fast the sacred rites and ceremonies."[49] Roman statesmen were fully aware of the truthfulness of the statement of a modern writer that, "wherever the religion of any state falls into disregard and contempt it is impossible for that state to subsist long." Now, Christianity was monotheistic, and threatened destruction to polytheism everywhere. And the Romans treated it as a crime because it was regarded as a form of seditious atheism whose teachings and principles were destructive of the established order of things. The Roman conception of the nature of the crime committed by an attack upon the national religion is well illustrated by the following sentence from Döllinger: "If an opinion unfavorable to the apotheosis of any member of the imperial dynasty happened to be dropped, it was dangerous in itself as falling within the purview of the law of high treason; and so it fell out in the case of Thrasea Pætus, who refused to believe in the deification of Poppæa." If it was high treason to refuse to believe in the deification of an emperor or an empress, what other crime could be imputed to him whose design was to destroy an entire religious system, and to pile all the gods and goddesses—Juno and Poppæa, Jupiter and Augustus—in common ruin?

From the foregoing, it may be readily seen that it is impossible to appreciate the legal aspects of the trial of Jesus before Pilate, unless it is constantly kept in mind that the Roman constitution, which was binding upon the whole empire, reserved to the state the right to permit or forbid the existence of new religious faiths and the exercise of rights of conscience in religious matters. Rome was perfectly willing to tolerate all religions as long as they were peaceful and passive in their relations with other religions. But when a new and aggressive faith appeared upon the scene, proclaiming the strange dogma that there was but one name under heaven whereby men might be saved, and demanding that every knee bow at the mention of that name, and threatening damnation upon all who refused, the majesty of Roman law felt itself insulted and outraged; and persecution, torture, and death were the inevitable result. The best and wisest of the Roman emperors, Trajan and the Antonines, devoted to the ax or condemned to crucifixion the early Christians, not because Christianity was spiritually false, but because it was aggressive and intolerant, and they believed its destruction necessary to the maintenance of the supremacy and sovereignty of the Roman State.

An interesting correspondence between Pliny and Trajan, while the former was governor of Bithynia, reveals the Roman conception of and attitude toward Christianity. Pliny wrote to Trajan: "In the meanwhile, the method I have observed toward those who have been brought before me as Christians is this: I asked them whether they were Christians; if they admitted it, I repeated the question twice, and threatened them with punishment; if they persisted, I ordered them to be at once punished, for I was persuaded, whatever the nature of their opinions might be, a contumacious and inflexible obstinacy certainly deserved correction. There were others also brought before me possessed with the same infatuation, but being Roman citizens, I directed them to be sent to Rome."

To this, Trajan replied: "You have adopted the right course, my dearest Secundus, in investigating the charges against the Christians who were brought before you. It is not possible to lay down any general rule for all such cases. Do not go out of your way to look for them. If, indeed, they should be brought before you, and the crime is proved, they must be punished; with the restriction, however, that where the party denies he is a Christian, and shall make it evident he is not, by invoking our gods, let him (notwithstanding any former suspicion) be pardoned upon his repentance."[50] Here the magnanimous Trajan called Christianity a crime, and this was the popular Roman conception of it during the first two centuries of its existence.

Now, it is true that Christianity was not on trial before Pilate; but the Author of Christianity was. And the same legal principles were extant and applicable that afterwards brought the Roman State and the followers of the Nazarene into mortal conflict. For the prisoner who now stood before the procurator to answer the charge of high treason asserted substantially the same claims and proclaimed the same doctrines that afterwards caused Rome to devote His adherents to flames and to wild beasts in the amphitheater. The record does not disclose that Pilate became fully acquainted at the trial of Jesus with His claims and doctrines. On the other hand, it is clear that he became convinced that the claim of Jesus to be "Christ a King" was not a pretension to earthly sovereignty. But, nevertheless, whatever might have been the information or the notions of the deputy of Tiberius, the teachings of Jesus were inconsistent and incompatible with the public law of the Roman State. Pilate was not necessarily called upon to enforce this law, since it was frequently the duty of Roman governors, as intimated by Trajan in his letter to Pliny, to exercise leniency in dealing with religious delinquents.

To summarize, then: it may be said that the Roman law applicable to the trial of Jesus was the *lex Julia Majestatis*, interpreted either in the light of claims to actual kingship made by Jesus, or to kingship of a religious realm whose character and existence were a menace to the religion and laws of Rome. In the light of the evidence adduced at the hearing before Pilate, these legal principles become mere abstract propositions, since there seems to have been neither necessity nor attempt to enforce them; but they were in existence, nevertheless, and were directly applicable to the trial of Jesus.

PONTIUS PILATE (MUNKACSY)

CHAPTER VII

PONTIUS PILATE

HIS Name.—The prænomen or first name of Pilate is not known. Rosadi calls him Lucius, but upon what authority is not stated. His nomen or family name indicates that he was connected either by descent or by adoption with the gens of the Pontii, a tribe first made famous in Roman history in the person and achievements of C. Pontius Telesinus, the great Samnite general. A German legend, however, offers another explanation. According to this story, Pilate was the natural son of Tyrus, King of Mayence. His father sent him to Rome as a hostage, and there he was guilty of murder. Afterwards he was sent to Pontus, where he distinguished himself by subduing certain barbarian tribes. In recognition of his services, it is said, he received the name Pontius. But this account is a pure fabrication. It is possible that it was invented by the 22d legion, which was assigned to Palestine at the time of the destruction of Jerusalem, and was afterwards stationed at Mayence. The soldiers of this legion might have been "either the bearers of this tradition or the inventors of the fable."

It is historically almost certain that Pilate was a native of Seville, one of the cities of Bætic Spain that enjoyed rights of Roman citizenship. In the war of annihilation waged by Agrippa against the Cantabrians, the father of Pilate, Marcus Pontius, acquired fame as a general on the side of Rome. He seems to have been a renegade to the cause of the Spaniards, his countrymen. And when Spain had been conquered by Rome, as a reward for service, and as a mark of distinction, he received the pilum (javelin), and from this fact his family took the name of Pilati. This is the common explanation of the origin of the cognomen Pilatus.

Others have sought to derive the word Pilate from *pileatus*, which, among the Romans, was the cap worn as a badge of servitude by manumitted slaves. This derivation would make Pontius Pilate a *libertus*, or the descendant of one.

Of his youth, very little is known. But it is believed that, after leaving Spain, he entered the suite of Germanicus on the Rhine and served through the German campaigns; and that, when peace was concluded, he went to Rome in search of fortune and in pursuit of pleasure.

His Marriage.—Soon after his arrival in Rome, Pilate was married to Claudia, the youngest daughter of Julia, the daughter of Augustus. Julia was a woman of the most dissolute and reckless habits. According to Suetonius, nothing so embittered the life of the Roman emperor as the shameful conduct of the mother of the wife of the procurator of Judea. He had reared her with the utmost care, had accustomed her to domestic employments such as knitting and spinning, and had sought to inculcate principles of purity and nobility of soul by requiring her to speak and act openly before the family, that everything which was said and done might be put down in a diary. His guardianship of the attentions paid her by young men was so strict that he once wrote a letter to Lucius Vinicius, a handsome young man of good family, in which he said: "You have not behaved very modestly, in making a visit to my daughter at Baiæ." Notwithstanding this good training, Julia became one of the lewdest and coarsest women in Rome. Augustus married her first to Marcellus; then, after the death of Marcellus, to Marcus Agrippa; and, finally, to Tiberius. But in spite of the noble matches that had been made for her, her lewdness and debaucheries became so notorious that Augustus was compelled to banish her from Rome. It is said that he was so much ashamed of her infamous conduct that for a long time he avoided all company, and even had thoughts of putting her to death. His sorrow and humiliation are shown from the circumstance that when one Phœbe, a freedwoman and confidante of hers, hanged herself about the time the decree of banishment was passed by the senate, he said: "I had rather be the father of Phœbe than of Julia." And whenever the name of Julia was mentioned to him, during her exile, Augustus was wont to exclaim: "Would I were wifeless, or had childless died."[51]

Such was the character of Julia, mother-in-law of Pilate. In exile, she bore Claudia to a Roman knight. In her fifteenth year, the young girl met the Spaniard in Rome and was courted by him. Nothing better illustrates the character of Pilate than his union with this woman with whose origin and bringing up he was well acquainted. It was a servile and lustful rather than a noble and affectionate eye which he cast upon her. Having won the favor of Tiberius and the consent of Claudia, the marriage was consummated. After the nuptial rites, tradition has it that Pilate desired to follow the bride in the imperial litter; but Tiberius, who had acted as one of the twelve witnesses required by the law, forced him back, and drawing a paper from his bosom, handed it to him and passed on. This paper contained his commission as procurator of Judea; and the real object of the suit paid to Claudia was attained.

Pilate proceeded at once to Cæsarea, the headquarters of the government of his province. His wife, who had been left behind, joined him afterwards. Cæsar's permission to do this was a most gracious concession, as it was not generally allowed that governors of provinces should take their wives with them. At first it was positively forbidden. But afterwards a *senatus consult*, which is embodied in the Justinian text, declared it better that the wives of proconsuls and procurators should not go with them, but ordaining that said officials might take their wives with them provided they made themselves personally responsible for any transgressions on their part. Notwithstanding the numerous restrictions of Roman law and custom, it is very evident that the wives of Roman officers frequently accompanied them to the provinces. From Tacitus we learn that at the time of the death of Augustus, Germanicus had his wife Agrippina with him in Germany; and afterwards, in the beginning of the reign of Tiberius, she was also with him in the East. Piso, the præfect of Syria, took his wife with him at the same time. These facts are historical corroborations of the Gospel accounts of the presence of Claudia in Jerusalem at the time of the crucifixion and of her warning dream to Pilate concerning the fate of the Master.

His Procuratorship.—Pontius Pilate was the sixth procurator of Judea. Sabinus, Coponius, Ambivus, Rufus, and Gratus had preceded him in the government of the province. Pilate's connection with the trial and crucifixion of Jesus will be dealt with in succeeding chapters of this volume. Only the chief acts of his public administration, in a purely political capacity, will be noticed here. One of the first of these acts serves well to illustrate the reckless and tactless character of the man. His predecessors in office had exercised great care in the matter of the religious prejudices of the Jews. They had studiously avoided exhibiting flags and other emblems bearing images of the emperor that might offend the sacred sentiments of the native population. Even Vitellius, the legate of Syria, when he was marching against the Arabian king Aretas, ordered his troops not to carry their standards into Jewish territory, but to march around it. Pilate, on the other hand, in defiance of precedent and policy, caused the garrison soldiers of Jerusalem to enter the city by night carrying aloft their standards, blazoned with the images of Tiberius. The news of this outrage threw the Jews into wild excitement. The people in great numbers flocked down to Cæsarea, where Pilate was still stopping, and begged him to remove the standards. Pilate refused; and for five days the discussion went on. At last he became enraged, summoned the people into the race course, had them surrounded by a detachment of soldiers, and served notice upon them that he would have them put to death if they did not become quiet and disperse. But, not in the least dismayed, they threw themselves upon the ground, laid bare their necks, and, in their turn, served notice upon Pilate that they, the children of Abraham, would rather die, and that they would die, before they would willingly see the Holy City defiled. The result was that Pilate finally yielded, and had the standards and images withdrawn from Jerusalem. Such was the Roman procurator and such the people with whom he had to deal. Thus the very first act of his procuratorship was a blunder which embarrassed his whole subsequent career.

A new storm burst forth when, on another occasion, Pilate appropriated funds from the Corban or sacred treasury to complete an aqueduct for bringing water to Jerusalem from the "Pools of Solomon." This was certainly a most useful enterprise; and, ordinarily, would speak well for the statesmanship and administrative ability of the procurator. But, in this instance, it was only another exhibition of tactless behavior in dealing with a stubborn and peculiar people. The Jews had a very great reverence for whatever was set apart for the Corban, and they considered it a form of awful impiety to devote its funds to secular purposes. Pilate, we must assume, was well acquainted with their religious scruples in this regard, and his open defiance of their prejudices was an illustration not of courage, but of weakness in administrative matters. Moreover, his final conduct in the matter of the aqueduct revealed a malignant quality in the temper of the man. On one occasion when he was getting ready to go to Jerusalem to supervise the building of this work, he learned that the people would again importune him, as in the case of the standards and the images. He then deliberately caused some of his soldiers to be disguised as Jewish citizens, had them armed with clubs and daggers, which they carried concealed beneath their upper garments; and when the multitude approached him to make complaints and to present their petitions, he gave a preconcerted signal, at which the assassins beat down and cut to pieces great numbers of the helpless crowds. Pilate was victorious in this matter; for the opposition to the building of the aqueduct was thus crushed in a most bloody manner. But hatred against Pilate was stirred up afresh and intensified in the hearts of the Jews.

A third act of defiance of the religious prejudices of the inhabitants of Jerusalem illustrates not only the obstinacy but the stupidity as well of the deputy of Cæsar in Judea. In the face of his previous experiences, he insisted on hanging up in Herod's palace certain gilt shields dedicated to Tiberius. The Jews remonstrated with him in vain for this new outrage upon their national feelings. They were all the more indignant because they believed that he had done it, "less for the honor of Tiberius than for the annoyance of the Jewish people." Upon the refusal of Pilate to remove the shields, a petition signed by the leading men of the nation, among whom were the four sons of Herod, was addressed to the emperor, asking for the removal of the offensive decorations. Tiberius granted the request and the shields were taken from Jerusalem and deposited in the temple of Augustus at Cæsarea— "And thus were preserved both the honor of the emperor and the ancient customs of the city."[52]

The instances above cited are recounted in the works of Josephus[53] and Philo. But the New Testament also contains intimations that Pilate was a cruel and reckless governor in his dealings with the Jews. According to St. Luke xiii. 1: "There were present at that season some that told him of the Galileans, whose blood Pilate had mingled with their sacrifices." Nothing definite is known of this incident mentioned by the Evangelist. But it probably refers to the fact that Pilate had put to the sword a number of Galileans while they were offering their sacrifices at Jerusalem.

His Character.—The estimates of the character of Pilate are as varied as the races and creeds of men. Both Josephus and Philo have handed down to posterity a very ugly picture of the sixth Roman procurator of Judea. Philo charges him with "corruptibility, violence, robberies, ill-treatment of the people, grievances, continuous executions without even the form of a trial, endless and intolerable cruelties." If we were to stop with this, we should have a very poor impression of the deputy of Tiberius; and, indeed at best, we can never either admire or love him. But there is a tender and even pathetic side to the character of Pilate, which is revealed to us by the Evangelists of the New Testament. The pure-hearted, gentle-minded authors of the Gospels, in whose writings there is not even a tinge of bitterness or resentment, have restored "for us the man within the governor, with a delicacy, and even tenderness, which make the accusing portrait of Philo and Josephus look like a hard, revengeful daub." Instead of painting him as a monster, they have linked conscience to his character and placed mercy in his heart, by their accounts of his repeated attempts to release Jesus. The extreme of pity and of pathos, derived from these exquisitely merciful side touches of the gentle biographers of the Christ, is manifested in the opinion of Tertullian that Pilate was virtually a Christian at heart.[54]

A further manifestation is the fact that the Abyssinian Church of Christians has canonized him and placed his name in the calendar on June 25th.

A still further revelation of this spirit of regarding Pilate merely as a sacred instrument in the hands of God is shown by the Apocryphal Gospel of Nicodemus which speaks of him as "uncircumcised in flesh but circumcised in heart."

Renan has called him a good administrator, and has sought to condone his brutal treatment of the Jews by pointing to the necessity of vigorous action in dealing with a turbulent and fanatical race. But the combined efforts of both sacred and secular apologists are still not sufficient to save the name of Pilate from the scorn and reprobation of mankind. That he was not a bad man in the worst sense of the term is manifest from the teachings of the Gospel narratives. To believe that he was wholly without conscience is to repudiate the revelations of these sacred writings. Of wanton cruelty and gratuitous wickedness, he was perhaps incapable. But the circumstances of his birth and breeding; his descent from a renegade father; his adventurous life in the army of Germanicus; his contact with and absorption of the skepticism and debauchery of Rome; his marriage to a woman of questionable virtue whose mother was notoriously coarse and lewd—all these things had given coloring to the character of Pilate and had stricken with inward paralysis the moral fiber of his manhood. And now, in the supreme moment of his life and of history, from his nerveless grasp fell the reins of fate and fortune that destiny had placed within his hands. Called upon to play a leading rôle in the mighty drama of the universe, his craven cowardice made him a pitiable and contemptible figure. A splendid example this, the conduct of Pilate, for the youth of the world, not to imitate but to shun! Let the young men of America and of all the earth remember that a crisis is allotted to every life. It may be a great one or a small one, but it will come either invited or unbidden. The sublime courage of the soul does not avoid, but seeks this crisis. The bravest and most holy aspirations leap at times like angels from the temple of the brain to the highest heaven. Never a physician who does not long for the skill that discovers a remedy for disease and that will make him a Pasteur or a Koch; never a poet that does not beseech the muse to inspire him to write a Hamlet or a Faust; never a general of armies who would not fight an Austerlitz battle. Every ambitious soul fervently prays for strength, when the great crisis comes, to swing the hammer of the Cyclop with the arm of the Titan. Let the young aspirant for the glories of the earth and the rewards of heaven remember that youth is the time for the formation of that courage and the gathering of that strength of which victory is born. Let him remember that if he degrades his physical and spiritual manhood in early life, the coming of the great day of his existence will make him another Pilate—cringing, crouching, and contemptible.

The true character of the Roman judge of Jesus is thus very tersely given by Dr. Ellicott: "A thorough and complete type of the later Roman man of the world: stern, but not relentless; shrewd and worldworn, prompt and practical, haughtily just, and yet, as the early writers correctly perceived, self-seeking and cowardly; able to perceive what was right, but without moral strength to follow it out."[55]

His End.—Pilate's utter recklessness was the final cause of his undoing. It was an old belief among the Samaritans that Moses buried the sacred vessels of the temple on Mt. Gerizim. An impostor, a sort of pseudo-prophet, promised the people that if they would assemble on the top of the mountain, he would unearth the holy utensils in their presence. The simple-minded Samaritans assembled in great numbers at the foot of the Mount, and there preparing to ascend, when Pilate on the pretense that they were revolutionists, intercepted them with a strong force of horse and foot. Those who did not immediately submit were either slain or put to flight. The most notable among the captives were put to death. The Samaritans at once complained to Vitellius, the legate in Syria at that time. Vitellius at once turned over the administration of Judea to Marcellus and ordered Pilate to leave for Rome in order to give an account to the emperor of the charges brought against him by the Jews.[56] Before he arrived in Italy, Tiberius had died; but Pilate never returned to the province over which he had ruled during ten bloody and eventful years.

"*Paradosis Pilati.*"—The death of Pilate is clouded in mystery and legend. Where and when he died is not known. Two apocryphal accounts are interesting, though false and ridiculous. According to one legend, the "Paradosis Pilati," the emperor Tiberius, startled and terrified at the universal darkness that had fallen on the Roman world at the hour of the crucifixion, summoned Pilate to Rome to answer for having caused it. He was found guilty and condemned to death; but before he was executed, he prayed to Jesus that he might not be destroyed in eternity with the wicked Jews, and pleaded ignorance as an excuse for having delivered the Christ to be crucified. A voice from heaven answered his prayer, and assured him that all generations would call him blessed, and that he should be a witness for Christ at his second coming to judge the Twelve Tribes of Israel. He was then executed; an angel, according to the legend, received his head; and his wife died from joy and was buried with him.

"*Mors Pilati.*"—According to another legend, the "Mors Pilati," Tiberius had heard of the miracles of healing wrought by Jesus in Judea. He ordered Pilate to conduct to Rome the man possessed of such divine power. But Pilate was forced to confess that he had crucified the miracle worker. The messenger sent by Tiberius met Veronica who gave him the cloth that had received the impress of the divine features. This was taken to Rome and given to the emperor, who was restored to health by it. Pilate was summoned immediately to stand trial for the execution of the Christ. He presented himself wearing the holy tunic. This acted as a charm upon the emperor, who temporarily relented. After a time, however, Pilate was thrown into prison, where he committed suicide. His body was thrown into the Tiber. Storms and tempests immediately followed, and the Romans were compelled to take out the corpse and send it to Vienne, where it was cast into the Rhone. But as the storms and tempests came again, the body was again removed and sent to Lucerne, where it was sunk in a deep pool, surrounded by mountains on all sides. Even then, it is said, the water of the pool began to boil and bubble strangely.

This tradition must have had its origin in an early attempt to connect the name of Pilate with Mt. Pilatus that overlooks Lake Lucerne. Another legend connected with this mountain is that Pilate sought to find an asylum from his sorrows in its shadows and recesses; that, after spending years in remorse and despair, wandering up and down its sides, he plunged into the dismal lake which occupies its summit. In times past, popular superstition was wont to relate how "a form is often seen to emerge from the gloomy waters, and go through the action of washing his hands; and when he does so, dark clouds of mist gather first round the bosom of the Infernal Lake (such as it has been styled of old) and then wrapping the whole upper part of the mountain in darkness, presage a tempest or hurricane which is sure to follow in a short space."[57]

The superstitious Swiss believed for many centuries that if a stone were thrown into the lake a violent storm would follow. For many years no one was permitted to visit it without special authority from the officers of Lucerne. The neighboring shepherds bound themselves by a solemn oath, which they renewed annually, never to guide a stranger to it.[58] The strange spell was broken, however, and the legend exploded in 1584, when Johannes Müller, curé of Lucerne, was bold enough to throw stones into the lake, and to stand by complacently to await the consequences.[59]

CHAPTER VIII

JESUS BEFORE PILATE

AT the close of their trial, according to Matthew[60] and Mark,[61] the high priest and the entire Sanhedrin led Jesus away to the tribunal of the Roman governor. It was early morning, probably between six and seven o'clock, when the accusing multitude moved from the judgment seat of Caiaphas to the Prætorium of Pilate. Oriental labor anticipates the day because of the excessive heat of noon; and, at daybreak, Eastern life is all astir. To accommodate the people and to enjoy the repose of midday, Roman governors, Suetonius tells us, mounted the *bema* at sunrise. The location of the judgment hall of Pilate in Jerusalem is not certainly known. It may have been in the Castle of Antonia, a frowning fortress that overlooked the Temple and its courts. Much more probably, however, it was the magnificent palace of Herod, situated in the northwest quarter of the city. This probability is heightened by the fact that it was a custom born of both pride and pleasure, for Roman procurators and proconsuls to occupy the splendid edifices of the local kings. The Roman proprætor of Sicily dwelt in the Castle of King Hiero; and it is reasonable to suppose that Pilate would have passed his time while at Jerusalem in the palace of Herod. This building was frequently called the "King's Castle," sometimes was styled the "Prætorium," and was often given the mixed name of "Herod's Prætorium." But, by whatever name known, it was of gorgeous architecture and magnificent proportions. Keim describes it as "a tyrant's stronghold and in part a fairy pleasure-house." A wall thirty cubits high completely encircled the buildings of the palace. Beautiful white towers crowned this wall at regular intervals. Three of these were named in honor of Mariamne, the wife; Hippicus, the friend; and Phasælus, the brother of the king. Within the inclosure of the wall, a small army could have been garrisoned. The floors and ceilings of the palace were decorated and adorned with the finest woods and precious stones. Projecting from the main building were two colossal marble wings, named for two Roman imperial friends, the Cæsareum and the Ægrippeum. To a person standing in one of the towers, a magnificent prospect opened to the view. Surrounding the castle walls were beautiful green parks, intercepted with broad walks and deep canals. Here and there splashing fountains gushed from brazen mouths. A hundred dovecots, scattered about the basins and filled with cooing and fluttering inmates, lent charm and animation to the scene. And to crown the whole, was the splendid panorama of Jerusalem stretching away among the hills and valleys. Such was the residence of the Roman knight who at this time ruled Judea. And yet, with all its regal splendor and magnificence, he inhabited it only a few weeks in each year. The Jewish metropolis had no fascination whatever for the tastes and accomplishments of Pilate. "The saddest region in the world," says Renan, who had been imbued, from long residence there, with its melancholy character, "is perhaps that which surrounds Jerusalem." "To the Spaniard," says Rosadi, "who had come to Jerusalem, by way of Rome, and who was also of courtly origin, there could have been nothing pleasing in the parched, arid and colorless nature of Palestine, much less in the humble, mystic, out-at-elbows existence of its people. Their superstition, which would have nothing of Roman idolatry, which was their sole belief, their all, appeared to him a reasonable explanation, and a legitimate one, of their disdain and opposition. He therefore detested the Jews, and his detestation was fully reciprocated." It is not surprising, then, that he preferred to reside at Cæsarea by the sea where were present Roman modes of thought and forms of life. He visited Jerusalem as a matter of official duty, "during the festivals, and particularly at Easter with its dreaded inspirations of the Jewish longing for freedom, which the festival, the air of spring and the great rendezvous of the nation, charmed into activity." In keeping with this custom, Pilate was now in the Jewish Capital on the occasion of the feast of the Passover.

Having condemned Him to death themselves, the Sanhedrin judges were compelled to lead Jesus away to the Prætorium of the Roman governor to see what he had to say about the case; whether he would reverse or affirm the condemnation which they had pronounced. Between dawn and sunrise, they were at the palace gates. Here they were compelled to halt. The Passover had commenced, and to enter the procurator's palace at such a time was to incur Levitic contamination. A dozen judicial blunders had marked the proceedings of their own trial in the palace of Caiaphas. And yet they hesitated to violate a purely ritual regulation in the matter of ceremonial defilement. This regulation was a prohibition to eat fermented food during the Passover Feast, and was sacred to the memory of the great deliverance from Egyptian bondage when the children of Israel, in their flight, had no time to ferment their dough and were compelled to consume it before it had been leavened. Their purposes and scruples were announced to Pilate; and, in a spirit of gracious and politic condescension, he removed the difficulty by coming out to meet them. But this action was really neither an inconvenience nor a condescension; for it was usual to conduct Roman trials in the open air. Publicity was characteristic of all Roman criminal proceedings. And, in obedience to this principle, we find that the proconsul of Achaia at Corinth, the city magistrates in Macedonia, and the procurators at Cæsarea and Jerusalem, erected their tribunals in the most conspicuous public places, such as the market, the race course, and even upon the open highway.[62] An example directly in point is, moreover, that of the procurator Florus who caused his judgment seat to be raised in front of the palace of Herod, A.D. 66, and, enthroned thereon, received the great men of Jerusalem who came to see him and gathered around his tribunal. To the same place, according to Josephus, the Jewish queen Bernice came barefoot and suppliant to ask favors of Florus.[63] The act of Pilate in emerging from the palace to meet the Jews was, therefore, in exact compliance with Roman custom. His judgment seat was doubtless raised immediately in front of the entrance and between the great marble wings of the palace. Pilate's tribune or *bema* was located in this space on the elevated spot called Gabaatha, an Aramaic word signifying an eminence, a "hump." The same place in Greek was called Lithostroton, and signified "The Pavement," because it was laid with Roman marble mosaic. The location on an eminence was in accordance with a maxim of Roman law that all criminal trials should be directed from a raised tribunal where everybody could see and understand what was being said and done. The ivory curule chair of the procurator, or perhaps the ancient golden royal chair of Archelaus was placed upon the tessellated pavement and was designed for the use of the governor. As a general thing, there was sitting room on the tribunal for the assessors, the accusers and the accused. But such courtesies and conveniences were not extended to the despised subjects of Judea; and Jesus, as well as the members of the Sanhedrin, was compelled to stand. The Latin language was the official tongue of the Roman empire, and was generally used in the administration of justice. But at the trial of Jesus it is believed that the Greek language was the medium of communication. Jesus had doubtless become acquainted with Greek in Galilee and probably replied to Pilate in that tongue. This is the opinion, at least, of both Keim[64] and Geikie.[65] The former asserts that there was no interpreter called at the trial of Christ. It is also reasonably certain that no special orator like Tertullus, who informed the governor against Paul, was present to accuse Jesus.[66] Doubtless Caiaphas the high priest played this important rôle.

When Pilate had mounted the *bema*, and order had been restored, he asked:

"What accusation bring ye against this man?"

This question is keenly suggestive of the presence of a judge and of the beginning of a solemn judicial proceeding. Every word rings with Roman authority and administrative capacity. The suggestion is also prominent that accusation was a more important element in Roman criminal trials than inquisition. This suggestion is reënforced by actual *dictum* from the lips of Pilate's successor in the same place: "It is not the manner of the Romans to deliver any man to die, before that he which is accused have the accusers face to face, and have license to answer for himself concerning the crime laid against him."[67]

The chief priests and scribes sought to evade this question by answering:

"If he were not a malefactor, we would not have delivered him up unto thee."[68]

They meant by this that they desired the procurator to waive his right to retry the case; accept their trial as conclusive; and content himself with the mere execution of the sentence. In this reply of the priests to the initial question of the Roman judge, is also revealed the further question of that conflict of jurisdiction between Jews and Romans that we have already so fully discussed. "If he were not a malefactor, we would not have delivered him up unto thee." These words from the mouths of the priests were intended to convey to the mind of Pilate the Jewish notion that a judgment by the Sanhedrin was all-sufficient; and that they merely needed his countersign to justify execution. But Pilate did not take the hint or view the question in that light. In a tone of contemptuous scorn he simply replied:

"Take ye him, and judge him according to your law."

This answer indicates that Pilate did not, at first, understand the exact nature of the proceedings against Jesus. He evidently did not know that the prisoner had been charged with a capital offense; else he would not have suggested that the Jews take jurisdiction of the matter. This is clearly shown from the further reply of the priestly accusers:

"It is not lawful for us to put any man to death."[69]

The advice of Pilate and the retort of the Jews have been construed in two ways. A certain class of critics have contended that the procurator granted to the Jews in this instance the right to carry out capital punishment, as others have maintained was the case in the execution of Stephen. This construction argues that Pilate knew at once the nature of the accusation.

Another class of writers contend that the governor, by this language, merely proposed to them one of the minor penalties which they were already empowered to execute. The objection to the first interpretation is that the Jews would have been delighted to have such power conferred upon them, and would have exercised it; unless it is true, as has been held, that they were desirous of throwing the odium of Christ's death upon the Romans. The second construction is entirely admissible, because it is consonant with the theory that jurisdiction in capital cases had been withdrawn from the Sanhedrin, but that the trial and punishment of petty offenses still remained with it. A third and more reasonable interpretation still is that when Pilate said, "Take ye him and judge him according to your law," he intended to give expression to the hatred and bitterness of his cynical and sarcastic soul. He despised the Jews most heartily, and he knew that they hated him. He had repeatedly outraged their religious feelings by introducing images and shields into the Holy City. He had devoted the Corban funds to unhallowed purposes, and had mingled the blood of the Galileans with their sacrifices. In short, he had left nothing undone to humiliate and degrade them. Now here was another opportunity. By telling them to judge Jesus according to their own laws, he knew that they must make a reply which would be wounding and galling to their race and national pride. He knew that they would have to confess that sovereignty and nationality were gone from them. Such a confession from them would be music to his ear. The substance of his advice to the Jews was to exercise their rights to a certain point, to the moment of condemnation; but to stop at the place where their sweetest desires would be gratified with the exercise of the rights of sovereignty and nationality.

Modern poetry supports this interpretation of ancient history. "The Merchant of Venice" reveals the same method of heaping ridicule upon a Jew by making him impotent to execute the law. Shylock, the Jew, in contracting a usurious loan, inserted a stipulation that if the debt should not be paid when due, the debtor must allow a pound of flesh to be cut from his body. The debt was not discharged at the maturity of the bond, and Shylock made application to the Doge to have the pound of human flesh delivered to him in accordance with the compact. But Portia, a friend of the debtor, though a woman, assumed the garb and affected the speech of a lawyer in his defense; and, in pleading the case, called tauntingly and exultingly to the Jew:

This bond doth give thee here no jot of blood;
The words expressly are, a pound of flesh:
Take then thy bond, take thou thy pound of flesh;
But, in the cutting it, if thou dost shed
One drop of Christian blood, thy lands and goods
Are by the laws of Venice confiscate
Unto the State of Venice.[70]

But whatever special interpretation may be placed upon the opening words passed between the priestly accusers and the Roman judge, it is clearly evident that the latter did not intend to surrender to the former the right to impose and execute a sentence of death. The substance of Pilate's address to the Jews, when they sought to evade his question concerning the accusation which they had to bring against Jesus, was this: I have asked for a specific charge against the man whom you have brought bound to me. You have given not a direct, but an equivocal answer. I infer that the crime with which you charge him is one against your own laws. With such offenses I do not wish to meddle. Therefore, I say unto you: "Take ye him and judge him according to your law." If I am not to know the specific charge against him, I will not assume cognizance of the case. If the accusation and the facts relied upon to support it are not placed before me, I will not sentence the man to death; and, under the law, you cannot.

The Jews were thus thwarted in their designs. They had hoped to secure a countersign of their own judgment without a retrial by the governor. They now found him in no yielding and accommodating mood. They were thus forced against their will and expectation to formulate specific charges against the prisoner in their midst. The indictment as they presented it, is given in a single verse of St. Luke:

"And they began to accuse him, saying, We found this fellow perverting the nation, and forbidding to give tribute to Cæsar, saying that he himself is Christ, a King."[71]

It is noteworthy that in this general accusation is a radical departure from the charges of the night before. In the passage from the Sanhedrin to the Prætorium, the indictment had completely changed. Jesus had not been condemned on any of the charges recorded in this sentence of St. Luke. He had been convicted on the charge of blasphemy. But before Pilate he is now charged with high treason. To meet the emergency of a change of jurisdiction, the priestly accusers converted the accusation from a religious into a political offense. It may be asked why the Sanhedrists did not maintain the same charges before Pilate that they themselves had considered before their own tribunal. Why did they not lead Jesus into the presence of the Roman magistrate and say: O Governor, we have here a Galilean blasphemer of Jehovah. We want him tried on the charge of blasphemy, convicted and sentenced to death. Why did they not do this? They were evidently too shrewd. Why? Because, in legal parlance, they would have had no standing in court. Why? Because blasphemy was not an offense against Roman law, and Roman judges would generally assume cognizance of no such charges.

The Jews understood perfectly well at the trial before Pilate the principle of Roman procedure so admirably expressed a few years later by Gallio, proconsul of Achaia, and brother of Seneca: "If it were a matter of wrong or wicked lewdness, O ye Jews, reason would that I should bear with you: but if it be a question of words and names, and of your law, look ye to it; for I will be no judge of such matters."[72] This attitude of Roman governors toward offenses of a religious nature perfectly explains the Jewish change of front in the matter of the accusation against Jesus. They merely wanted to get themselves into a Roman court on charges that a Roman judge would consent to try. In the threefold accusation recorded by the third Evangelist, they fully accomplished this result.

The first count in the indictment, that He was perverting the nation, was vague and indefinite, but was undoubtedly against Roman law, because it was in the nature of sedition, which was one of the forms of treason under

Roman jurisprudence. This charge of perverting the nation was in the nature of the revival of the accusation of sedition which they had first brought forward by means of the false witnesses before their own tribunal, and that had been abandoned because of the contradictory testimony of these witnesses.

The second count in the indictment, that He had forbidden to give tribute to Cæsar, was of a more serious nature than the first. A refusal, in modern times, to pay taxes or an attempt to obstruct their collection, is a mild offense compared with a similar act under ancient Roman law. To forbid to pay tribute to Cæsar in Judea was a form of treason, not only because it was an open defiance of the laws of the Roman state, but also because it was a direct denial of Roman sovereignty in Palestine. Such conduct was treason under the definitions of both Ulpian and Cicero. The Jews knew the gravity of the offense when they sought to entrap Jesus in the matter of paying tribute to Cæsar. They believed that any answer to the question that they had asked, would be fatal to Him. If He advised to pay the imperial tribute, He could be charged with being an enemy to His countrymen, the Jews. If He advised not to pay the tribute, He would be charged with being a rebellious subject of Cæsar. His reply disconcerted and bewildered them when He said: "Render therefore unto Cæsar the things which are Cæsar's; and unto God the things that are God's."[73] In this sublime declaration, the Nazarene announced the immortal principle of the separation of church and state, and of religious freedom in all the ages. And when, in the face of His answer, they still charged Him with forbidding to pay tribute to Cæsar, they seem to have been guilty of deliberate falsehood. Keim calls the charge "a very flagrant lie." Both at Capernaum,[74] where Roman taxes were gathered, and at Jerusalem,[75] where religious dues were offered, Jesus seems to have been both a good citizen and a pious Jew. "Jésus bon citoyen" (Jesus a good citizen) is the title of a chapter in the famous work of Bossuet entitled "Politique tirée de l'Ecriture sainte." In it the great French ecclesiastic describes very beautifully the law-abiding qualities of the citizen-prophet of Galilee. In pressing the false charge that he had advised not to pay taxes to Rome, the enemies of Jesus revealed a peculiar and wanton malignity.

The third count in the indictment, that the prisoner had claimed to be "Christ a King," was the last and greatest of the charges. By this He was deliberately accused of high treason against Cæsar, the gravest offense known to Roman law. Such an accusation could not be ignored by Pilate as a loyal deputy of Tiberius. The Roman monarch saw high treason in every word and act that was uncomplimentary to his person or dangerous to his power. Fifty-two prosecutions for treason, says Tacitus, took place during his reign.

The charges of high treason and sedition against Jesus were all the more serious because the Romans believed Palestine to be the hotbed of insurrection and sedition, and the birthplace of pretenders to kingly powers. They had recently had trouble with claimants to thrones, some of them from the lowest and most ignoble ranks. Judas, the son of Hezekiah, whom Herod had caused to be put to death, proclaimed royal intentions, gathered quite a multitude of adherents about him in the neighborhood of Sepphoris in Galilee, raised an insurrection, assaulted and captured the palace of the king at Sepphoris, seized all the weapons that were stored away in it, and armed his followers with them. Josephus does not tell us what became of this royal pretender; but he does say that "he became terrible to all men, by tearing and rending those that came near him."[76]

In the province of Perea, a certain Simon, who was formerly a slave of Herod, collected a band of followers, and had himself proclaimed king by them. He burned down the royal palace at Jericho, after having plundered it. A detachment under the command of the Roman general Gratus made short work of the pretensions of Simon by capturing his adherents and putting him to death.[77]

Again, a certain peasant named Athronges, formerly a shepherd, claimed to be a king, and for a long time, in concert with his four brothers, annoyed the authorities of the country, until the insurrection was finally broken up by Gratus and Ptolemy.[78]

In short, during the life of Jesus, Judea was passing through a period of great religious and political excitement. The Messiah was expected and a king was hoped for; and numerous pretenders appeared from time to time. The Roman governors were constantly on the outlook for acts of sedition and treason. And when the Jews led Jesus into the presence of Pilate and charged Him with claiming to be a king, the recent cases of Judas, Simon, and Athronges must have arisen in his mind, quickened his interest in the pretensions of the prisoner of the Jews, and must have awakened his sense of loyalty as Cæsar's representative. The lowliness of Jesus, being a carpenter, did not greatly allay his fears; for he must have remembered that Simon was once a slave and that Athronges was nothing more than a simple shepherd.

When Pilate had heard the accusations of the Jews, he deliberately arose from his judgment seat, gathered his toga about him, motioned the mob to stand back, and beckoned Jesus to follow him into the palace. St. John alone tells us of this occurrence.[79]

At another time, in the Galilean simplicity and freedom of His nature, the Prophet of Nazareth had spoken with a tinge of censure and sarcasm of the rulers of the Gentiles that lorded it over their subjects,[80] and had declared that "they that wear soft clothing are in kings' houses."[81] Now the lowly Jewish peasant was entering for the first time a palace of one of the rulers of the Gentiles in which were soft raiment and royal purple. The imagination is helpless to picture the historical reflections born of the memories of that hour. A meek and lowly carpenter enters a king's palace on his way to an ignominious death upon the cross; and yet the greatest kings of all the centuries that followed were humble worshipers in their palaces before the cross that had been the instrument of his torture and degradation. Such is the irony of history; such is the mystery of God's providence; such is the mystic ebb and flow of the tides and currents of destiny and fate.

Of the examination of Jesus inside the palace, little is known. Pilate, it seems, brushed the first two charges aside as unworthy of serious consideration; and proceeded at once to examine the prisoner on the charge that he pretended to be a king. "If," Pilate must have said, "the fellow pretends to be a king, as Simon and Athronges did before him; if he says that Judea has a right to have a king other than Cæsar, he is guilty of treason, and it is my solemn duty as deputy of Tiberius to ascertain the fact and have him put to death."

The beginning of the interrogation of Jesus within the palace is reported by all the Evangelists in the same words. Addressing the prisoner, Pilate asked: "Art thou the King of the Jews?" "Jesus answered him, Sayest thou this thing of thyself, or did others tell it thee of me?"[82]

This was a most natural and fitting response of the Nazarene to the Roman. It was necessary first to understand the exact nature of the question before an appropriate answer could be made. Jesus simply wished to know whether the question was asked from a Roman or a Jewish, from a temporal or a spiritual standpoint. If the interrogation was directed from a Roman, a temporal point of view, His answer would be an emphatic negative. If the inquiry had been prompted by the Jews, it was then pregnant with religious meaning, and called for a different reply; one that would at once repudiate pretensions to earthly royalty, and, at the same time, assert His claims to the Messiahship and heavenly sovereignty.

"Pilate answered, Am I a Jew? Thine own nation and the chief priests have delivered thee unto me: What hast thou done?"

To this Jesus replied: "My kingdom is not of this world: if my kingdom were of this world, then would my servants fight, that I should not be delivered to the Jews: but now is my kingdom not from hence."[83]

This reply of the Master is couched in that involved, aphoristic, strangely beautiful style that characterized His speech at critical moments in His career. Its import is clear, though expressed in a double sense: first from the Roman political, and then from the Jewish religious side.

First He answered negatively: "My kingdom is not of this world."

By this He meant that there was no possible rivalry between Him and Cæsar. But, in making this denial, He had used two words of grave import: My Kingdom. He had used one word that struck the ear of Pilate with electric force: the word Kingdom. In the use of that word, according to Pilate's reasoning, Jesus stood self-convicted. For how, thought Pilate, can He pretend to have a Kingdom, unless He pretends to be a king? And then, as if to cow and intimidate the prisoner, as if to avoid an unpleasant issue of the affair, he probably advanced threateningly upon the Christ, and asked the question which the Bible puts in his mouth: "Art thou a king then?"

Rising from the simple dignity of a man to the beauty and glory and grandeur of a God, Jesus used the most wonderful, beautiful, meaningful words in the literature of the earth: "Thou sayest that I am a king. To this end was I born, and for this cause came I into the world, that I should bear witness unto the truth. Everyone that is of the truth heareth my voice."[84]

This language contains a perfectly clear description of the kingdom of Christ and of His title to spiritual sovereignty. His was not an empire of matter, but a realm of truth. His kingdom differed widely from that of Cæsar. Cæsar's empire was over the bodies of men; Christ's over their souls. The strength of Cæsar's kingdom was in citadels, armies, navies, the towering Alps, the all-engirdling seas. The strength of the kingdom of the Christ was and is and will ever be in sentiments, principles, ideas, and the saving power of a divine word. But, as clever and brilliant as he must have been, Pilate could not grasp the true meaning of the words of the Prophet. The spiritual and intellectual grandeur of the Galilean peasant was beyond the reach of the Roman lord and governor. In a cynical and sarcastic mood, Pilate turned to Jesus and asked: "What is truth?"[85]

This pointed question was the legitimate offspring of the soul of Pilate and a natural product of the Roman civilization of his age. It was not asked with any real desire to know the truth; for he turned to leave the palace before an answer could be given. It was simply a blank response born of mental wretchedness and doubt. If prompted by any silent yearning for a knowledge of the truth, his conduct indicated clearly that he did not hope to have that longing satisfied by the words of the humble prisoner in his charge. "What is truth?" An instinctive utterance this, prompted by previous sad reflections upon the wrecks of philosophy in search of truth.

We have reason to believe that Pilate was a man of brilliant parts and studious habits. His marriage into the Roman royal family argued not only splendid physical endowments, but rare intellectual gifts as well. Only on this hypothesis can we explain his rise from obscurity in Spain to a place in the royal family as husband of the granddaughter of Augustus and foster daughter of Tiberius. Then he was familiar, if he was thus endowed and accomplished, with the despairing efforts of his age and country to solve the mysteries of life and to ascertain the end of man. He had doubtless, as a student, "mused and mourned over Greece, and its search of truth intellectual—its keen and fruitless search, never-ending, ever beginning, across wastes of doubt and seas of speculation lighted by uncertain stars." He knew full well that Roman philosophy had been wrecked and stranded amidst the floating débris of Grecian thought and speculation. He had thought that the *ultima ratio* of Academicians and Peripatetics, of Stoics and Epicureans had been reached. But here was a new proposition—a kingdom of truth whose sovereign had as subjects mere vagaries, simple mental conceptions called truths—a kingdom whose boundaries were not mountains, seas, and rivers, but clouds, hopes, and dreams.

What did Pilate think of Jesus? He evidently regarded Him as an amiable enthusiast, a harmless religious fanatic from whom Cæsar had nothing to fear. While alone with Jesus in the palace, he must have reasoned thus with himself, silently and contemptuously: The mob outside tells me that this man is Rome's enemy. Foolish thought! We know who Cæsar's enemies are. We have seen and heard and felt the enemies of Rome—barbarians from beyond the Danube and the Rhine—great strong men, who can drive a javelin not only through a man, but a horse, as well. These are Cæsar's enemies. This strange and melancholy man, whose subjects are mere abstract truths, and whose kingdom is beyond the skies, can be no enemy of Cæsar.

Believing this, he went out to the rabble and pronounced a verdict of acquittal: "I find in him no fault at all."

Pilate had tried and acquitted Jesus. Why did he not release Him, and, if need be, protect Him with his cohort from the assaults of the Jews? Mankind has asked for nearly two thousand years why a Roman, with the blood of a Roman in him, with the glorious prestige and stern authority of the Roman empire at his back, with a Roman legion at his command, did not have the courage to do the high Roman act. Pilate was a moral and intellectual coward of arrant type. This is his proper characterization and a fitting answer to the world's eternal question.

The Jews heard his sentence of acquittal in sullen silence. Desperately resolved to prevent His release, they began at once to frame new accusations.

"And they were the more fierce, saying, He stirreth up the people, teaching throughout all Jewry, beginning from Galilee to this place."[86]

This charge was intended by the Jews to serve a double purpose: to strengthen the general accusation of high treason recorded by St. Luke; and to embitter and poison the mind of the judge against the prisoner by telling Pilate that Jesus was from Galilee. In ancient times Galilee was noted as the hotbed of riot and sedition. The Galileans were brave and hardy mountaineers who feared neither Rome nor Judea. As champions of Jewish nationality, they were the fiercest opponents of Roman rule; and in the final catastrophe of Jewish history they were the last to be driven from the battlements of Jerusalem. As advocates and preservers of the purity of the primitive Jewish faith, they were relentless foes of Pharisaic and Sadducean hypocrisy as it was manifested by the Judean keepers of the Temple. The Galileans were hated, therefore, by both Romans and Judeans; and the Sanhedrists believed that Pilate would make short work of Jesus if he learned that the prisoner was from Galilee. But a different train of thought was excited in the mind of the Roman governor. He was thinking about one thing, and they about another. Pilate showed himself throughout the trial a craven coward and contemptible timeserver. From beginning to end, his conduct was a record of cowardice and subterfuge. He was constantly looking for loopholes of escape. His heart's desire was to satisfy at once both his conscience and the mob. The mention of Galilee was a ray of light that fell across the troubled path of the cowardly and vacillating judge. He believed that he saw an avenue of escape. He asked the Jews if Jesus was a Galilean. An affirmative reply was given. Pilate then determined to rid himself of responsibility by sending Jesus to be tried by the governor of the province to which He belonged. He felt that fortune favored his design; for Herod, Tetrarch of Galilee, was at that very moment in Jerusalem in attendance upon the Passover feast. He acted at once upon the happy idea; and, under the escort of a detachment of the Prætorian Cohort, Jesus was led away to the palace of the Maccabees where Herod was accustomed to stop when he came to the Holy City.

CHAPTER IX

JESUS BEFORE HEROD

IT was still early morning when Jesus, guarded by Roman soldiers and surrounded by a jeering, scoffing, raging multitude of Jews, was conducted to the palace of the Maccabees on the slope of Zion, the official residence of Herod when he came to Jerusalem to attend the sacred festivals. This place was to the northeast of the palace of Herod and only a few streets distant from it. The journey must have lasted therefore only a few minutes.

But who was this Herod before whom Jesus now appeared in chains? History mentions many Herods, the greatest and meanest of whom was Herod I, surnamed the Great, who ordered the massacre of the Innocents at Bethlehem. At his death, he bequeathed his kingdom to his sons. But being a client-prince, a *rex socius*, he could not finally dispose of his realm without the consent of Rome. Herod had made several wills, and, at his death, contests arose between his sons for the vacant throne of the father. Several embassies were sent to Rome to argue the rights of the different claimants. Augustus granted the petitioners many audiences; and, after long delay, finally confirmed practically the last will of Herod. This decision gave Judea, Samaria, and Idumea, with a tribute of six hundred talents, to Archelaus. Philip received the regions of Gaulanitis, Auranitis, Trachonitis, Batanea, and Iturea, with an income of one hundred talents. Herod Antipas was given the provinces of Galilee and Perea, with an annual tribute of two hundred talents and the title of Tetrarch. The title of Ethnarch was conferred upon Archelaus.

Herod Antipas, Tetrarch of Galilee, was the man before whom Jesus, his subject, was now led to be judged. The pages of sacred history mention the name of no more shallow and contemptible character than this petty princeling, this dissolute Idumæan Sadducee. Compared with him, Judas is eminently respectable. Judas had a conscience which, when smitten with remorse, drove him to suicide. It is doubtful whether Herod had a spark of that celestial fire which we call conscience. He was a typical Oriental prince whose chief aim in life was the gratification of his passions. The worthlessness of his character was so pronounced that it excited a nauseating disgust in the mind of Jesus, and disturbed for a moment that serene and lofty magnanimity which characterized His whole life and conduct. To Herod is addressed the only purely contemptuous epithet that the Master is ever recorded to have used. "And he said unto them, Go ye, and tell *that fox*, Behold, I cast out devils, and I do cures to-day and to-morrow, and the third day I shall be perfected."[87]

The son of a father who was ten times married and had murdered many of his wives; the murderer himself of John the Baptist; the slave of a lewd and wicked woman—what better could be expected than a cruel, crafty, worthless character, whose attributes were those of the fox?

But why was Jesus sent to Herod? Doubtless because Pilate wished to shift the responsibility from his own shoulders, as a Roman judge, to those of the Galilean Tetrarch. A subsidiary purpose may have been to conciliate Herod, with whom, history says, he had had a quarrel. The cause of the trouble between them is not known. Many believe that the murder of the Galileans while sacrificing in the Temple was the origin of the unpleasantness. Others contend that this occurrence was the result and not the cause of the quarrel between Pilate and Herod. Still others believe that the question of the occupancy of the magnificent palace of Herod engendered ill feeling between the rival potentates. Herod had all the love of gorgeous architecture and luxurious living that characterized the whole Herodian family. And, besides, he doubtless felt that he should be permitted to occupy the palace of his ancestors on the occasion of his visits to Jerusalem. But Pilate would naturally object to this, as he was the representative of almighty Rome in a conquered province and could not afford to give way, in a matter of palatial residence, to a petty local prince. But, whatever the cause, the unfriendliness between them undoubtedly had much to do with the transfer of Jesus from the Prætorium to the palace of the Maccabees.

"And when Herod saw Jesus, he was exceeding glad: for he was desirous to see him for a long season, because he had heard many things of him; and he hoped to have seen some miracle done by him."[88]

This passage of Scripture throws much light upon Herod's opinion and estimate of Jesus. Fearing that he was the successor and imitator of Judas the Gaulonite, Herod at first sought to drive Him from his province by sending spies to warn Him to flee. The courageous and contemptuous reply of Jesus, in which he styled Herod "that fox," put an end to further attempts at intimidation.

The notions of the Galilean Tetrarch concerning the Galilean Prophet seem to have changed from time to time. Herod had once regarded Jesus with feelings of superstitious dread and awe, as the risen Baptist. But these apprehensions had now partially passed away, and he had come to look upon the Christ as a clever impostor whose claims to kingship and Messiahship were mere vulgar dreams. For three years, Galilee had been ringing with the fame of the Miracle-worker; but Herod had never seen his famous subject. Now was his chance. And he anticipated a rare occasion of magic and merriment. He doubtless regarded Jesus as a clever magician whose performance would make a rich and racy programme for an hour's amusement of his court. This was no doubt his dominant feeling regarding the Nazarene. But it is nevertheless very probable that his Idumæan cowardice and superstition still conjured images of a drunken debauch, the dance of death, and the bloody head; and connected them with the strange man now before him.

No doubt he felt highly pleased and gratified to have Jesus sent to him. The petty and obsequious vassal king was caught in Pilate's snare of flattery. The sending of a noted prisoner to his judgment seat by a Roman procurator was no ordinary compliment. But Herod was at once too serious and too frivolous to assume jurisdiction of any charges against this prisoner, who had offended both the religious and secular powers of Palestine. To condemn Jesus would be to incur the ill will and resentment of his many followers in his own province of Galilee. Besides, he had already suffered keenly from dread and apprehension, caused by the association of the names of John and Jesus, and he had learned that from the blood of one murdered prophet would spring the message and mission of another still more powerful and majestic. He was, therefore, unwilling to embroil himself and his dominions with the heavenly powers by condemning their earthly representatives.

Again, though weak, crafty and vacillating, he still had enough of the cunning of the fox not to wish to excite the enmity of Cæsar by a false judgment upon a noted character whose devoted followers might, at any moment, send an embassy to Rome to make serious and successful charges to the Emperor. He afterwards lost his place as Tetrarch through the suspicions of Caligula, who received news from Galilee that Herod was conspiring against him.[89] The premonitions of that unhappy day probably now filled the mind of the Idumæan.

On the other hand, Herod was too frivolous to conduct from beginning to end a solemn judicial proceeding. He evidently intended to ignore the pretensions of Jesus, and to convert the occasion of His coming into a festive hour in which languor and drowsiness would be banished from his court. He had heard much of the miracles of the prisoner in his presence. Rumor had wafted to his ears strange accounts of marvelous feats. One messenger had brought news that the Prophet of Nazareth had raised from the dead a man named Lazarus from Bethany, and also the son of the widow of Nain. Another had declared that the laws of nature suspended themselves on occasion at His behest; that when He walked out on the sea, He did not sink; and that He stilled the tempests with a mere motion of His hand. Still another reported that the mighty magician could take mud from the pool and restore sight; that a woman, ill for many months, need only touch the hem of His garment to be made whole again; and that if He but touched the flesh of a leper, it would become as tender and beautiful as that of a newborn babe. These reports had doubtless been received by Herod with sneers and mocking. But he gathered from them that Jesus was a clever juggler whose powers of entertainment were very fine; and this was sufficient for him and his court.

"Then he questioned with him in many words; but he answered him nothing."[90]

Herod thus opened the examination of Jesus by interrogating Him at length. The Master treated his insolent questions with contemptuous scorn and withering silence. No doubt this conduct of the lowly Nazarene greatly surprised and nettled the supercilious Idumæan. He had imagined that Jesus would be delighted to give an exhibition of His skill amidst royal surroundings. He could not conceive that a peasant would observe the contempt of silence in the presence of a prince. He found it difficult, therefore, to explain this silence. He probably mistook it for stupidity, and construed it to mean that the pretensions of Jesus were fraudulent. He doubtless believed that his captive would not work a miracle because He could not; and that in His failure to do so were exploded His claims to kingship and Messiahship. At all events, he was evidently deeply perplexed; and this perplexity of the Tetrarch, in its turn, only served to anger the accusing priests who stood by.

"And the chief priests and scribes stood and vehemently accused him."[91]

This verse from St. Luke clearly reveals the difference in the temper and purposes of the Sanhedrists on the one hand, and of Herod on the other. The latter merely intended to make of the case of Jesus a farcical proceeding in which the jugglery of the prisoner would break the monotony of a day and banish all care during an idle hour. The priests, on the other hand, were desperately bent upon a serious outcome of the affair, as the words "vehemently accused" suggest. In the face of their repeated accusations, Jesus continued to maintain a noble and majestic silence.

Modern criticism has sought to analyze and to explain the behavior of Christ at the court of Herod. "How comes it," asks Strauss, "that Jesus, not only the Jesus without sin of the orthodox school, but also the Jesus who bowed to the constituted authorities, who says 'Give unto Cæsar that which is Cæsar's'—how comes it that he refuses the answer due to Herod?" The trouble with this question is that it falsely assumes that there was an "answer due to Herod." In the first place, it must be considered that Herod was not Cæsar. In the next place, we must remember that St. Luke, the sole Evangelist who records the event, does not explain the character of the questions asked by Herod. Strauss himself says that they "displayed simple curiosity." Admitting that Jesus acknowledged the jurisdiction of Herod, was He compelled to answer irrelevant and impertinent questions? We do not know what these questions were. But we have reason to believe that, coming from Herod, they were not such as Jesus was called upon to answer. It is very probable that the prisoner knew His legal rights; and that He did not believe that Herod, sitting at Jerusalem, a place without his province, was judicially empowered to examine Him. If He was not legally compelled to answer, we are not surprised that Jesus refused to do so as a matter of graciousness and accommodation; for we must not forget that the Man-God felt that He was being questioned by a vulgar animal of the most cunning type.

But what is certain from the Scriptural context is that Herod felt chagrined and mortified at his failure to evoke from Jesus any response. He was enraged that his plans had been foiled by one of his own subjects, a simple Galilean peasant. To show his resentment, he then resorted to mockery and abuse.

"And Herod with his men of war set him at nought, and mocked him, and arrayed him in a gorgeous robe, and sent him again to Pilate."[92]

We are not informed by St. Luke what special charge the priests brought against Jesus at the judgment seat of Herod. He simply says that they "stood and vehemently accused him." But we are justified in inferring that they repeated substantially the same accusations which had been made before Pilate, that He had claimed to be Christ a King. This conclusion best explains the mockery which they sought to heap upon Him; for in ancient times, when men became candidates for office, they put on white gowns to notify the people of their candidacy. Again, Tacitus assures us that white garments were the peculiar dress of illustrious persons; and that the tribunes and consuls wore them when marching before the eagles of the legions into battle.[93]

The meaning of the mockery of Herod was simply this: Behold O Pilate, the illustrious candidate for the kingship of the Jews! Behold the imperial gown of the royal peasant pretender!

The appearance before Herod resulted only in the humiliation of Jesus and the reconciliation of Pilate and Herod.

"And the same day Pilate and Herod were made friends together: for before they were at enmity between themselves."[94]

CHAPTER X

JESUS AGAIN BEFORE PILATE

THE sending of Jesus to Herod had not ended the case; and Pilate was undoubtedly very bitterly disappointed. He had hoped that the Galilean Tetrarch would assume complete jurisdiction and dispose finally of the matter. On the contrary, Herod simply mocked and brutalized the prisoner and had him sent back to Pilate. The Roman construed the action of the Idumæan to mean an acquittal, and he so stated to the Jews.

"And Pilate, when he had called together the chief priests and the rulers and the people, Said unto them, Ye have brought this man unto me, as one that perverteth the people: and, behold, I, having examined him before you, have found no fault in this man touching those things whereof ye accuse him: No, nor yet Herod: for I sent you to him; and, lo, nothing worthy of death is done unto him. I will therefore chastise him, and release him."[95]

The proposal to scourge the prisoner was the second of those criminal and cowardly subterfuges through which Pilate sought at once to satisfy his conscience and the demands of the mob. The chastisement was to be a sop to the rage of the rabble, a sort of salve to the wounded pride of the priests who were disappointed that no sentence of death had been imposed. The release was intended as a tribute to justice, as a soothing balm and an atoning sacrifice to his own outraged sense of justice. The injustice of this monstrous proposal was not merely contemptible, it was execrable. If Jesus was guilty, He should have been punished; if innocent, he should have been set free and protected from the assaults of the Jews.

The offer of scourging first and then the release of the prisoner was indignantly rejected by the rabble. In his desperation, Pilate thought of another loophole of escape.

The Evangelists tell us that it was a custom upon Passover day to release to the people any single prisoner that they desired. St. Luke asserts that the governor was under an obligation to do so.[96] Whether this custom was of Roman or Hebrew origin is not certainly known. Many New Testament interpreters have seen in the custom a symbol of the liberty and deliverance realized by Israel in its passage from Egypt at the time of the first great Passover. Others have traced this custom to the Roman practice of releasing a slave at the Lectisternia, or banquets to the gods.[97] Aside from its origin, it is interesting as an illustration of a universal principle in enlightened jurisprudence of lodging somewhere, usually with the chief executive of a race or nation, a power of pardon which serves as an extinction of the penal sanction. This merciful principle is a pathetic acknowledgment of the weakness and imperfection of all human schemes of justice.

Pilate resolved to escape from his confusion and embarrassment by delivering Jesus to the people, who happened to appear in great numbers at the very moment when Christ returned from Herod. The multitude had come to demand the usual Passover deliverance of a prisoner. The arrival of the crowd of disinterested strangers was inopportune for the priests and elders who were clamoring for the life of the prisoner in their midst. They marked with keen discernment the resolution of the governor to release Jesus. They were equal to the emergency, and began to whisper among the crowd that Barabbas should be asked.

"And they had then a notable prisoner, called Barabbas. Therefore when they were gathered together, Pilate said unto them, Whom will ye that I release unto you? Barabbas, or Jesus which is called Christ? For he knew that for envy they had delivered him."[98]

Pilate believed that the newly arrived multitude would be free from the envy of the priests, and that they would be satisfied with Jesus whom they had, a few days before, welcomed into Jerusalem with shouts of joy. When they demanded Barabbas, he still believed that if he offered them the alternative choice of a robber and a prophet, they would choose the latter.

"But the chief priests and elders persuaded the multitude that they should ask Barabbas, and destroy Jesus. The governor answered and said unto them, Whether of the twain will ye that I release unto you? They said, Barabbas. Pilate saith unto them, What shall I do then with Jesus which is called the Christ? They all say unto him, Let him be crucified."[99]

"Barabbas, or Jesus which is called the Christ?" Such was the alternative offered by a Roman governor to a Jewish mob. Barabbas was a murderer and a robber. Jesus was the sinless Son of God. An erring race wandering in the darkness of sin and perpetually tasting the bitterness of life beneath the sun, preferred a criminal to a prophet. And to the ghastliness of the choice was added a touch of the irony of fate. The names of both the prisoners were in signification the same. Barabbas was also called Jesus. And Jesus Barabbas meant Jesus the Son of the Father. This frightful coincidence was so repugnant to the Gospel writers that they are generally silent upon it. In this connection, Strauss remarks: "According to one reading, the man's complete name was ἰησοῦς βαρραβας, which fact is noted only because Olshausen considers it noteworthy. Barabbas signifies 'son of the father,' and consequently Olshausen exclaims: 'All that was essential to the Redeemer appears ridiculous in the assassin!' and he deems applicable the verse: '*Ludit in humanis divina potentia rebus.*' We can see nothing in Olshausen's remark but a *ludus humanæ impotentiæ.*"[100]

Amidst the tumult provoked by the angry passions of the mob, a messenger arrived from his wife bearing news that filled the soul of Pilate with superstitious dread. Claudia had had a dream of strange and ill-boding character.

"When he was set down on the judgment seat, his wife sent unto him, saying, Have thou nothing to do with that just man: For I have suffered many things this day in a dream because of him."[101]

This dream of Pilate's wife is nothing strange. Profane history mentions many similar ones. Calpurnia, Cæsar's wife, forewarned him in a dream not to go to the senate house; and the greatest of the Romans fell beneath the daggers of Casca and Brutus, because he failed to heed the admonition of his wife.

In the apocryphal report of Pilate to the emperor Tiberius of the facts of the crucifixion, the words of warning sent by Claudia are given: "Beware said she to me, beware and touch not that man, for he is holy. Last night I saw him in a vision. He was walking on the waters. He was flying on the wings of the winds. He spoke to the tempest and to the fishes of the lake; all were obedient to him. Behold! the torrent in Mount Kedron flows with blood, the statues of Cæsar are filled with the filth of Gemoniæ, the columns of the Interium have given away and the sun is veiled in mourning like a vestal in the tomb. O, Pilate, evil awaits thee if thou wilt not listen to the prayer of thy wife. Dread the curse of the Roman Senate, dread the powers of Cæsar."

This noble and lofty language, this tender and pathetic speech, may appear strange to those who remember the hereditary stigma of the woman. If this dream was sent from heaven, the recollection is forced upon us that the medium of its communication was the illegitimate child of a lewd woman. But then her character was probably not worse than that of Mary Magdalene, who was very dear to the Master and has been canonized not only by the church, but by the reverence of the world.

It is certain, however, that the dream of Claudia had no determining effect upon the conduct of Pilate. Resolution and irresolution alternately controlled him. Fear and superstition were uppermost in both mind and heart. The Jews beheld with anxious and discerning glance the manifestation of the deep anguish of his soul. They feared that the governor was about to pronounce a final judgment of acquittal. Exhibiting fierce faces and frenzied feelings, they moved closer to him and exclaimed: "We have a law, and by our law he ought to die, because he made himself the Son of God."[102]

Despairing of convicting Jesus on a political charge, they deliberately revived a religious one, and presented to Pilate substantially the same accusation upon which they had tried the prisoner before their own tribunal.

"He made himself the Son of God!" These words filled Pilate's mind with a strange and awful meaning. In the mythology and ancient annals of his race, there were many legends of the sons of the gods who walked the earth in human form and guise. They were thus indistinguishable from mortal men. It was dangerous to meet them; for to offend them was to provoke the wrath of the gods, their sires. These reflections, born of superstition, now swept through Pilate's mind with terrific force; and the cries of the mob, "He made himself the Son of God," called from out the deep recesses of his memory the half-forgotten, half-remembered stories of his childhood. Could not Jesus, reasoned Pilate, be the son of the Hebrew Jehovah as Hercules was the son of Jupiter? Filled with superstitious dread and trembling with emotion, Pilate called Jesus inside the Temple a second time; and, looking with renewed awe and wonder, asked: "Whence art thou?"[103] But Jesus answered him nothing.

Pilate came forth from the judgment hall a second time determined to release the prisoner; but the Jews, marking his decision, began to cry out: "Away with him, away with him, crucify him!"[104] Maddened by the relentless importunity of the mob, Pilate replied scornfully and mockingly:

"Shall I crucify your king?"

The cringing, hypocritical priests shouted back their answer:

"We have no king but Cæsar."[105]

And on the kingly idea of loyalty to Roman sovereignty they framed their last menace and accusation. From the quiver of their wrath they drew the last arrow of spite and hate, and fired it straight at the heart of Jesus through the hands of Pilate:

"If thou let this man go, thou art not Cæsar's friend: whosoever maketh himself a king speaketh against Cæsar."[106]

This last maneuver of the mob sealed the doom of the Christ. It teaches also most clearly that Pilate was no match for the Jews when their religious prejudices were aroused and they were bent on accomplishing their desires. They knew Pilate and he knew them. They had been together full six years. He had been compelled to yield to them in the matter of the standards and the eagles. The sacred Corban funds had been appropriated only after blood had been shed in the streets of Jerusalem. The gilt shields of Tiberius that he had placed in Herod's palace were taken down at the demands of the Jews and carried to the temple of Augustus at Cæsarea. And now the same fanatical rabble was before him demanding the blood of the Nazarene, and threatening to accuse him to Cæsar if he released the prisoner. The position of Pilate was painfully critical. He afterwards lost his procuratorship at the instance of accusing Jews. The shadow of that distant day now fell like a curse across his pathway. Nothing was so terrifying to a Roman governor as to have the people send a complaining embassy to Rome. It was especially dangerous at this time. The imperial throne was filled by a morbid and suspicious tyrant who needed but a pretext to depose the governor of any province who silently acquiesced in traitorous pretensions to kingship. Pilate trembled at these reflections. His feelings of self-preservation suggested immediate surrender to the Jews. But his innate sense of justice, which was woven in the very fiber of his Roman nature, recoiled at the thought of Roman sanction of judicial murder. He resolved, therefore, to propitiate and temporize. The frenzied rabble continued to cry: "Crucify him! Crucify him!" Three times, in reply, Conscience sent to Pilate's trembling lips the searching question: "Why, what evil hath he done?" "Crucify him! Crucify him!" came back from the infuriated mob.

Pilate finally resolved to do their bidding and obey their will. But he seems to have secretly cherished the hope that scourging, which was the usual preliminary to crucifixion, might be made to satisfy the mob. But this hope was soon dispelled; and he found himself compelled to yield completely to their wishes by delivering the prisoner to be crucified. Before this final step, however, which was an insult to the true courage of the soul and an outrage upon all the charities of the heart, he resolved to apply a soothing salve to wounded conscience. He resolved to perform a ceremonial cleansing act. Calling for a basin of water, he washed his hands before the multitude, saying: "I am innocent of the blood of this just person: see ye to it."[107]

This was a simple, impressive, theatrical act; but little, mean, contemptible, cowardly. He washed his hands when he should have used them. He should have used them as Brutus or Gracchus or Pompeius Magnus would have done, in pointing his legion to the field of duty and of glory. He should have used them as Bonaparte did when he put down the mob in the streets of Paris. But he was too craven and cowardly; and herein is to be found the true meaning of the character and conduct of Pilate. He believed that Jesus was innocent; and that the accusations against Him were inspired by the envy of His countrymen. He had declared to the Jews in an emphatic verdict of acquittal that he found in Him no fault at all. And yet this very sentence, "I find in him no fault at all," was the beginning of that course of cowardly and criminal vacillation which finally sent Jesus to the cross. "Yet was this utterance," says Innes, "as it turned out, only the first step in that downward course of weakness the world knows so well: a course which, beginning with indecision and complaisance, passed through all the phases of alternate bluster and subserviency; persuasion, evasion, protest, and compromise; superstitious dread, conscientious reluctance, cautious duplicity, and sheer moral cowardice at last; until this Roman remains photographed forever as the perfect feature of the unjust judge, deciding 'against his better knowledge, not deceived.'"

"Then released he Barabbas unto them: and when he had scourged Jesus, he delivered him to be crucified. Then the soldiers of the governor took Jesus into the common hall, and gathered unto him the whole band of soldiers. And they stripped him, and put on him a scarlet robe. And when they had platted a crown of thorns, they put it upon his head, and a reed in his right hand: And they bowed the knee before him, and mocked him, saying, Hail, King of the Jews! And they spit upon him, and took the reed, and smote him on the head. And after that they had mocked him, they took the robe off from him, and put his own raiment on him, and led him away to crucify him."[108]

Thus ended the most memorable act of injustice recorded in history. At every stage of the trial, whether before Caiaphas or Pilate, the prisoner conducted Himself with that commanding dignity and majesty so well worthy of His origin, mission, and destiny. His sublime deportment at times caused His judges to marvel greatly. And through it all, He stood alone. His friends and followers had deserted Him in His hour of greatest need. Single-handed and unaided, the Galilean peasant had bared His breast and brow to the combined authority, to the insults and outrages, of both Jerusalem and Rome. "Not a single discordant voice was raised amidst the tumultuous clamour: not a word of protest disturbed the mighty concord of anger and reviling; not the faintest echo of the late hosannas, which had wrung with wonder, fervour, and devotion, and which had surrounded and exalted to the highest pitch of triumph the bearer of good tidings on his entry into the Holy City. Where were the throngs of the hopeful and believing, who had followed His beckoning as a finger pointing toward the breaking dawn of truth and regeneration? Where were they, what thinking and why silent? The bands at the humble and poor, of the afflicted and outcast who had entrusted to His controlling grace the salvation of soul and body—where were they, what thinking and why silent? The troops of women and youths, who had drawn fresh strength from the spell of a glance or a word from the Father of all that liveth—where were they, what thinking and why silent? And the multitudes of disciples and enthusiasts who had scattered sweet-scented boughs and joyous utterances along the road to Sion, blessing Him that came in the name of the Lord—where were they, what thinking and why silent? Not a remembrance, not a sign, not a word of the great glory so lately His. Jesus was alone."

CHRIST LEAVING THE PRÆTORIUM (DORÉ)

CHAPTER XI

LEGAL ANALYSIS AND SUMMARY OF THE ROMAN TRIAL OF JESUS

IN the preceding pages of this volume we have considered the elements of both Law and Fact as related to the Roman trial of Jesus. Involved in this consideration were the powers and duties of Pilate as procurator of Judea and as presiding judge at the trial; general principles of Roman provincial administration at the time of Christ; the legal and political status of the subject Jew in his relationship to the conquering Roman; the exact requirements of criminal procedure in Roman capital trials at Rome and in the provinces at the date of the crucifixion; the Roman law applicable to the trial of Jesus; and the facts of said trial before Pilate and Herod.

We are now in a position to analyze the case from the view point of the juristic agreement or nonagreement of Law and Fact; and to determine by a process of judicial dissection and re-formation, the presence or absence of essential legal elements in the proceedings. We have learned what should have been done by Pilate acting as a Roman judge in a criminal matter involving the life of a prisoner. We have also ascertained what he actually did. We are thus enabled to compare the requirements with the actualities of the case; and to ascertain the resemblances in the proceedings against Jesus to a legally conducted trial under Roman law.

But, in making this summary and analysis, a most important consideration must be constantly held in mind: that, in matters of review on appeal, errors will not be presumed; that is, errors will not be considered that do not appear affirmatively upon the record. The law will rather presume and the court will assume that what should have been done, was done. In conformity with this principle, the presumption must be indulged that Pilate acted in strict obedience to the requirements of Roman law in trying Jesus, unless the Gospels of the New Testament, which constitute the record in the case, either affirmatively or by reasonable inference, disclose the absence of such obedience. A failure to note this presumption and to keep this principle in mind, has caused many writers upon this subject to make erroneous statements concerning the merits and legal aspects of the trial of Christ.

Laymen frequently assert the essential principle of this presumption without seeming to be aware of it. Both Keim and Geikie declare that assessors or assistants were associated with Pilate in the trial of Jesus. The Gospel records nowhere even intimate such a thing; and no other original records are in existence to furnish such information. And yet one of the most celebrated of the biblical critics, Dr. Theodor Keim, writing on the trial of Christ by Pilate, says: "Beside him, upon benches, were the council or the assessors of the court, sub-officials, friends, Roman citizens, whose presence could not be dispensed with, and who were not wanting to the procurators of Judea, although our reports do not mention them."[109] To the same effect, Dr. Cunningham Geikie thus writes: "The assessors of the court—Roman citizens—who acted as nominal members of the judicial bench, sit beside Pilate—for Roman law required their presence."[110]

These statements of the renowned writers just quoted are justified not only on the ground of logical historical inference, but also on the principle of actual legal presumption. The closest scrutiny of the New Testament narratives nowhere discovers even an intimation that a bench of judges helped Pilate to conduct the trial of Jesus. And yet, as Geikie says, "Roman law required their presence," and the legal presumption is that they were in and about the Prætorium ready to lend assistance, and that they actually took part in the proceedings. This inference is strengthened by the fact that Pilate, after he had learned the nature of the accusation against Jesus, called Him into the palace to examine Him. Why did Pilate do this? Why did he not examine the prisoner in the presence of His accusers in the open air? Geikie tells us that there was a judgment hall in the palace in which trials were usually conducted.[111] Is it not possible, nay probable, that the assessors and Pilate were assembled at an early hour in this hall to hear the usual criminal charges of the day, or, perhaps, to try the accusation against Jesus, of whose appearance before them they had been previously notified; and that, when the governor heard that the religious scruples of the Jews would not permit them to enter the judgment hall during the Passover feast, he went out alone to hear the accusation against the prisoner; and that he then returned with the accused into the hall where the bench of judges were awaiting him, to lay before them the charges and to further examine the case? It is admitted that this theory and the statement of Geikie that there was a hall in the palace where trials were generally held, are seemingly refuted by the fact that Roman trials were almost always conducted in the open air. But this was not invariably true; and the case of Pilate and his court might have been an exception.

It has been sought to lay particular stress upon the doctrine of legal presumption that what should have been done, was done, unless the record affirmatively negatives the fact, because it is impossible to appreciate fully the legal aspects of the trial of Jesus, unless this doctrine is understood and kept constantly in view.

A casual perusal of the New Testament narratives leaves the impression upon the mind of the reader that the proceedings against Jesus before Pilate were exceedingly irregular and lacking in all the essential elements of a regular trial. As a matter of fact, this impression may be grounded in absolute truth. It may be that the action of Pilate was arbitrary and devoid of all legal forms. This possibility is strengthened by the consideration that Jesus was not a Roman citizen and could not, therefore, demand the strict observance of forms of law in His trial. A Jewish provincial, when accused of crime, stood before a Roman governor with no other rights than the plea of justice as a defense against the summary exercise of absolute power. In other words, in the case of Jesus, Pilate was not bound to observe strictly rules of criminal procedure prescribed by Roman law. He could, if he saw fit, dispense with forms of law and dispose of the case either equitably or as his whims suggested. Nor was there a right of appeal in such a case, from the judgment of the procurator to the emperor at Rome. The decision of the governor against a provincial was final. The case of Paul before Felix and before Festus was entirely different. Paul was a Roman citizen and, as such, was entitled to all the rights involved in Roman citizenship, which included the privilege of an appeal to Cæsar against the judgment of a provincial officer; and he actually exercised this right.[112] It was incumbent, therefore, upon Roman officials to observe due forms of law in proceeding against him. And St. Luke, in Acts xxiv., indicates the almost exact precision and formality of a Roman trial, in the case of Paul.

But the fact that Jesus was not a Roman citizen does not prove that due forms of law were not observed in His trial. It is hardly probable, as before observed, that despotism and caprice were tolerated at any time, in any part of the Roman world. And, besides, Roman history and jurisprudence are replete with illustrations of complete legal protection extended by Roman officials to the non-Roman citizens of subject states. It is, moreover, a legitimate and almost inevitable inference, drawn from the very nature of the Roman constitution and from the peculiar character of Roman judicial administration, that no human life belonging to a citizen or subject of Rome would be permitted to be taken without due process of law, either imperial or local.

In forming an opinion as to the existence or non-existence of a regular trial of Jesus before Pilate, the meager details of the New Testament histories must not alone be relied upon. Nor must it be forgotten that the Gospel writers were not lawyers or court officers reporting a case to be reviewed on appeal. They were laymen writing a general account of a judicial transaction. And the omissions in their narratives are not to be considered as either discrepancies or falsehoods. They simply did not intend to tell everything about the trial of Jesus; and the fact that they do not record the successive steps of a regular trial does not mean that these steps were not observed.

It is respectfully submitted that if a modern layman should write a newspaper or book account of one of the great criminal trials of this century, with no intention of making it a strictly judicial report, this account would not reveal the presence of more essential legal elements than are disclosed by the reports of the Evangelists of the proceedings against Jesus.

The majority of writers on the subject express the opinion that the appearance of the Christ before the Roman governor was nothing more than a short hearing in which a few questions were asked and answers made; that the proceedings were exceedingly brief and informal; and that the emergencies of the case rather than forms of law guided the judgment and controlled the conduct of Pilate. As a layman, the author of these volumes would take the same view. But as a lawyer, treating the subject in a judicial manner, and bound by legal rules, regulations, and presumptions, in reviewing the merits of the case, he feels constrained to dissent from the prevalent opinion and to declare that the New Testament records, though meager in details, exhibit all the essential elements of an ordinary criminal trial, whether conducted in ancient or modern times. He further asserts that if the affirmative statements of the Evangelists that certain things were done be supplemented by the legal presumption that still other things were done because they should have been done, and because the record does not affirmatively declare that they were not done, an almost perfect judicial proceeding can be developed from the Gospel reports of the trial of Jesus before Pilate. These reports disclose the following essential elements of all ancient and modern criminal trials:

1. The Indictment, or *Nominis Delatio*.

"What accusation bring ye against this man?"

"And they began to accuse him, saying, We found this fellow perverting the nation, and forbidding to give tribute to Cæsar, saying that he himself is Christ a King."

2. The Examination, or *Interrogatio*.

"Art thou the King of the Jews?"

"Art thou a King then?"

3. The Defense, or *Excusatio*.

"My kingdom is not of this world: if my kingdom were of this world then would my servants fight, that I should not be delivered to the Jews: but now is my kingdom not from hence.... To this end was I born and for this cause came I into the world, that I should bear witness unto the truth. Everyone that is of the truth heareth my voice."

4. The Acquittal, or *Absolutio*.

"I find in him no fault at all."

Here we have clearly presented the essential features of a criminal trial: the Indictment, the Examination of the charge, the Defense, and the Judgment of the tribunal, which, in this case, was an Acquittal.

To demonstrate that Pilate intended to conduct the proceedings against Jesus seriously and judicially, at the beginning of the trial, let us briefly review the circumstances attendant upon the successive steps just enumerated. And to this end, let us proceed in order:

1. The Indictment, or *Nominis Delatio*.

When Pilate had seated himself in the ivory curule chair of the procurator of Judea, at an early hour on Friday morning, the day of the crucifixion of Jesus, a Jerusalem mob, led by the Sanhedrin, confronted him with the prisoner. His first recorded words are: "What accusation bring ye against this man?" As before suggested, this question is very keenly indicative of the presence of the judge and of the beginning of a solemn judicial proceeding. Every word rings with Roman authority and strongly suggests administrative action.

The accusing priests sought to evade this question by answering: "If he were not a malefactor, we would not have delivered him up unto thee."

If Pilate had adopted the Jewish view of the merits of the matter, that his countersign was the only thing necessary to justify the final condemnation and punishment of the prisoner; or, if he had been indifferent to the legal aspects of the case, he would simply have granted their request at once, and would have ordered the prisoner to execution. But this was not the case; for we are assured that he insisted on knowing the nature of the accusation before he would assume jurisdiction of the affair. The mere information that He was a "malefactor" did not suffice. The conduct of the Roman judge clearly indicated that accusation was a more important element of Roman criminal procedure than was inquisition. To meet the emergency, the Jews were compelled, then, to make the formal charge, that:

"We found this fellow perverting the nation, and forbidding to give tribute to Cæsar, saying that he himself is Christ a King."

Here we have presented the indictment, the first step in a criminal proceeding; and it was presented not voluntarily, but because a Roman judge, acting judicially, demanded and forced its presentment.

2. The Examination, or *Interrogatio*.

Not content with knowing the nature of the charges against the prisoner, Pilate insisted on finding out whether they were true or not. He accordingly took Jesus inside the palace and interrogated Him. With true judicial tact, he brushed aside the first two accusations as unimportant, and came with pointed directness to the material question:

"Art thou the King of the Jews?"

This interrogation bears the impress of a judicial inquiry, touching a matter involving the question of high treason, the charge against the prisoner. It clearly indicates a legal proceeding in progress. And when Jesus made reply that seemed to indicate guilt, the practiced ear of the Roman judge caught the suggestion of a criminal confession, and he asked impatiently:

"Art thou a King then?"

This question indicates seriousness and a resolution to get at the bottom of the matter with a view to a serious judicial determination of the affair.

3. The Defense, or *Excusatio*.

In reply to the question of the judge, the prisoner answered:

"My kingdom is not of this world."

This language indicates that Jesus was conscious of the solemnity of the proceedings; and that He recognized the right of Pilate to interrogate Him judicially. His answer seemed to say: "I recognize your authority in matters of this life and this world. If my claims to kingship were temporal, I fully appreciate that they would be treasonable; and that, as the representative of Cæsar, you would be justified in delivering me to death. But my pretensions to royalty are spiritual, and this places the matter beyond your reach."

The defense of Jesus was in the nature of what we call in modern pleading a Confession and Avoidance: "A plea which admits, in words or in effect, the truth of the matter contained in the Declaration; and alleges some new matter to avoid the effect of it, and shows that the plaintiff is, notwithstanding, not entitled to his action."

It may be analyzed thus:

Confession: Inside the palace, Pilate asked Jesus the question: "Art thou the King of the Jews?" According to St. Matthew, Jesus answered: "Thou sayest";[113] according to St. Mark: "Thou sayest it";[114] according to St. Luke: "Thou sayest it";[115] according to St. John: "Thou sayest that I am a king."[116]

All these replies are identical in signification, and mean: Thou sayest it, because I am really a king. In other words, He simply confessed that He was a king. Then came His real defense.

Avoidance: "My kingdom is not of this world: if my kingdom were of this world, then would my servants fight, that I should not be delivered to the

Jews: but now is my kingdom not from hence.... To this end was I born and for this cause came I into the world, that I should bear witness of the truth. Everyone that is of the truth heareth my voice."

After having confessed claims to kingship, and having thereby made Himself momentarily liable on the charge of high treason, He at once avoids the effect of the declaration by alleging new matter which exempted Him from the operation of the *crimen Læsæ Majestatis*. He boldly declares His kingship, but places His kingdom beyond the skies in the realm of truth and spirit. He asserts a bold antithesis between the Empire of Cæsar and the Kingdom of God. He cheerfully acknowledges the procuratorship of Pilate in the first, but fearlessly proclaims His own Messiahship in the second.

4. The Acquittal, or *Absolutio*.

It is more than probable that Pilate's heathen soul mocked the heavenly claims of the lowly prisoner in his presence, but his keenly discerning Roman intellect marked at once the distinction between an earthly and a heavenly kingdom. He saw clearly that their boundaries nowhere conflicted, and that treasonable contact was impossible. He judged that Jesus was simply a gentle enthusiast whose pretensions were harmless. Accordingly, he went out to the mob and pronounced a verdict of "not guilty." Solemnly raising his hand, he proclaimed the sentence of acquittal:

"I find in him no fault at all."

This language is not the classical legal phraseology of a Roman verdict of acquittal. The Latin word for a single ballot was *absolvo*; the words of a collective judgment of a bench of judges was *non fecisse videtur*. The language of St. John, though that of a layman, is equally as effectual, if not so formal and judicial.

More than any other feature of the case, the verdict of acquittal, "I find in him no fault at all," indicates the regularity and solemnity of a judicial proceeding. Standing alone, it would indicate the close of a regular trial in which a court having jurisdiction had sat in judgment upon the life or liberty of an alleged criminal.

If to these essential elements of a trial which the Gospel records affirmatively disclose be added other necessary elements of a regular Roman trial which legal presumption supplies, because these records do not deny their existence, we have then in the proceedings against Jesus all the important features of Roman criminal procedure involving the question of life or death. That several essential elements are absent is evident from a reasonable construction of the statements of the Evangelists. That which most forcibly negatives the existence of a regular trial was the precipitancy with which the proceedings were conducted before Pilate. We have seen that ten days were allowed at Rome after the *nominis receptio* to secure testimony and prepare the case before the beginning of the trial. This rule was certainly not observed at the trial of Jesus. But several irregularities which are apparent from a perusal of the Gospel histories may be explained from the fact that Jesus was not a Roman citizen and was not, therefore, entitled to a strict observance of Roman law in the proceedings against him.

The foregoing analysis and summary apply only to the proceedings of the first appearance of Jesus before Pilate. It was at this time that the real Roman trial took place. All subsequent proceedings were irregular, tumultuous and absolutely illegal. The examination of Jesus by Herod cannot, strictly speaking, be called a trial. The usual explanation of the sending of the prisoner to Herod is that Pilate learned that He was a native and citizen of Galilee; and that, desiring to rid himself of an embarrassing subject, he determined to transfer the accused from the *forum apprehensionis* to the *forum originis vel domicilii*. It has frequently been asserted that it was usual in Roman procedure to transfer a prisoner from the place of arrest to the place of his origin or residence. There seems to be no authority for this contention. It may or may not have been true as a general proposition. But it was certainly not true in the case of the transfer of Jesus to Herod. In the first place, when Pilate declared, "I find no fault in him at all," a verdict of acquittal was pronounced, and the case was ended. The proceedings had taken form of *res adjudicata*, and former jeopardy could have been pleaded in bar of further prosecution. It might be differently contended if Pilate had discovered that Jesus was from Galilee before the proceedings before him were closed. But it is clear from St. Luke, who alone records the occurrence of the sending of the prisoner to Herod, that the case was closed and the verdict of acquittal had been rendered before Pilate discovered the identity of the accused.[117] It was then too late to subject a prisoner to a second trial for the same offense.

Rosadi denies emphatically that Herod had jurisdiction of the offense charged against Jesus. In this connection, he says: "His prosecutors insisted tenaciously upon His answering to a charge of *continuous* sedition, as lawyers call it. This offence had been begun in Galilee and ended in Jerusalem—that is to say, in Judæa. Now it was a rule of Roman law, which the procurator of Rome could neither fail to recognize nor afford to neglect, that the competence of a court territorially constituted was determined either by the place in which the arrest was made, or by the place in which the offence was committed. Jesus had been arrested at the gates of Jerusalem; His alleged offence had been committed for the most part, and as far as all the final acts were concerned, in the city itself and in other localities of Judæa. In continuous offences competence was determined by the place in which the last acts going to constitute the offence had been committed. Thus no justification whatever existed for determining the court with regard to the prisoner's origin. But this investigation upon a point of Roman law is to all intents superfluous, because either Pilate, when he thought of Herod, intended to strip himself of his inalienable judicial power, and in this case he ought to have respected the jurisdiction and competence of the Grand Sanhedrin and not to have busied himself with a conflict as to cognizance which should only have been discussed and resolved by the Jewish judicial authorities; or else he had no intention of abdicating his power, and in this case he ought never to have raised the question of competence between himself, Governor of Judæa, and Herod, Regent of Galilee, but between himself and the Roman Vice-Governor of Galilee, his colleague, if there had been such an one. It is only between judges of the same judicial hierarchy that a dispute as to territorial competence can arise. Between magistrates of different States there can only exist a contrast of power and jurisdiction. The act of Pilate cannot then be interpreted as a scruple of a constitutional character. It is but a miserable escape for his irresolution, a mere endeavour to temporize."

The second and final appearance of Jesus before Pilate bears little resemblance to a regular trial. The characteristic elements of an ordinary Roman criminal proceeding are almost wholly wanting. The pusillanimous cowardice of the procurator and the blind fury of the mob are the chief component parts. A sort of wild phantasmagoria sweeps through the multitude and circles round the tribunal of the governor. Pilate struggles with his conscience, and seeks safety in subterfuge. He begins by declaring to the assembled priests and elders that neither he nor Herod has found any fault in the man; and then, as a means of compromise and conciliation, makes the monstrous proposal that he will first scourge and then release the prisoner. This infamous proposal is rejected by the mob. The cowardly procurator then adopts another mean expedient as a way of escape. He offers to deliver Jesus to them as a Passover gift. Him they refuse and Barabbas, the robber, is demanded. Pilate's terror is intensified by superstitious dread, when the mob begins to cry: "He made himself the Son of God!" From out the anguish of his soul, the voice of Justice sends to his quivering lips the thrice-repeated question: "Why, what evil hath he done?" The mob continues to cry: "Crucify him! Crucify him!"

And as a final assault upon his conscience and his courage, the hypocritical priests warn him that he must not release a pretender to kingship, for such a man is an enemy to Cæsar. The doom of the Nazarene is sealed by this last maneuver of the rabble. Then, as a propitiation to the great God of truth and justice, and as balm to his hurt and wounded conscience, he washes his hands in front of them and exclaims: "I am innocent of the blood of this just person: see ye to it."

The crucifixion followed Pilate's final determination; and thus ended the most famous trial in the history of the world. It began with the arrest of Jesus in Gethsemane at midnight, and ended with His crucifixion on Golgotha on the afternoon of the same day. As we have seen, it was a double trial, conducted within the jurisdictions of the two most famous systems of jurisprudence known to mankind. In both trials, substantially the right issue was raised. Before the Sanhedrin, the prisoner was charged with blasphemy and convicted. Regarding Jesus as a mere man, a plain Jewish citizen, this judgment was "substantially right in point of law", but was unjust and outrageous because forms of criminal procedure which every Jewish prisoner was entitled to have observed, were completely ignored.

The proceedings before Pilate, we have reason to believe, were conducted, in a general way, with due regard to forms of law. But the result was judicial murder, because the judge, after having acquitted Jesus, delivered Him to be crucified. "I find in him no fault at all" was the verdict of Pilate. But this just and righteous sentence was destroyed and obliterated by the following: "And they were instant with loud voices, requiring that he might be crucified. And the voices of them and of the chief priests prevailed. And Pilate gave sentence that it should be as they required."[118]

A horrible travesty on justice, this! "*Absolvo*" and "*Ibis ad crucem*," in the same breath, were the final utterances of a Roman judge administering Roman law in the most memorable judicial transaction known to men.

The treatment of this great theme would be incomplete and unsatisfactory unless reference were made to the peculiar views of some who believe that political rather than legal considerations should govern in determining the justice or the injustice of the proceedings against Jesus before Pilate. A certain class of critics insist on regarding the Roman governor in the light of an administrator rather than a judge, and contend that the justice of his conduct and the righteousness of his motives should be tested by principles of public policy rather than by strict legal rules. It is insisted by such persons that various considerations support this contention. It is pointed out that Pilate exercised the unlimited jurisdiction of the military *imperium*, and was not, therefore, strictly bound by legal rules; that Jesus was not a Roman citizen, and, for this reason, was not entitled to the strict observance of forms of law; and that the stubborn, rebellious and turbulent temper of the Jewish people required the strong hand of a military governor, enforcing political obedience by drastic measures, rather than the action of a judge punctiliously applying rules of law. These peculiar views subject the conduct of Pilate to the pressure of public necessity rather than to the test of private right, and insist that sympathy rather than censure should hold the scales in which his deeds are weighed.

This view of the case was presented in the last generation by Sir James Fitz-James Stephen in a book of extraordinary strength and brilliancy entitled "Liberty, Equality, Fraternity." It was written in answer to John Stuart Mill, and is, without doubt, the most powerful assault in the English language on what men have been pleased to call in modern times "liberty of conscience." In his letters and essays, Mr. Mill, according to the interpretation of Mr. Stephen, "condemns absolutely all interference with the expression of opinion." When tried by this standard, the Athenian dicasts, who condemned Socrates; Marcus Aurelius, who persecuted the Christians; Pontius Pilate, who crucified Jesus; and Philip II, who sanctioned the tortures of the Spanish Inquisition, were simply violators of rights of personal opinion and of freedom of conscience. If you deny the right of liberty of conscience, Mr. Mill contends, you must not censure Marcus Aurelius and other persecutors of Christianity. On the contrary, you must approve such persecution; and you must go further, and find "a principle which would justify Pontius Pilate." This challenge was boldly accepted by Mr. Stephen, who says:

"Was Pilate right in crucifying Christ? I reply, Pilate's paramount duty was to preserve the peace in Palestine, to form the best judgment he could as to the means required for that purpose, and to act upon it when it was formed. Therefore, if and in so far as he believed in good faith and on reasonable grounds that what he did was necessary for the preservation of the peace of Palestine, he was right. It was his duty to run the risk of being mistaken, notwithstanding Mr. Mill's principle as to liberty. He was in the position of a judge whose duty it is to try persons duly brought before him for trial at the risk of error."[119]

This contention is founded upon the inexorable doctrine that what is, is right; that revolution, though righteous, must be nipped in the bud and destroyed; and that rights of private conscience must not be tolerated if they tend to disturb the peace of the community at large. The inevitable logic of the theory of Mr. Stephen is that the established order of things in Palestine under Roman rule was right, and that it was the duty of the Roman governor to regard all attempts at innovation or revolution in religion or government as a breach of the peace which was to be promptly suppressed by vigorous measures. There is undoubtedly a certain amount of truth in this contention, in so far as it implies that under a just and orderly plan of government, the rights of the commonwealth to peace and security are greater than the claims of the individual to liberty of conscience which conflict with and tend to destroy those rights. It is a truth, at once sovereign and fundamental, in both law and government, that the rights of the collective body are greater than those of any individual member; and that when the rights of the whole and those of a part of the body politic conflict, the rights of the part must yield and, if necessity requires it, be destroyed. Upon no other basis can the doctrine of majorities in politics and the right of Eminent Domain in law, rest. But the application of the principles involved in this theory must always be made with proper limitations, and with a due regard to the rights of minorities and individuals; else government becomes an engine of despotism instead of an expression of political freedom. A claim of privilege which every member of the community has a right to make, must be respected by the collective body; otherwise, a common right has been violated and destroyed. The complete recognition of this principle is imperative and fundamental, and is the corner stone of political freedom in free institutions among men.

But the trouble with the contention of Mr. Stephen is that it proceeds upon a wrong hypothesis. He intimates that Pilate might have "believed in good faith that what he did was necessary for the preservation of the peace of Palestine." This is a purely gratuitous and unhistorical suggestion. The Gospel records nowhere justify such an assumption. The very opposite is taught by these sacred writings. It is true that Caiaphas contended that it was expedient that one man should die rather than that the whole nation should perish. But this was a Jewish, not a Roman opinion. The Evangelical narratives are unanimous in declaring that Pilate believed Jesus to be innocent and that "for envy" He had been accused by His countrymen.

It is cheerfully conceded that occasions may present themselves, in the tumult and frenzy of revolution, when the responsible authorities of government may put to death a person whose intentions are innocent, but whose acts are incentives to riot and bloodshed. This may be done upon the principle of self-preservation, which is the first law of government as well as of nature. But no such necessity arose in the case of Jesus; and no such motives are ascribed by the Evangelists to Pilate. They very clearly inform us that the action of the Roman governor in delivering the prisoner to be crucified was prompted by private and not public considerations. He had no fears that Jesus would precipitate a revolution dangerous to the Roman state. He simply wished to quiet the mob and retain his position as procurator of Judea. The facts of history, then, do not support the contention of Mr. Stephen.

Continuing, in another place, the same eminent writer says: "The point to which I wish to direct attention is that Pilate's duty was to maintain peace and order in Judea and to maintain the Roman power. It is surely impossible to contend seriously that it was his duty, or that it could be the duty of any one in his position, to recognize in the person brought to his judgment seat, I do not say God Incarnate, but the teacher and preacher of a higher form of morals and a more enduring form of social order than that of which he himself was the representative. To a man in Pilate's position the morals and the social order which he represents are for all practical purposes final and absolute standards. If, in order to evade the obvious inference from this, it is said that Pilate ought to have respected the principle of religious liberty as propounded by Mr. Mill, the answer is that if he had done so he would have run the risk of setting the whole province in a blaze. It is only in very modern times, and under the influence of modern sophisms, that belief and action have come to be so much separated in these parts of the world that the distinction between the temporal and spiritual department of affairs even appears to be tenable; but this is a point for future discussion.

"If this should appear harsh, I would appeal again to Indian experience. Suppose that some great religious reformer—say, for instance, some one claiming to be the Guru of the Sikhs, or the Imam in whose advent many Mahommedans devoutly believe—were to make his appearance in the Punjab or the North-West Provinces. Suppose that there was good reason to believe—and nothing is more probable—that whatever might be the preacher's own personal intentions, his preaching was calculated to disturb the public peace and produce mutiny and rebellion: and suppose further (though the supposition is one which it is hardly possible to make even in imagination), that a British officer, instead of doing whatever might be necessary, or executing whatever orders he might receive, for the maintenance of British authority, were to consider whether he ought not to become a disciple of the Guru or Imam. What course would be taken towards him? He would be instantly dismissed with ignominy from the service which he would disgrace, and if he acted up to his convictions, and preferred his religion to his Queen and country, he would be hanged as a rebel and a traitor."[120]

These theories and illustrations are not only plausible but entirely reasonable when viewed in the light of the facts which they assume to be true. But here again, we must insist that they do not harmonize with the actual facts of the case to which they are intended to apply. In the extract above quoted, three suppositions are suggested. The first one is immaterial. Let us analyze the other two in the light of the Gospel histories. The second supposition is this: "Suppose that there was good reason to believe—and nothing is more probable—that whatever might be the preacher's own personal intentions, his preaching was calculated to disturb the public peace and produce mutiny and rebellion." What passage of Scripture, it may be asked, justifies this parallel with the case of Jesus before Pilate? There is, in fact, absolutely none. The nearest approach to one is Matthew xxvii. 24: "When Pilate saw that he could prevail nothing, but that rather a tumult was made, he took water, and washed his hands before the multitude, saying, I am innocent of the blood of this just person: see ye to it." The "tumult" here referred to means nothing more than the manifestation of agitated feelings on the part of the mob, who were enraged at the prospect of an acquittal by the governor. It does not remotely refer to the danger of a popular rebellion which might endanger the security and safety of Rome. To admit this supposition would be to elevate the motives of Pilate in consenting to the crucifixion of Jesus to the level of solicitude for the welfare of his country. This would not be justified by the record, which clearly reveals that Pilate was moved by personal selfishness rather than by a sense of official duty.

The third and last supposition above mentioned is this: "And suppose, further (though the supposition is one which it is hardly possible to make even in imagination), that a British officer, instead of doing whatever might be necessary, or executing whatever orders he might receive, for the maintenance of British authority, were to consider whether he ought not to become a disciple of the Guru or Imam." Here again, we may ask, what passage of Scripture supports this parallel of a Mohammedan Guru before a British officer with Jesus Christ before Pontius Pilate? Where is it anywhere stated, or by reasonable inference implied, that Pilate considered whether he ought not to become a disciple of Jesus? The celebrated English author has simply argued his case from a radically defective record of fact.

On the other hand, let us draw what we conceive to be a true parallel. Let us take an illustration nearer home. Suppose that the Governor General of the Philippine Islands was clothed with authority of life and death as a judge in criminal matters pertaining to the affairs of those islands. Suppose that a Mohammedan preacher should appear somewhere in the archipelago where Mohammedans are numerous, and begin to proclaim a new religious faith which was opposed not only to the ordinary tenets of Islamism, but also to the Christian religion which is the dominant faith of the rulers of the Philippines. Suppose that the coreligionists of this Mohammedan prophet should seize him, bring him before the Governor General, and lodge against him a threefold charge: That he was stirring up sedition in the islands; that he had advised the Filipinos not to pay taxes due to the United States government; and that he had said and done things that were treasonable against the United States. Suppose that the Governor General, after personal examination, became satisfied that the Mohamammedan preacher was an innocent enthusiast, that the charges against him were false, and were due to the envy and hatred of his fellow-Mohammedans; that to quiet the passions, and satisfy the demands of the mob, he proposed to scourge him first and then release him; that, in the face of the vehement accusations of the rabble, he hesitated and vacillated for several hours; and that finally, when the Mohammedans threatened to send a complaint to President Roosevelt which might endanger his position, he ordered his innocent prisoner to death. Suppose this should happen beneath the American flag, what would be the judgment of the American people as to the merits of the proceedings? Would the Governor General retain his office by such a course of conduct?

But let us view it in another light. Let us assume that the Governor General believed that the Mohammedan preacher was innocent and that his "personal intentions" were not remotely hostile or treasonable, but felt that his preaching might stir up rebellion dangerous to the power of the American government in the Philippines; and that it was his duty as the guardian of American honor and security, to put the native preacher to death; and this not to punish past criminal conduct, but to prevent future trouble by a timely execution. Suppose that the Governor General should do this while sitting as a judge, would it not be judicial murder? Suppose that he should do it while acting as an administrator, would it be less an assassination? Would it not stamp with indelible shame the administration that should sanction or tolerate it? Would the press of America not denounce the act as murder, declare that despotism reigned in our Eastern possessions, and demand the removal and punishment of the man who had disgraced his office and brought odium upon the administrative justice of his country?

In closing the Roman trial of Jesus, let us repeat what we have already said: that the conduct of Pilate, when the prisoner was first brought before him, seems to have been marked by judicial regularity and solemnity; that the Roman procurator seems to have deported himself in a manner worthy of his office; that, in the beginning, he appears to have resolved to observe due forms of law in the proceedings, to the end that justice might be attained; and that, after a comparatively regular trial, he pronounced an absolute verdict of acquittal. Thus far the course of Pilate is manly and courageous. But with the return of the prisoner from Herod, unmanliness and cowardice begin.

This last act of the great drama presents a pitiable spectacle of Roman degeneracy. A Roman governor of courtly origin, clothed with *imperium*, with a Prætorian Cohort at his command, and the military authority and resources of an empire at his back, cringes and crouches before a Jerusalem mob. The early Christian writers characterized Pilate with a single term (ἀνανδρία), "unmanliness." They were right. This word is a summary, accurate and complete, of the character of the man.

There is inherent in the highest and noblest of the human species a quality of courage which knows no fear; that prefers death and annihilation to dishonor and disgrace; that believes, with Cæsar, that it is better to die at once than to live always in fear of death; and, with Mahomet, that Paradise will be found in the shadow of the crossing of swords. This quality of courage is peculiar to no race of men and to no form of civilization. It has existed everywhere and at all times. It causes the spirit of man to tread the earth like a lion and to mount the air like an eagle. The ancient barbarians of Gaul believed that lightning was a menace from the skies; and amidst the very fury of the storm, from their great bows they sent arrows heavenward as a defiance to the gods. This quality of courage, which is natural to man, Pilate lacked. And when we think of his cowardly, cringing, crouching, vacillating conduct before a few fanatical priests in Jerusalem, another scene at another time comes up before us. The Tenth Legion rises in mutiny and defies Julius Cæsar. The mighty Roman summons his rebellious soldiers to the Field of Mars, reads to them the Roman riot act, and threatens to dismiss them not only from his favor but from Roman military service. The veterans of a hundred Gallic battlefields are subdued and conquered by the tone and glance of a single man; and with tearful eyes, beg forgiveness, and ask to be permitted to follow once again him and his eagles to the feast of victory and of death. Imagine, if you can, Cæsar in the place of Pilate. it is not difficult to conceive the fare of a vulgar rabble who persisted in annoying such a Roman by demanding the blood of an innocent man.

But the cowardice and pusillanimity of the Roman governor are not properly illustrated by comparison with the courage and magnanimity of a Roman general. At the trial of Jesus, Pilate was acting in a judicial capacity, and was essentially a judge. His character, then, may be best understood by contrasting it with another judge in another age and country. His craven qualities will then be manifest.

The greatest of the English jurists and judges was Sir Edward Coke. His legal genius was superb and his judicial labors prodigious. During the greater part of his professional career he slept only six hours, "and from three in the morning till nine at night he read or took notes of the cases tried in Westminster Hall with as little interruption as possible." He was great not only as a judge, but as an advocate as well. The consummate skill with which he argued the intricate cases of Lord Cromwell and Edward Shelley, brought him a practice never before equaled in England, and made him renowned as the greatest lawyer of the times. His erudition was profound, his powers of advocacy brilliant, his personal and judicial courage was magnificent. He not only repeatedly defied and ridiculed his colleagues on the bench, but more than once excited the wrath and braved the anger of the king. He fearlessly planted himself upon the ancient and inalienable rights of Englishmen; and, time and time again, interposed his robe at office between the privileges of the Commons and the aggressions of the Crown. He boldly declared that a royal proclamation could not make that an offense which was not an offense before. His unswerving independence was well illustrated in a case brought before him in 1616. The question at issue was the validity of a grant made by the king to the Bishop of Lichfield of a benefice to be held *in commendam*. King James, through his attorney-general, Bacon, commanded the chief justice to delay judgment till he himself had discussed the question with the judges. Bacon, at Coke's request, sent a letter containing the same command to each of the judges. Coke then obtained their signatures to a paper declaring that the instructions of the attorney-general were illegal, and that they were bound to proceed with the case. The king became very angry, summoned the judges before him in the council chamber, declared to them his kingly prerogative, and forbade them to discuss his royal privileges in ordinary arguments before their tribunal. Coke's colleagues fell upon their knees, cowed and terrified, before the royal bigot and despot, and begged his pardon for having expressed an opinion that had excited his displeasure. But Coke refused to yield, and, when asked if, in the future, he would delay a case at the king's order, he bravely replied that on all occasions and under any emergency, he would do nothing unworthy of himself or his office as an English citizen and judge. And rather than prostitute the high prerogatives of his court, he indignantly and contemptuously hurled his judicial mantle into the face of the Stuart king. How much grander and nobler was the conduct of Coke, the Englishman, than that of Pilate, the cowardly, pusillanimous Roman! Both were judges, both stood in the shadow of the majesty and menace of a throne, both were threatened with royal wrath, both held high judicial places under the governments of the most vast and glorious empires that this world has known. Coke preferred the dictates of his conscience to the decrees of his king; and his name remains forever enshrined in the minds and memories of men as the noblest type of a brave and righteous judge. For a miserable mess of Roman political pottage, Pilate forfeited his birthright to the most splendid and illustrious example of judicial integrity and courage in the history of the earth; and his name remains forever a hissing and reproach, as the worst specimen of the corrupt and cowardly judge that mankind has known.

If it be objected that the position of Pilate was more painful and precarious than that of Coke, because the Roman was confronted by a wild and furious mob, reply must then be made that both the spirit and letter of Roman laws forbade surrender by Roman governors and administrators of the principles of justice to the blind passions of the multitude. This spirit was, in a later age, set forth in the laws of Justinian, when reproduction was made of the proclamations of the emperors Diocletian and Maximian, on the occasion of a public riot, that "the vain clamors of the people are not to be heeded, seeing that it is in no wise necessary to pay any attention to the cries of those desiring the acquittal of the guilty, or the condemnation of the innocent."[121]

Pilate yielded to the demands of the mob when his country's laws forbade it. His intellect willed the execution of an innocent man when his conscience condemned it. "Such was the man whose cowardice, made manifest in the most supreme and memorable act of injustice the world has ever known, was destined to earn him eternal infamy. To him and to no others pointed the poet as

'colui
Che fece per viltate il gran rifiuto;'

to him, the prototype of that long train of those who were never quite alive, who vainly sought glory in this world, vainly dreaded infamy; who, ever wavering betwixt good and evil, washed their hands; who, like the neutral angels of the threshold, were neither faithful nor rebellious; who are equally despised by pity and justice; who render themselves

'A Dio spiacenti ed ai nemici sui.'

And what man other than Pilate was ever placed so typically, in such accordance with the eyes of the poet, between the Son of God and His enemies, between justice and mercy, between right and wrong, between the Emperor and the Jews, and has refused either issue of the dilemma?

"Was it Celestine, Diocletian, or Esau? But they of two things chose the one; and who knows but that they chose the better? A hermitage and a mess of pottage may under many aspects be better worth than the papacy renounced by Celestine, than the empire abdicated by Diocletian, or than the birthright bartered by Esau. But Pilate refused to choose, and his refusal was great—great enough to justify the antonomasia of Dante—and it was cowardly. He refused not only the great gift of free will in a case when a free choice was his absolute duty. When admitted, like the fallen angels, to the great choice between good and evil, he did not cleave for ever to the good, as did St. Michael, or to the evil, as did Lucifer, but he refused a power which for him was the fount of duty and which cost the life of a man and the right of an innocent."

But was Pilate alone guilty of the crime of the crucifixion? Were the Jews wholly blameless? This raises the question: Who were the real crucifiers of the Christ, the Jews or the Romans? That the Jews were the instigators and the Romans the consummators of the crucifixion is evident from the Gospel narratives. The Jews made the complaint, and the Romans ordered and effected the arrest of the prisoner in Gethsemane. Having tried Him before their own tribunal, the Jews then led Jesus away to the Roman governor, and in the Prætorium accused Him and furnished evidence against Him. But the final act of crucifying was a Roman act. It is true that Jewish elements were present in the crucifixion of Jesus. The death draught offered Him on the cross suggests a humane provision of Hebrew law. This drink was usury administered among the Hebrews "so that the delinquent might lose clear consciousness through the ensuing intoxication." Again, the body of Jesus was removed from the cross and buried before it was night. This was in deference to an ancient custom of the Jews to bury criminals before sunset who had first been executed by stoning for the crime of blasphemy and had then been subjected to the indignity of being hung upon a tree, in conformity with a Mosaic ordinance contained in Deut. xxi. 22. But these two incidents exhaust the Jewish features of the crucifixion; and, besides, these elements were merely physical. The spiritual or moral features, involving turpitude and crime, are entirely different considerations from those that are simply historical. The question still arises: Who were the morally guilty parties? Who were the directly responsible agents of the crucifixion, the Jews or the Romans? Upon whom should the greater blame rest, if both were guilty? A passage from St. John seems to indicate that the Jews were the bearers of the greater sin. Replying to a question of Pilate concerning the procurator's power to crucify Him, "Jesus answered, Thou couldest have no power at all against me, except it were given thee from above; therefore he that delivered me unto thee hath the greater sin."[122] According to many commentators, Jesus referred to Caiaphas; according to others, He spoke of Judas as the person who had the greater sin. But in any case it is certain that He did not intend to involve the whole Jewish nation in the crime of His arrest and execution. The language of the scriptural context indicates a single person. Pilate, on the one hand, is made the silent instrument in the hands of God for the accomplishment of the designs of Heaven. Caiaphas, on the other hand, is probably referred to as the one having the greater sin, because, being the high priest of the Sanhedrin, he better understood the questions involved in the religious charge of blasphemy, and was, therefore, the greater sinner against the laws of God, in the matter of the injustice then being perpetrated.

THE CRUCIFIXION (MUNKACSY)

Aside from the religious questions involved, and speaking in the light of history and law, our own judgment is that the real crucifiers of the Christ were the Romans, and that Pilate and his countrymen should bear the greater blame. It is true that the Jews were the instigators, the accusers. But Pilate was the judge whose authority was absolute. The Jews were powerless to inflict the death penalty. Pilate had the final disposition of all matters of life and death. In short, he could have prevented the crucifixion of Jesus. He did not do so; and upon him and his countrymen should rest the censure of Heaven and the execration of mankind.

But, admitting that the priests of the Sanhedrin were equally guilty with Pilate and the Romans, does it follow that all Jews of the days of Jesus who were not participants in the crime against him, should suffer for the folly and criminal conduct of a mere fragment of a Saducean sect? Is it not true that the Jewish people, as a race, were not parties to the condemnation and execution of the Christ? Is it not reasonable to suppose that the masses in Palestine were friendly to the democratic Reformer who was the friend of the poor, the lame, and the blind? Did not the reception of his miracles and his triumphal entry into Jerusalem indicate His popularity with the plain people? Is it not historically true that the great body of the Jewish population in Judea, in Galilee, in Samaria, and in Perea, was unfriendly to the members of the Sanhedrin, and regarded them as political renegades and religious delinquents? Is it not reasonably certain that a large majority of the countrymen of Jesus were his ardent well-wishers and sincerely regretted his untimely end? Is it possible to conceive that these friends and well-wishers were the inheritors of the curse of Heaven because of the crime of Golgotha? If not, is it rational to suppose that their innocent descendants have been the victims of this curse?

The cruel and senseless notion of the implacable wrath of Deity has prevailed in all the ages as an explanation of the destruction of Jerusalem and the dispersion and persecution of the Jews. It is worse than nonsense to see in this event anything but the operation of vulgar physical forces of the most ordinary kind. The fall of Jerusalem was a most natural and consequential thing. It was not even an extraordinary historical occurrence, even in Jewish history. Titus did not so completely destroy Jerusalem as did Nebuchadnezzar before him. Razing cities to the ground was a customary Roman act, a form of pastime, a characteristic Roman proceeding in the case of stubborn and rebellious towns. Scipio razed Carthage and drove Carthaginians into the most remote corners of the earth. Was any Roman or Punic god interested in this event? Cæsar destroyed many Gallic cities and scattered Gauls throughout the world. Was any deity concerned about these things?

Roman admiration was at times enkindled, but Roman clemency was never gained by deeds of valor directed against the arms of Rome. Neither Hannibal nor Mithradates, Vercingetorix nor Jugurtha, the grandest of her enemies, received any mercy at her hands. To oppose her will, was to invite destruction; and the sequel was a mere question of "the survival of the fittest." The most turbulent, rebellious and determined of all the imperial dependencies was the province of Judea. The Jews regarded the Romans as idolaters; and, instead of obeying them as masters, despised and defied them as barbarians. When this spirit became manifest and promised to be perpetual, the dignity of the Roman name as well as the safety of the Roman State, demanded the destruction of Jerusalem and the dispersion of the Jews. And destruction and dispersion followed as naturally as any profane effect follows any vulgar cause.

The Irish, another splendid race, are being dispersed throughout the earth by the English domination of Ireland. Is anybody so keenly discerning as to see in Irish dispersion a divine or superhuman agency? Is it not, after all, the simple operation of the same brutal, physical forces that destroyed Carthage and Jerusalem, and, in a latter century, dismembered Poland?

But the advocates of the divine wrath theory quote Scriptures and point to prophecy in support of their contention. Then Scriptures must be pitted against Scriptures. The last prayer of the Master on the cross must be made to repeal every earlier Scriptural prophecy or decree. "Father, forgive them, for they know not what they do," is the sublimest utterance in the literature of the world. It is the epitome of every Christian virtue and of all religious truth. This proclamation from the cross repealed the Mosaic law of hereditary sin; placed upon a personal basis responsibility for offenses against God and man; and served notice upon future generations that those who "know not what they do" are entitled to be spared and forgiven. To believe that God ignored the prayer of Christ on the cross; and that the centuries of persecution of the Jews which followed, were but the fulfillment of prophecy and fate, is to assail the Messiahship of Jesus and to question the goodness and mercy of Jehovah. Jesus knew the full meaning of His prayer and was serious unto death. To believe that the Father rejected the petition of the Son is to destroy the equality of the persons of the Trinity by investing one with the authority and power to review, revise, and reject the judgments and petitions of the others. If the Christian doctrine be true that Christ was God "manifest in the flesh"; if the doctrine of the Trinity be true that God the Father, God the Son, and God the Holy Ghost, are one and the same, eternal and inseparable, then the prayer of Jesus on the cross was not a petition, but a declaration that the malefactors of the crucifixion, who, in the blindness of ignorance, had helped to kill the Son of Man, would receive at the Last Day the benefits of the amnesty of the Father of mercy and forgiveness.

If the perpetrators of the great injustice of the Sanhedrin and of the Prætorium are to be forgiven because they knew not what they did, is there any justice, human or divine, in persecuting their innocent descendants of all lands and ages? "When Sir Moses Montefiore was taunted by a political opponent with the memory of Calvary and described by him as one who sprang from the murderers who crucified the world's Redeemer, the next morning the Jewish philanthropist, whom Christendom has learned to honor, called upon his assailant and showed him the record of his ancestors which had been kept for two thousand years, and which showed that their home had been in Spain for two hundred years before Jesus of Nazareth was born." This half-humorous anecdote illustrates the utter absurdity and supreme injustice of connecting the modern Jew with ancient tragic history. The elemental forces of reason, logic, courage and sympathy, wrapped up and interwoven in every impulse and fiber of the human mind and heart, will be forever in rebellion against the monstrous doctrine of centuries of shame, exile and persecution visited upon an entire race, because of the sins and crimes of a handful of their progenitors who lived more than a thousand years before.

But, if the visitation of the sins of the fathers upon the sons is to be maintained, and perpetuated as a form of divine, if not of human justice, then, why not, at least, be consistent in the application of the principle? Many philosophers and critics have detected a striking kinship between the teachings of Socrates and those of Jesus. A celebrated historian closes a chapter of the history of Greece with this sentence: "Thus perished the greatest and most original of the Grecian philosophers (Socrates), whose uninspired wisdom made the nearest approach to the divine morality of the Gospel."[123] The indictments against the philosopher of Athens and the Prophet of Nazareth were strikingly similar. Socrates was charged with corrupting Athenian youth; Jesus, with perverting the nation. Socrates was charged with treason against Athens; Jesus, with treason against Rome. Both were charged with blasphemy; the Athenian, with blasphemy of the Olympic gods; the Nazarene, with blaspheming Jehovah. Both sealed with their blood the faith that was in them. If the descendants of the crucifiers of the Christ are to be persecuted, brutalized, and exiled for the sins of the fathers, why not apply the same pitiless law of hereditary punishment to the descendants of the Athenian dicasts who administered hemlock to the greatest sage of antiquity? Why not persecute all the Greeks of the earth, wherever found, because of the injustice of the Areopagus?

Coming back from antiquity and the Greeks to modern times in America, let us express the hope that all forms of race prejudice and persecution will soon cease forever. It is a truth well known of all intelligent men that racial prejudice against the Jew has not completely vanished from the minds and hearts of Gentiles; that political freedom in an enlightened age has not brought with it full religious tolerance and social recognition; that the Jew enjoys the freedom of the letter, but is still under the ban of the spirit. It is not necessary to go to Russia to prove this contention. In 1896, Adolf von Sonnenthal, the greatest of modern actors, who has covered the Austrian stage with glory, celebrated the fortieth anniversary of his entrance into theatrical life. The City Council of Vienna refused to extend him the freedom of the city, because he was a Jew. In 1906, Madame Bernhardt, the most marvelous living woman, while acting in Canada, was insulted by having spoiled eggs thrown upon the stage amidst shouts of "Down with the Jewess!" This outrage called forth a letter of apology, which appeared in public print, from Sir Wilfred Laurier, Prime Minister of the Dominion. In the summer of 1907, the sister of Senator Isidor Rayner, of Maryland, was refused admission to an Atlantic City hotel because she was a Jewess. Be it remembered that these several acts of prejudice and persecution did not happen in the Middle Ages, or under the government of the Romanoffs. Two of them occurred at the beginning of the twentieth century, beneath the flags of two of the freest and most civilized nations of the globe. What have Americans to say of the exclusion of a virtuous, refined, intelligent sister of a great American senator from an American hotel for no other reason than that she was a Jewess; that is, that she was of the same race with the Savior of mankind?

There is certainly no place for religious intolerance and race prejudice beneath our flag. Fake and hypocritical our religion, if while professing faith in Jesus we continue to persecute those for whom He prayed! In vain did Washington, marching in Liberty's vanguard, "lead Freedom's eaglets to their feast"; in vain the proclamation of the Declaration of Independence and the adoption of the Constitution at Philadelphia, a hundred years ago; in vain the bonfires and orations of the nation's natal day, if our boasted liberties are to exist in theory, but not in practice, in fancy, but not in fact!

Let no persecutor of the Jew lay the unction to his soul that he is justified by the tragedy of Golgotha; for he who persecutes in the name of religion is a spiritual barbarian, an intellectual savage. Let this same persecutor not make the mistake of supposing that the Jews are wholly responsible for the persecution that has been heaped upon them. Before he falls into the foolish blunder of such a supposition, let him ponder the testimony of several Gentile experts upon the subject. Let him read "The Scattered Nation," a brilliant lecture on the Jew by the late Zebulon Vance, of North Carolina, in which occurs this sentence: "If the Jew is a bad job, in all honesty we should contemplate him as the handiwork of our own civilization." Let him find Shakespearean confirmation of this statement in "The Merchant of Venice," Act III, Scene i. If the Jew-baiter objects that this is the imagination of a poet, let us then point him to the testimony of a great historian and statesman to prove to him that the Gentile is in great measure responsible for the causes that have produced Jewish persecution.

In the British House of Commons, on April 17, 1873, a bill for the removal of the disabilities of the Jews was the subject of parliamentary discussion. Lord Macaulay took part in the debate and spoke as follows:

The honorable member for Oldham tells us that the Jews are naturally a mean race, a money-getting race; that they are averse to all honorable callings; that they neither sow nor reap; that they have neither flocks nor herds; that usury is the only pursuit for which they are fit; that they are destitute of all elevated and amiable sentiments.

Such, sir, has in every age been the reasoning of bigots. They never fail to plead in justification of persecution the vices which persecution has engendered. England has been legally a home to the Jews less than half a century, and we revile them because they do not feel for England more than a half patriotism.

We treat them as slaves, and wonder that they do not regard us as brethren. We drive them to mean occupations, and then reproach them for not embracing honorable professions. We long forbade them to possess land, and we complain that they chiefly occupy themselves in trade. We shut them out from all the paths of ambition, and then we despise them for taking refuge in avarice.

During many ages we have, in our dealings with them, abused our immense superiority of force, and then we are disgusted because they have recourse to that cunning which to the natural and universal defence of the weak against the violence of the strong. But were they always a mere money-changing, money-getting, money-hoarding race? Nobody knows better than my honorable friend, the member for the University of Oxford, that there is nothing in their national character which unfits them for the highest duties of citizens.

He knows that, in the infancy of civilization, when our island was as savage as New Guinea, when letters and art were still unknown to Athens, when scarcely a thatched hut stood on what was afterwards the site of Rome, this contemned people had their fenced cities and cedar palaces, their splendid Temple, their fleets of merchant ships, their schools of sacred learning, their great statesmen and soldiers, their natural philosophers, their historians and their poets.

What nation ever contended more manfully against overwhelming odds for its independence and religion? What nation ever, in its last agonies, gave such signal proofs of what may be accomplished by a brave despair? And if, in the course of many centuries, the depressed descendants of warriors and sages have degenerated from the qualities of their fathers; if, while excluded from the blessings of law and bowed down under the yoke of slavery, they have contracted some of the vices of outlaws and slaves, shall we consider this is a matter of reproach to them? Shall we not rather consider it as a matter of shame and remorse to ourselves? Let us do justice to them. Let us open to them the door of the House of Commons. Let us open to them every career in which ability and energy can be displayed. Till we have done this, let us not presume to say that there is no genius among the countrymen of Isaiah, no heroism among the descendants of the Maccabees.

If the persecutor of the Jew is not moved by the eloquence of Macaulay or by the satire and sarcasm of Shakespeare, then let him call the roll of Hebrew great names and watch the mighty procession as it moves. Abraham among patriarchs; Moses among lawgivers; Isaiah and Jeremiah among prophets; Philo, Maimonides, Spinoza, and Mendelsohn among philosophers; Herschel, Sylvester, Jacobi, and Kronecker among mathematicians and astronomers; Josephus, Neander, Graetz, Palgrave, and Geiger among historians; Mendelssohn, Meyerbeer, Offenbach, Goldmark, Joachim, Rubinstein, and Strauss among musicians; Sonnenthal, Possart, Rachel, and Bernhardt among actors and actresses; Disraeli, Gambetta, Castelar, Lasker, Crémieux, and Benjamin among statesmen; Halevi and Heine among poets; Karl Marx and Samuel Gompers among labor leaders and political economists; the Rothschilds, Bleichrörders, Schiffs, and Seligmans among financiers; Auerbach and Nordau among novelists; Sir Moses Montefiore and Baron Hirsch among philanthropists!

But there are no Cæsars, no Napoleons, no Shakespeares, no Aristotles among them, you say? Maybe so; but what of that? Admitting that this is true, is anything proved by the fact? These characters represented mountain peaks of intellect, and were the isolated products of different races and different centuries. It may be justly observed that, of their kind, no others were comparable to them. But if the "mountain-peak" theory is to govern as to the intellectuality of races, will it be seriously contended that any one of the last-mentioned characters was equal in either spiritual or intellectual grandeur to the Galilean peasant, Jesus of Nazareth? If colossal forms of intellect and soul be invoked, does not the Jew still lead the universe?

Jesus was the most perfect product of Jewish spiritual creation, the most precious gem of human life. The most brilliant and civilized nations of the earth worship Him as God, "manifest in the flesh, justified by the Spirit, seen of angels, preached unto the Gentiles, believed on in the world, received up into glory."[124]

Both skeptics and believers of all ages have alike pronounced His name with reverence and respect. Even the flippant, sarcastic soul of Voltaire was awed, softened and subdued by the sweetness of His life and the majesty of His character.[125]

"If the life and death of Socrates are those of a sage," said Rousseau, "the life and death of Jesus are those of a God."[126]

"Jesus of Nazareth," says Carlyle, "our divinest symbol! Higher has the human thought not yet reached. A symbol of quite perennial, infinite character, whose significance will ever demand to be anew inquired into, and anew made manifest."[127]

"Jesus Christ," says Herder, "is in the noblest and most perfect sense, the realized ideal of humanity."[128]

"He is," says Strauss, "the highest object we can possibly imagine with respect to religion, the Being without whose presence in the mind perfect piety is impossible."[129]

"The Christ of the Gospels," says Renan, "is the most beautiful incarnation of God in the most beautiful of forms. His beauty is eternal; His reign will never end."[130]

Max Nordau betrays secret Jewish pride in Jesus when he says: "Jesus is soul of our soul, even as he is flesh of our flesh. Who, then, could think of excluding him from the people of Israel? St. Peter will remain the only Jew who has said of the Son of David, 'I know not the man.' Putting aside the Messianic mission, this man is ours. He honors our race, and we claim him as we claim the Gospels—flowers of Jewish literature and only Jewish."

"Is it a truth," asks Keim, "or is it nothing but words, when this virtuous God-allied human life is called the noblest blossom of a noble tree, the crown of the cedar of Israel? A full vigorous life in a barren time, a new building among ruins, an erect strong nature among broken ones, a Son of God among the godless and the God-forsaken, one who was joyous, hopeful, generous among those who were mourning and in despair, a freeman among slaves, a saint among sinners—by this contradiction to the facts of the time, by this gigantic exaltation above the depressed uniformity of the century, by this compensation for stagnation, retrogression, and the sickness of death in progress, health, force and color of eternal youth—

finally, by the lofty uniqueness of what he achieved, of his purity, of his God-nearness—he produces, even with regard to endless new centuries that have *through him* been saved from stagnation and retrogression, the impression of mysterious solitariness, superhuman miracle, divine creation."[131]

"Between Him and whoever else in the world," said Napoleon at St. Helena, "there is no possible term of comparison."[132]

Throughout Napoleonic literature two names constantly recur as exhibiting the Corsican's ideals of spiritual and intellectual perfection. These names are those of Jesus Christ and Julius Cæsar. Napoleon's stupendous genius and incomprehensible destiny formed the basis of a secret conviction within his soul that with Jesus and Cæsar displaced, he himself would be the grandest ornament of history. But in the mind of the emperor there was no element of equality or comparison between Jesus and Cæsar. The latter he regarded as the crown and consummation of Roman manhood, the most superb character of the ancient world. The former he believed to be divine.

It was the custom of Napoleon while in exile at St. Helena to converse almost daily about the illustrious men of antiquity and to compare them with himself. On one occasion while talking upon his favorite theme with an officer, one of the companions of his exile, he suddenly stopped and asked: "But can you tell me who Jesus Christ was?" In reply, the officer candidly confessed that he had never thought much about the Nazarene. "Well, then," said Napoleon, "I will tell you." The illustrious captive then compared Jesus with the heroes of antiquity and finally with himself. The comparison demonstrated how paltry and contemptible was everything human when viewed in the light of the divine character and sublime achievements of the Man of Nazareth. "I think I understand somewhat of human nature," said Napoleon, "and I tell you all these were men, and I am a man, but not one is like Him; Jesus Christ was more than man. Alexander, Cæsar, Charlemagne, and myself founded great empires; but upon what did the creations of our genius depend? Upon force. Jesus alone founded His empire upon love, and to this very day millions would die for Him."[133]

We have every reason to believe that the homage paid the character of Jesus by Napoleon was not merely the product of his brain, but was also the humble tribute of his heart. When the disasters of the Russian campaign broke upon his fortunes, when "the infantry of the snow and the cavalry of the wild blast scattered his legions like winter's withered leaves," the iron-hearted, granite-featured man who had "conquered the Alps and had mingled the eagles of France with the eagles of the crags," only laughed and joked. But, while contemplating the life and death of Jesus, he became serious, meditative and humble. And when he came to write his last will and testament, he made this sentence the opening paragraph: "I die in the Roman

Catholic Apostolical religion, in the bosom of which I was born more than fifty years ago."[134] The Christianity of Napoleon has been questioned. It is respectfully submitted that only an ungenerous criticism will attribute hypocrisy to this final testimony of his religious faith. The imperial courage, the grandeur of character, and the loftiness of life of the greatest of the emperors negative completely the thought of insincerity in a declaration made at a time when every earthly inducement to misrepresentation had passed forever.

But Jesus was not the Christ, the Savior of warrior-kings alone, in the hour of death. On the battlefield of Inkerman an humble soldier fell mortally wounded. He managed to crawl to his tent before he died. When found he was lying face downward with the open Bible beside him. His right hand was glued with his lifeblood to Chapter XI., Verse 25 of St. John. When the hand was lifted, these words, containing the ever-living promise of the Master, could be clearly traced: "I am the resurrection and the life: he that believeth in me, though he were dead, yet shall he live."

PART II
GRÆCO-ROMAN PAGANISM

JUPITER (ANTIQUE SCULPTURE)

CHAPTER I

GRÆCO-ROMAN PAGANISM

EXTENT of the Roman Empire at the Time of Christ.—The policy of ancient Rome was to extend and hold her possessions by force of arms. She made demands; and if they were not complied with, she spurned the medium of diplomacy and appealed for arbitrament to the god of battles. Her achievements were the achievements of war. Her glories were the glories of combat. Her trophies were the treasures of conquered provinces and chained captives bowed in grief and shame. Her theory was that "might makes right"; and in vindication and support of this theory she imbued her youth with a martial spirit, trained them in the use of arms from childhood to manhood, and stationed her legions wherever she extended her empire. Thus, military discipline and the fortune of successful warfare formed the basis of the prosperity of Rome.

At the period of which we write, her invincible legions had accomplished the conquest of the civilized earth. Britain, Gaul, Spain, Italy, Illyria, Greece, Asia Minor, Africa, Egypt, and the islands of the Mediterranean—six hundred thousand square leagues of the most fertile territory in the world— had been subdued to the Roman will and had become obedient to Roman decrees. "The empire of the Romans," says Gibbon, "filled the world, and when that empire fell into the hands of a single person, the world became a safe and dreary prison for his enemies. The slave of imperial despotism, whether he was compelled to drag his gilded chain in Rome and the Senate, or to wear out a life of exile on the barren rock of Seriphus, or on the frozen banks of the Danube, expected his fate in silent despair. To resist was fatal, and it was impossible to fly. On every side he was encompassed by a vast extent of sea and land, which he could never hope to traverse without being discovered, seized, and restored to his irritated master. Beyond the frontiers, his anxious view could discover nothing, except the ocean, inhospitable deserts, hostile tribes of barbarians, of fierce manners and unknown language, or dependent kings who would gladly purchase the emperor's protection by the sacrifice of an obnoxious fugitive. 'Wherever you are,' said Cicero to the exiled Marcellus, 'remember that you are equally within the power of the conqueror.'"

In obedience to a universal law of development and growth, when the Roman empire had reached the limits of physical expansion, when Roman conquest was complete, when Roman laws and letters had reached approximate perfection, and when Roman civilization had attained its crown and consummation, Roman decline began. The birth of the empire marked the beginning of the end. It was then that the shades of night commenced to gather slowly upon the Roman world; and that the Roman ship of state began to move slowly but inevitably, upon a current of indescribable depravity and degeneracy, toward the abyss. The Roman giant bore upon his shoulders the treasures of a conquered world; and Bacchus-like, reeled, crowned and drunken, to his doom.

No period of human history is so marked by lust and licentiousness as the history of Rome at the beginning of the Christian era. The Roman religion had fallen into contempt. The family instinct was dead, and the marital relation was a mockery and a shame. The humane spirit had vanished from Roman hearts, and slavery was the curse of every province of the empire. The destruction of infants and the gladiatorial games were mere epitomes of Roman brutality and degeneracy. Barbarity, corruption and dissoluteness pervaded every form of Roman life.

A perfect picture of the depravity of the times about which we write may be had from a perusal of the Roman satirists, Tacitus and Juvenal. The ordinary Roman debauchee was not the sole victim of their wrath. They chiseled the hideous features of the Cæsars with a finer stroke than that employed by Phidias and Praxiteles in carving statues of the Olympic gods.

The purpose of Part II of this volume is to give coloring and atmosphere to the picture of the trial and crucifixion of Jesus by describing: (1) The Græco-Roman religion; and (2) the Græco-Roman social life, during the century preceding and the century following the birth of the Savior.

1.—THE GRÆCO-ROMAN RELIGION

Origin and Multiplicity of the Roman Gods.—The Romans acquired their gods by inheritance, by importation, and by manufacture. The Roman race sprang from a union of Etruscans, Latins, and Sabines; and the gods of these different tribes, naturalized and adopted, were the first deities of Rome. Chief among them were Janus, Jupiter, Juno, and Minerva. Other early Roman deities were Sol, the Sun, and Luna the Moon, both of Sabine origin; Mater Matuta, Mother of Day; Divus Pater Tiberinus, or Father Tiber; Fontus, the god of fountains; Vesta, the goddess of the hearth; and the Lares and Penates, household gods.

These primitive Italian divinities were at first mere abstractions, simple nature-powers; but later they were Hellenized and received plastic form. The Greeks and Romans had a common ancestry and the amalgamation of their religions was an easy matter. The successive steps in the process of blending the two forms of worship are historical. From Cumæ, one of the oldest Greek settlements in Italy, the famous Sibylline books found their way to Rome; and through these books the Greek gods and their worship established themselves in Italy. The date of the arrival of several of the

Hellenic deities is well ascertained. The first temple to Apollo was vowed in the year 351 A.U.C. To check a lingering epidemic of pestilence and disease, the worship of Æsculapius was introduced from Epidaurus into Rome in the year 463. In 549, Cybele, the Idæan mother, was imported from Phrygia, in the shape of a black stone, and was worshiped at Rome by order of the Sibylline books.

In various ways, the Hellenization of the Roman religion was accomplished. The Decemviri, to whom the consulting of the Sibylline books was intrusted, frequently interpreted them to mean that certain foreign gods should be invited at once to take up their residence in Rome.

The introduction of Greek literature also resulted in the importation of Greek gods. The tragedies of Livius Andronicus and the comedies of Nævius, founded upon Greek legends of gods and heroes, were presented in Rome in the later years of the third century B.C. Fragments of Greek literature also began to make their way into the Capital about this time. Philosophers, rhetoricians, and grammarians flocked from Greece to Italy and brought with them the works of Homer, Hesiod and the Greek philosophers, whose writings were permeated with Greek mythology.

Grecian sculpture was as potent as Grecian literature in transforming and Hellenizing the religion of Rome. The subjugation of the Greek colonies in the south of Italy and the conquests of Greek cities like Syracuse and Corinth in the East, brought together in Rome the masterpieces of the Greek sculptors.

A determined effort was made from time to time by the patriotic Romans to destroy Hellenic influence and to preserve in their original purity early Roman forms of worship. But all attempts were futile. The average Roman citizen, though practical and unimaginative, was still enamored of the beautiful myths and exquisite statues of the Greek gods. And it was only by Hellenizing their own deities that they could bring themselves into touch and communion with the Hellenic spirit. The æsthetical and fascinating influence of the Greek language, literature and sculpture, was overwhelming. "At bottom, the Roman religion was based only on two ideas—the might of the gods who were friendly to Rome, and the power of the ceremonies over the gods. How could a religion, so poverty-stricken of thought, with its troops of phantom gods, beingless shadows and deified abstractions, remain unscathed and unaltered when it came in contact with the profusion of the Greek religion, with its circle of gods, so full of life, so thoroughly anthropomorphised, so deeply interwoven into everything human?"[135]

Not only from Greece but from every conquered country, strange gods were brought into Italy and placed in the Roman pantheon. When a foreign city was besieged and captured, the Romans, after a preliminary ceremony, invited the native gods to leave their temples and go to Rome where, they were assured, they would have much grander altars and would receive a more enthusiastic worship. It was a religious belief of the ancient masters of the world that gods could be enticed from their allegiance and induced to emigrate. In their foreign wars, the Romans frequently kept the names of their own gods secret to prevent the enemy from bribing them.

The gods at Rome increased in number just in proportion that the empire expanded. The admission of foreign territory brought with it the introduction of strange gods into the Roman worship.

When the Romans needed a new god and could not find a foreign one that pleased them, they deliberately manufactured a special deity for the occasion. In the breaking up and multiplication of the god-idea, they excelled all the nations of antiquity. It was the duty of the pontiffs to manufacture a divinity whenever an emergency arose and one was needed. The god-casting business was a regular employment of the Decemviri and the Quindecemviri; and a perusal of the pages of Roman history reveals these god-makers actively engaged in their workshops making some new deity to meet some new development in Roman life.

The extent of the polytheistic notions of the ancient Romans is almost inconceivable to the modern mind. Not only were the great forces of nature deified, but the simplest elements of time, of thought, and action. Ordinary mental abstractions were clothed with the attributes of gods. Mens (Mind), Pudicitia (Chastity), Pietas (Piety), Fides (Fidelity), Concordia (Concord), Virtus (Courage), Spes (Hope), and Voluptas (Pleasure), were all deities of the human soul, and were enthusiastically worshiped by the Romans. A single human action was frequently broken into parts each of which had a little god of its own. The beginning of a marriage had one deity and its conclusion, another. Cunina was the cradle-goddess of a child. Statilinus, Edusa, Potnia, Paventia, Fabelinus and Catius were other goddesses who presided over other phases of its infancy. Juventas was the goddess of its youth; and, in case of loss of parents, Orbona was the goddess that protected its orphanage.

Any political development in the Roman state necessitated a new divinity to mark the change. In the early periods of their history, the Romans used cattle as a medium of exchange in buying and bartering. Pecunia was then the goddess of such exchange. But when, in later times, copper money came into use, a god called Æsculanus was created to preside over the finances; and when, still later, silver money began to be used, the god Argentarius was called into being to protect the coinage. This Argentarius was naturally the son of Æsculanus.

Not only the beneficent but the malign forces of nature were deified. Pests, plagues, and tempests had their special divinities who were to be placated. "There were particular gods for every portion of a dwelling—the door, the threshold of the door, and even the hinges of the door. There was a special god for each different class—even the most menial and the most immoral; and a special divinity for those who were afflicted in a peculiar manner, such as the childless, the maimed or the blind. There was the god of the stable, and the goddess of the horses; there were gods for merchants, artists, poets and tillers of the soil. The gods must be invoked before the harvest could be reaped; and not even a tree could be felled in the forest without supplicating the unknown god who might inhabit it."[136]

The extreme of the Roman divinity-making process was the deification of mere negative ideas. Tranquillitas Vacuna was the goddess of "doing nothing."

Not only were special actions and peculiar ideas broken up and subdivided with an appropriate divinity for each part or subdivision, but the individual gods themselves were subdivided and multiplied. It is said that there were three hundred Jupiters in Rome. This means that Jupiter was worshiped under three hundred different forms. Jupiter Pluvius, Jupiter Fulgurator, Jupiter Tonans, Jupiter Fulminator, Jupiter Imbricitor, Jupiter Serenator, were only a few designations of the supreme deity of the Romans.

It will thus be seen that polytheism was insatiable in its thirst for new and strange gods. When the god-casting business was once begun, there was no end to it. And when the Roman empire had reached its greatest expansion, and Roman public and private life had attained to complete development, the deities of the Roman religion were innumerable. No pantheon could hold them, and no Roman could remember the names of all. Temples of the gods were everywhere to be found throughout the empire; and where there were no altars or temples, certain trees, stones and rocks were decorated with garlands and worshiped as sacred places which the gods were supposed to frequent. Thus the Roman world became crowded with holy places, and the gods and goddesses became an innumerable host. Petronius makes a countrywoman from a district adjoining Rome declare that it was much easier to find a god in her neighborhood than a man. We shall see that the multiplicity of the gods was finally the cause of the decay and ruin of the Roman religion.

The Roman Priesthood.—The Roman priesthood was composed of several orders of pontiffs, augurs, keepers of the Sibylline books, Vestal virgins, epulos, salians, lupercals, etc.

Fifteen pontiffs exercised supreme control in matters of religion. They were consecrated to the service of the gods; and all questions of doubtful religious interpretation were submitted to the judgment of their tribunal.

Fifteen learned and experienced augurs observed the phenomena of nature and studied the flight of birds as a means of directing the actions of the state.

Fifteen keepers of the Sibylline books read the pages of their treasures and from them divined coming events.

Six Vestals, immaculate in their virginity, guarded the Roman sacred fire, and presided at the national hearthstone of the Roman race.

Seven epulos conducted the solemn processions and regulated the religious ceremonies at the annual festivals of the gods.

Fifteen flamens were consecrated to the service of separate deities. Those of Jupiter, Mars, and Quirinus were held in the highest esteem. The Flamen Dialis, or priest of Jupiter, was loaded down with religious obligations and restrictions. He was not permitted to take an oath, to ride, to have anything tied with knots on his person, to look at a prisoner, see armed men, or to touch a dog, a goat, or raw flesh, or yeast. He was not allowed to bathe in the open air; nor could he spend the night outside the city. He could resign his office only on the death of his wife. The Salians were priests of Mars, who, at festivals celebrated in honor of the war-god, danced in heavy armor, and sang martial hymns.

Roman Forms of Worship.—Roman worship was very elaborate and ceremonial. It consisted of sacrifices, vows, prayers, and festivals. With the exception of the ancient Hebrews, the Romans were the greatest formalists and ritualists of antiquity. Every act of Roman public and private life was supposed to be framed in accordance with the will of the gods. There was a formula of prayer adapted to every vicissitude of life. Cæsar never mounted his chariot, it is said, that he did not repeat a formula three times to avert dangers.

A painful exactness in the use of words was required in the offering of a Roman prayer. A syllable left out or a word mispronounced, or the intervention of any disturbing cause of evil import, would destroy the merit of the formula. The Romans believed that the voice of prayer should not be interrupted by noises or bad omens. And that the sound of evil augury might not be heard at the moment of supplication, they were in the habit of covering their ears. Musical notes of favorable import were not objectionable, and frequently flutes were played while the prayer was being offered to chase away disturbing sounds. At other times, the priests had special assistants whose duty it was to maintain silence during the recital of the formula. But, if the ceremony was successful, if the language had been correctly pronounced, without the omission or addition of a word; if all disturbing causes and things of evil omen had been alienated from the services, then the granting of the prayer was assured, regardless of the motive or intention of the person praying. It should be remembered that piety and faith were not necessary to the efficacy of Roman prayer. Ceremonial precision, rather than purity of heart, was pleasing to the Roman gods. A peculiar element entered into the religions of both the ancient Romans and the ancient Hebrews. It was the principle of contract in an almost purely juristic sense. Both the Romans and the Hebrews believed that if the divine law was obeyed to the letter, their deities were under the strictest obligation to grant their petitions.

Under the Roman form of worship, a peculiar act of supplication was performed by the suppliant who kissed his right hand, turned round in a circle by the right, and then seated himself upon the ground. This was done in obedience to one of the laws of Numa. The circular movement of the earth, it was thought, was symbolized by the turning round in a circle; and the sitting down indicated that the suppliant was confidant that his prayer would be granted.

The Romans believed that prayers were more efficacious if said in the immediate presence and, if possible, in actual contact with the image of the god. The doorkeepers of the temple were frequently besieged by suppliants who begged to be admitted into the inclosures of the sacred places where they might pray to the deity on the spot.

On account of the vast numbers of the gods, the Romans were sometimes at a loss to know which one to address in prayer. Unlike the Greeks, they had no preferences among their deities. Each was supplicated in his turn according to the business in hand. But they were frequently in doubt as to the name of the god who had control of the subject-matter of their petitions. In such cases, the practical genius of the Roman people served them well. They had recourse to several expedients which they believed would insure success. When in doubt as to the particular divinity which they should address in supplication, they would, at times, invoke, in the first place, Janus, the god of all good beginnings, the doorkeeper, so to speak, of the pantheon, who, it was believed, would deliver the prayer to the proper deity. At other times, in such perplexity, they would address their petitions to a group of gods in which they knew the right one was bound to be. It sometimes happened that they did not know whether the deity to be supplicated was a god or goddess. In such an emergency, they expressed themselves very cautiously, using the alternative proviso: "Be thou god or goddess." At other times, in cases of extreme doubt, they prayed to all the deities at once; and often, in fits of desperation, they dismissed the entire pantheon and addressed their prayers to the Unknown God.

Another mode of propitiating the gods was by sacrifice. Animals, the fruits of the fields, and even human beings were devoted to this purpose. In the matter of sacrifice, the practical genius of the Roman people was again forcibly manifested. They were tactful enough to adapt the sacrifice to the whims and tastes of the gods. A provision of the Twelve Tables was that "such beasts should be used for victims as were becoming and agreeable to each deity." The framers of these laws evidently believed that the gods had keenly whetted appetites and discriminating tastes in the matter of animal sacrifice. Jupiter Capitolinus was pleased with an offering of white cattle with gilded horns, but would not accept rams or bulls. Mars, Neptune and Apollo were, on the other hand, highly delighted with the sacrifice of bulls. It was also agreeable to Mars to have horses, cocks, and asses sacrificed in his honor. An intact heifer was always pleasing to the goddess Minerva. A white cow with moon-shaped horns delighted Juno Calendaris. A sow in young was sacrificed to the great Mother; and doves and sparrows to Venus. Unweaned puppies were offered as victims of expiation to the Lares and Penates. Black bulls were usually slaughtered to appease the infernal gods.

The most careful attention was given to the selection of the victims of sacrifice from the flocks and herds. Any serious physical defect in the animal disqualified. A calf was not fit for slaughter if its tail did not reach to the joint of the leg. Sheep with cloven tongues and black ears were rejected. Black spots on a white ox had to be rubbed white with chalk before the beast was available for sacrifice.

Not only animals were sacrificed, but human beings as well, to appease the wrath of the gods in time of awful calamity. In early Roman history, gray-headed men of sixty years were hurled from the Pons Sublicius into the Tiber as an offering to Saturn. In the year 227 B.C., the pontiffs discovered from the Sibylline books that the Gauls and Greeks were to attack and capture the city. To fulfill the prophecy and, at the same time to avert the danger, the senate decreed that a man and woman of each of these two nations should be buried alive in the forum as a form of constructive possession. This was nothing but a human sacrifice to the gods.

Again, two of Cæsar's soldiers, who had participated in a riot in Rome, were taken to the Campus Martius and sacrificed to Mars by the pontiffs and the Flamen Martialis. Their heads were fixed upon the Regia, as was the case in the sacrifice of the October-horse. As an oblation to Neptune, Sextus Pompeius had live men and horses thrown into the sea at the time when a great storm was destroying the fleet of the enemy.

A near approach to human sacrifice was the custom of sprinkling the statue of Jupiter Latiaris with the blood of gladiators. A priest caught the blood as it gushed from the wound of the dying gladiator, and dashed it while still warm at the face of the image of the god.

Suetonius tells us that after the capture of Perugia, Augustus Cæsar slaughtered three hundred prisoners as an expiatory sacrifice to Julius Cæsar.

Thus at the beginning of the Christian era, human beings were still being sacrificed on the altars of superstition.

Ascertaining the Will of the Gods.—Various methods were employed by the Romans in ascertaining the will of the gods. Chief among these were the art of divination from the flight of birds and from the inspection of the entrails of animals; also from the observation of lightning and the interpretation of dreams. The Romans had no oracles like those of the Greeks, but they frequently sent messengers to consult the Delphic oracle.

Nothing is stranger or more disgusting in all the range of religious history than the practice of the Roman haruspices. That the ancient masters of the world should have felt themselves obliged to search in the belly of a beast for the will of Jupiter is one of the abominable enigmas of Pagan superstition. The inspection of the entrails of victims was a Tuscan science, early imported from Etruria, and naturalized at Rome. Tuscan haruspices accompanied the Roman armies everywhere, and determined by their skill whether a battle should be fought or a retreat ordered. When it was doubtful what to do, an animal was slaughtered, and the heart, lungs, liver, tongue, spleen, kidneys and caul were closely inspected with the aid of a small needle or knife. Various conditions and appearances of these parts were considered as signs of the pleasure or disfavor of the gods. Largely developed veins on the adverse side were considered tokens of extreme displeasure and an indication of pending misfortune. It was also considered gravely ominous when the head or protuberance in the right lobe of the liver was wanting. The Romans were too practical and indomitable, however, to allow a single bad omen to frustrate a great enterprise. If the inspection of the entrails of the first animal was not favorable, they slaughtered still others until a propitious sign was observed. At times, a score of beasts were slain before the gods gave assent to the enterprise in hand.

Divination from the flight and notes of birds was another method employed by the Romans in finding out the will of the gods. And it may be remarked that this was certainly a more rational and elevated form of divination than that which we have just discussed. An eagle swooping down from the skies would certainly be a more natural and pleasing suggestion of the thoughts and attributes of Jove than the filthy interior of the entrails of a bull.

The elements of divination from the flight of birds were derived either from the significant notes and sounds of their voices, or from the manner in which their wings were flapped or their flight conducted. If the bird flew from the left to the right of the augur, it was considered a happy omen; if the flight was in the opposite direction, the enterprise in hand had to be abandoned or at least delayed. Augury by flight was usually applied to eagles and vultures, while woodpeckers, ravens, crows, and screech owls announced the will of the gods by note. The direction from which the note came, usually determined the nature of the augury. But, in the case of the screech owl, the sounds were always of evil omen, from whatever side they came. And those who have been so unfortunate as to hear its mournful, desolate and God-forsaken tones will not be disposed to censure either the Romans or their gods for the low esteem in which they held this bird.

Again, it was a principle of Roman augury that auspices could be neutralized or overcome. If a crow furnished an omen, and an eagle gave another which was opposed to it, the first sign was wiped out, because the eagle was a larger and nobler bird than the crow. And, as in the case of prayer, so also in the matter of the auspices, a disturbing sound would destroy the effect of the augury. The squeak or cry of a mouse would destroy a message from Jupiter conveyed in the scream of an eagle.

But the most potent manifestation of the divine mind, among the ancient Romans, was that derived from thunder and lightning. Lightning to them was the sovereign expression of the will of the gods; and a single flash blotted out every other sign and token. It was an irrevocable presage and could not be remotely modified or evaded. It came directly from the hand of the deity and was an emphatic revelation of the divine mind. All places struck by lightning were considered sacred and were consecrated to the god who had sent the bolt. Upon the spot where it fell, an altar was raised and an inclosure formed. The service of consecration consisted in burying the lightning, that is, in restoring the earth thrown up by it, and in the sacrifice of a two-year-old sheep. All such places were considered hallowed spots and it was impious and sacrilegious to touch them or even look at them. The gods deprived of reason those who destroyed the altars and sacred inclosures of these places.

These various methods of ascertaining the will of the deities were employed in every important transaction of Roman public and private life. At times, all of them coöperated on occasions of vast import and when the lives and destinies of great men were involved.

The following single paragraph from Suetonius contains allusions to all the modes of divination which we have just discussed:

After the death of Cæsar, upon his return from Apollonia as he was entering the city, on a sudden, in a clear and bright sky a circle resembling the rainbow surrounded the body of the sun; and immediately afterwards, the tomb of Julia, Cæsar's daughter, was struck by lightning. In his first consulship whilst he was observing the auguries, twelve vultures presented themselves as they had done to Romulus. And when he offered sacrifice, the livers of all the victims were folded inward in the lower part; a circumstance which was regarded by those present, who had skill in things of that nature, as an indubitable prognostic of great and wonderful fortune.[137]

The interpretation of dreams also formed an important part in the determination of the will of the gods, not only among the Romans, but among all ancient nations. The literature of antiquity, both sacred and profane, is filled with dreams. Whether the biographer is Matthew or Plutarch, dreams appear on the pages of both. Chrysippus made a collection of prophetical dreams in order to explain their meaning. Both Galen and Hippocrates believed that dreams were sent by the gods to men. Artemidorus wrote a treatise on the subject, and in it he assures us that it was compiled at the express bidding and under the direction of Apollo himself.

It was in a dream that Joseph was warned not to put away Mary his wife.[138] It was also in a dream that an angel voice warned him to flee into Egypt with the infant Savior to escape the murderous designs of Herod.[139] Nearly every great event, both in Greek and Roman history, seems to have been heralded or attended by dreams. The following account is given by Suetonius of the dreams of Quintus Catulus and Marcus Cicero presaging the reign of Augustus:

Quintus Catulus had a dream, for two nights successively after his dedication of the Capitol. The first night he dreamt that Jupiter out of several boys of the order of the nobility who were playing about his altar, selected one, into whose bosom he put the public seal of the commonwealth, which he held in his hand; but in his vision the next night, he saw in the bosom of Jupiter Capitolinus, the same boy; whom he ordered to be removed, but it was forbidden by the God, who declared that it must be brought up to become the guardian of the state. The next day, meeting Augustus, with whom till that hour he had not the least acquaintance, and looking at him with admiration, he said he was extremely like the boy he had seen in his dream. Some gave a different account of Catulus's first dream, namely that Jupiter, upon several noble lads requesting of him that they might have a guardian, had pointed to one amongst them, to whom they were to prefer their requests; and putting his fingers to the boy's mouth to kiss, he afterwards applied them to his own.

Marcus Cicero, as he was attending Caius Cæsar to the Capitol, happened to be telling some of his friends a dream which he had the preceding night, in which he saw a comely youth let down from heaven by a golden chain, who stood at the door of the Capitol, and had a whip put into his hands by Jupiter.

And immediately upon sight of Augustus, who had been sent for by his uncle Cæsar to the sacrifice, and was as yet perfectly unknown to most of the company, he affirmed that it was the very boy he had seen in his dream. When he assumed the manly toga, his senatorian tunic becoming loose in the seam on each side, fell at his feet. Some would have this to forebode, that the order of which that was the badge of distinction, would some time or other be subject to him.[140]

Omens also played an important rôle in molding the destiny of the Roman state. In his "Life of Cæsar Augustus," Suetonius says:

Some signs and omens he regarded as infallible. If in the morning, his shoe was put on wrong, the left instead of the right, that boded some disaster. If when he commenced a long journey, by land or sea, there happened to fall a mizzling rain, he held it to be a good sign of a speedy and happy return. He was much affected likewise with anything out of the common course of nature. A palm-tree which chanced to grow up between some stones in the court of his house, he transplanted into a court where the images of the Household Gods were placed, and took all possible care to make it thrive. In the island of Capri, some decayed branches of an old ilex, which hung drooping to the ground, recovered themselves upon his arrival; at which he was so delighted, that he made an exchange with the Republic of Naples, of the Island of Ischia, for that of Capri. He likewise observed certain days; as never to go from home the day after the Numdinæ, nor to begin any serious business upon the nones; avoiding nothing else in it, as he writes to Tiberius, than its unlucky name.[141]

Any unusual happening and all the striking phenomena of nature were regarded by the Romans as prodigies or omens indicative of the will of the gods. The nature of the occurrence indicated the pleasure or the wrath of the deity. An eclipse of the sun and the moon, a shooting star, a rainbow of peculiar color, showers of stones and ashes, were regarded as awful prodigies, and generally threw the Roman Senate into a panic. On such occasions, the pontifical college called a hurried meeting. The augurs and haruspices were summoned to immediate duty; and everything was done to ascertain the will of the gods and to do their bidding. A two-headed snake or a three-legged chicken, such as we frequently see to-day, would have shaken the whole Roman religious system to the center.

Such was the credulity of the Roman people, that the most improbable and impossible stories, mere rumors born of lying imposture, were heard and believed. "Idols shed tears or sweated blood, oxen spoke, men were changed into women, cocks into hens, lakes or brooks ran with blood or milk, mice nibbled at the golden vessels of the temples, a swarm of bees lighted on a temple or in a public place." All such alleged occurrences required sacrifices and expiatory rites to conquer the fury and regain the favor of the gods.

Fall of the Early Roman Religion.—At the beginning of the Christian era, the old Roman religion, founded upon the institutions of Numa, had almost come to an end. The invasion of Italy by the Greek gods was the first serious assault upon the early Roman faith. The elegant refinement and fascinating influence of Greek literature, philosophy and sculpture, had incrusted with a gorgeous coating the rude forms of the primitive Roman worship. But, as time advanced, the old gods grew stale and new deities were sought. The human soul could not forever feed upon myths, however brilliant and bewitching. The mysterious and melancholy rites of Isis came to establish themselves by the side of those of Janus and Æsculapius. The somber qualities of the Egyptian worship seemed to commend it. Even so good and grand a man as Marcus Aurelius avowed himself an adorer of Serapis; and, during a sojourn in Egypt, he is reported to have conducted himself like an Egyptian citizen and philosopher while strolling through the temples and sacred groves on the banks of the Nile.[142]

The effect of the repeated changes from one form of religious faith to another was to gradually destroy the moral fiber of Roman worship and to shatter Roman faith in the existence and stability of the gods. The first manifestation of that disintegration which finally completely undermined and destroyed the temple of Roman worship was the familiarity with which the Romans treated their gods. Familiarity with gods, as with men, breeds contempt. A striking peculiarity of both the Roman and Greek mythologies was the intimate relationship that existed between gods and human beings. Sometimes it took the form of personal intercourse from which heroes sprang, as was the case with Jupiter and Alcmene, of whom Hercules was born. At other times, deities and human beings traveled together on long voyages, as was the case with Minerva and Telemachus on their trip to the island of Calypso. These were instances of what the Greeks regarded as that natural and sympathetic relationship that not only could but should exist between them and their divinities. But in time the Romans entered upon a career of frivolous fellowship and familiarity with their gods which destroyed their mutual respect, and hastened the dissolution of the bonds that had hitherto held them together. They began to treat their divinities as men, deserving of honor indeed, but nevertheless human beings with all the frailties and attributes of mortals. "Arnobius speaks of morning serenades sung with an accompaniment of fifes, as a kind of reveille to the sleeping gods, and of an evening salutation, in which leave was taken of the deity with the wishing him a good night's rest."

The Lectisternia or banquets of the gods were ordinary religious functions to which the deities themselves were invited. These feasts were characterized at times by extreme exclusiveness. It was not right, thought the Romans, to degrade and humiliate the greater gods by seating them at the banquet board with smaller ones. So, a right royal fête was annually arranged in the Capitol in honor of Jupiter, Juno, and Minerva. The statue of the great god was placed reclining on a pillow; and the images of the two goddesses were seated upon chairs near him. At other times, the functions were more democratic, and great numbers of the gods were admitted, as well as a few select and distinguished mortals. On such occasions, the images of the gods were placed in pairs on cushions near the table. The Romans believed that the spirit of the god actually inhabited or occupied the statue. This we learn from Lucian. The happy mortals who were fortunate enough to be present at the banquet, actually believed that they were seated among the gods. Livy tells us that once the gods turned on their cushions and reversed themselves at the table, and that mice then came and devoured the meats.[143]

The Roman historians very seriously inform us that special invitations were extended the gods to attend these banquets. They fail to tell us, however, whether R.S.V.P. or any other directions were inserted in the cards of invitation. We are left completely in the dark as to the formality employed by the deities to indicate their acceptance or rejection of the proffered honor.

The purpose of the Lectisternia was at first undoubtedly to promote hospitality and fellowship, and to conciliate the good will of the gods. But finally such intimacy ripened into contempt and all kinds of indecencies began to be practiced against the deities. Speaking of the actions of certain Romans, Seneca says: "One sets a rival deity by the side of another god; another shows Jupiter the time of day; this one acts the beadle, the other the anointer, pretending by gesture to rub in the ointment. A number of coiffeurs attend upon Juno and Minerva, and make pretence of curling with their fingers, not only at a distance from their images, but in the actual temple. Some hold the looking-glass to them; some solicit the gods to stand security for them; while others display briefs before them, and instruct them in their law cases." This rude conduct was practiced by men. But Seneca, continuing, says: "Women, too, take their seats at the Capitol pretending that Jupiter is enamored of them, and not allowing themselves to be intimidated by Juno's presence."[144]

Roman Skepticism.—Of contempt of the gods, which was due to many causes, skepticism was born. The deities of every race had been brought to Rome and placed in the pantheon; and there, gazing into each other's faces, had destroyed each other. The multiplicity of the gods was the chief agency in the destruction of the Roman faith and ritual. The yoke and burden of endless ceremonials had been borne for centuries and were now producing intolerable irritation and nauseating disgust. The natural freedom of the soul was in open rebellion and revolt against the hollow forms and rigid exactions of the Roman ritual. The eagle of the human intellect was already preparing to soar above the clouds of superstition. Cicero gave expression to the prevalent sentiments of educated Romans of his day when he wrote:

I thought I should be doing an immense benefit both to myself and to my countrymen if I could entirely eradicate all superstitious errors. Nor is there any fear that true religion can be endangered by the demolition of this superstition; for as this religion which is united with the knowledge of nature is to be propagated, so, also, are all the roots of superstition to be destroyed; for that presses upon and pursues and persecutes you wherever you turn yourself, whether you consult a diviner or have heard an omen or have immolated a victim, or beheld a flight of birds; whether you have seen a Chaldæan or a soothsayer; if it lightens or thunders, or if anything is struck by lightning; if any kind of prodigy occurs; some of which things must be frequently coming to pass, so that you can never rise with a tranquil mind.

The completion of Roman conquest in the reign of Augustus was another potent influence in the destruction of the old Roman religion. The chief employment of the Roman gods had ever been as servants of the Roman state in the extension of the Roman empire. Their services were now no longer needed in this regard, and their ancient worshipers were ready to repudiate and dismiss them. The Hebrew characteristic of humility and resignation in the presence of divine displeasure was not a Roman trait. The ancient masters of the world reserved the right to object and even to rebel when the gods failed to do their duty after appropriate prayers had been said and proper ceremonies had been performed. Sacrilege, as the result of disappointment, was a frequent occurrence in Roman religious life. Bitter defiance of the heavenly powers sometimes followed a defeat in battle or a failure in diplomacy. Augustus, as supreme pontiff, chastised Neptune, the god of the sea, because he lost his fleet in a storm, by forbidding the image of the god to be carried in the procession of the next Circensian games. The emperor Julian was regarded as a most pious potentate, but he did not hesitate to defy the gods when he became displeased. At the time of the Parthian war, he was preparing to sacrifice ten select and beautiful bulls to Mars the Avenger, when nine of them suddenly lay down while being led to the altar, and the tenth broke his band. The fury of the monarch was aroused, and he swore by Jupiter that he would not again offer a sacrifice to Mars.[145] Claudius, the commander of the Roman fleet at Drepanum, ordered the sacred pullets to be thrown into the sea because they would not eat. When Germanicus was sick in Asia, his devoted admirers offered frequent prayers to the gods for his recovery. When the report of his death reached Rome, the temples of the unaccommodating deities were stoned, and their altars were overturned.[146]

The same feeling of angry resentment and defiance may be discerned in inscriptions on the graves of relatives prematurely snatched away by death. An epitaph on the monument of a child of five years was this: "To the unrighteous gods who robbed me of my life." Another on the tombstone of a maiden of twenty, named Procope, read as follows: "I lift my hand against the god who has deprived me of my innocent existence."[147]

The soil of familiarity, contempt and sacrilege which we have just described, was most fertile ground for the growth of that rank and killing skepticism which was destroying the vitals of the Roman faith at the time of Christ. This unbelief, it is true, was not universal. At the time of the birth of the Savior, the Roman masses still believed in the gods and goddesses of the Greek and Roman mythologies. Superstition was especially prevalent in the country districts of both Greece and Italy. Pausanias, who lived about the middle of the second century of the Christian era, tells as that in his time the olden legends of god and hero were still firmly believed by the common people. As he traveled through Greece, the cypresses of Alcmæon, the stance of Amphion, and the ashes of the funeral piles of Niobe's children were pointed out to him. In Phocis, he found the belief still existing that larks laid no eggs there because of the sin of Tereus.[148] Plutarch, who lived about the middle of the first century of our era, tells us that the people were still modeling the gods in wax and clay, as well as carving them in marble and were worshiping them in contempt and defiance of philosophers and statesmen.[149] But this credulity was limited to the ignorant and unthinking masses. The intellectual leaders of both the Greek and Roman races had long been in revolt against the absurdity and vulgarity of the myths which formed the foundation of their popular faiths. The purity and majesty of the soul felt keenly the insult and outrage of enforced obedience to the obscene divinities that Homer and Hesiod had handed down to them. Five hundred years before Christ, Pindar, the greatest lyric poet of Greece, had denounced the vulgar tales told of the deities, and had branded as blasphemous the story of the cannibal feast spread for the gods by the father of Pelops. Xenophanes, also, in the sixth century before Christ, had ridiculed the mythical tales of the Homeric poems, and had called attention to the purely human character of popular religions. He had pointed out that the Ethiopians painted the images of their deities black, and gave them flat noses, in the likeness of themselves; that the Thracians, on the other hand, created their gods blue-eyed and red; and that, in general, every race had reflected its own physical peculiarities in the creation of its gods. He declared it to be his opinion that if the beasts of the field should attempt to produce a likeness of the gods, the horses would produce a resemblance of themselves, and that oxen and lions would ascribe to their own divinities their own images and peculiarities.

The whole structure of the Roman religion, built upon myths and adorned with fables, was ill fitted to stand the tests of analysis and criticism. It was destined to weaken and crumble the moment it was subjected to serious rational inquiry. Such inquiry was inevitable in the progress of that soul-growth which the centuries were sure to bring. Natural philosophy and historical study began to dissolve the sacred legends and to demand demonstration and proof where faith had before sufficed. Skeptical criticism began to dissect the formulæ of prayer and to analyze the elements of augury and sacrifice. Reason began to revolt against the proposition that Jupiter was justified in rejecting a petition because a syllable had been omitted or a word mispronounced. Men began to ask: "What explanation could be given of the strange changes of mind in the gods, often threatening evil on the first inspection of the victim, and at the second promising good? How did it happen that a sacrifice to Apollo gave favorable, and one to Diana unfavorable signs? Why did the Etruscan, the Elan, the Egyptian, and the Punic inspectors of sacrifice interpret the entrails in an entirely different manner? Again, what connection in nature was there between a fissure in the liver of a lamb, and a trifling advantage to a man, an inheritance to be expected, or the like? And on a man's intending to sacrifice, did a change, corresponding to his circumstances, take place in the entrails of the beast; so that, supposing another person had selected the same victim, he would have found the liver in a quite different condition?"

The gods themselves became subjects of inspection and analysis. Their origin and nature were studied historically, and were also reviewed in the light of natural and ethical products. Three hundred years before Christ, Evhemere of Messina boldly declared that the gods were simply ancient kings deified by fear and superstition after death. Anaxagoras sought to identify the several deities with the forces and phenomena of nature, thus converting the pantheon into an observatory, or into a physical and chemical laboratory. Metrodorus contended that the gods were deifications of mere abstract ethical precepts.

Instances are recorded in history, from time to time, where the philosophers attempted to explain to the people the natural meaning of those things which they believed were pregnant with supernatural import. On a certain occasion, a ram with one horn was found on the farm of Pericles, and, from this circumstance, an Athenian diviner, named Lampon, predicted that the party of the orator would triumph over the opposite faction and gain control of the government. Whereupon Anaxagoras dissected the skull, and demonstrated to the people the natural cause of the phenomenon in the peculiar shape of the animal's brain. But this reformer finally suffered the fate of other innovators, was prosecuted for impiety, and was only saved by the influence of Pericles.

At the beginning of the Christian era, the religion of Rome was privately ridiculed and repudiated by nearly all statesmen and philosophers of the empire, although they publicly professed it on grounds of public policy. Seneca, a contemporary of Jesus, advised observance of rites appointed by law, on patriotic grounds. "All which things," he says, "a wise man will observe as being commanded by the laws, but not as being pleasing to the gods." Again he says: "All that ignoble rabble of gods which the superstition of ages has heaped up, we shall adore in such a way as to remember that their worship belongs rather to custom than to reality." Ridiculing the popular notions of the matrimonial relations of the deities, the same eminent philosopher says: "And what of this, that we unite the gods in marriage, and that not even naturally, for we join brothers and sisters? We marry Bellona to Mars, Venus to Vulcan, Salacia to Neptune. Some of them we leave unmarried, as though there were no match for them, which is surely needless, especially when there are certain unmarried goddesses, as Populonia, or Fulgora, or the goddess Rumina, for whom I am not astonished that suitors have been wanting."

The prevailing skepticism of the times is well illustrated in a dialogue which Cicero introduces into his first Tusculan Disputation between M, which may be interpreted Marcus, and A, which may be translated Auditor:

> MARCUS: Tell me, are you not afraid of the three-headed Cerberus in the infernal regions, and the roaring of Cocytus, and the passage over Acheron, and Tantalus, dying with thirst, while water laves his chin, and Sisyphus,
>
> "Who sweats with arduous toil in vainThe steepy summit of the mount to gain?"
>
> Perhaps you are also afraid of the inexorable judges, Minos and Rhadamanthus, because before them neither L. Crassus nor M. Antonius can defend you, and because appearing before Grecian judges, you will not be permitted to employ Demosthenes, but must plead for yourself before a very great crowd. All these things, perhaps, you fear, and therefore regard death as an eternal evil.
>
> AUDITOR: Do you think I'm such a fool as to give credence to such things?
>
> MARCUS: What! You don't believe in them?
>
> AUDITOR: Truly, not in the least.
>
> MARCUS: I am deeply pained to hear that.

AUDITOR: Why?

MARCUS: Because, if occasion had offered, I could very eloquently have denounced them, myself.[150]

The contemptuous scorn of the cultivated Romans of his time is frequently revealed in the writings of Cicero. He refers more than once to the famous remark of Cato, who said that he could not explain why the haruspices did not laugh in each other's faces when they began to sacrifice.

At this point, it is worthy of observation that the prevalent unbelief was not limited to a simple denial of the existence of mythical divinities and of the efficacy of the worship rendered them. Roman skepticism sought to destroy the very foundation of all religious belief by denying not only the existence of the gods, but also the immortality of the soul. Cicero is said to have been the only great Roman of his time who believed that death was not the end. Students of Sallust are familiar with his account of the conspiracy of Cataline in which it is related that Julius Cæsar, in a speech before the Roman senate, opposed putting the traitor to death because that form of punishment was too mild, since beyond the grave there was neither joy nor sorrow.[151]

Antagonism to the doctrine of the immortality of the soul reached a melancholy refinement in the strange contention that life after death was a cruel thought. Pliny expresses this sentiment admirably when he says:

What folly it is to renew life after death. Where shall created beings find rest if you suppose that shades in hell and souls in heaven continue to have any feeling? You rob us of man's greatest good—death. Let us rather find in the tranquillity which preceded our existence the pledge of the repose which is to follow it.

When skepticism had destroyed their faith in the gods, and had robbed them of the consolations of religion, educated Romans sought refuge and solace in Greek philosophy. Stoicism and Epicureanism were the dominant spiritual and intellectual forces of the Roman empire at the time of Christ. Epicureanism was founded by Epicurus, who was born of an Athenian family in the Island of Samos about 342 B.C. Stoicism originated with Zeno, a native of Cittium in Cyprus, born about the year 340 B.C.

The original design of the system of Epicurus was to found a commonwealth of happiness and goodness in opposition to the purely intellectual aristocracy of Plato and Aristotle. Men were beginning to tire of speculation and dialectics, and to long for a philosophy built upon human feeling and sensibility. As a touchstone of truth, it was proposed to substitute sensation for intellect. Whatever was pleasing to the natural and healthful senses was to be taken to be true. The pursuit of happiness was to be the chief aim of the devotees of this system. The avoidance of mental pain and physical suffering, as well as the cultivation of all pleasurable emotions, were to be the leading features of every Epicurean programme. In the beginning, Epicureanism inculcated principles of virtue as a means of happiness. The mode of life of the first followers of Epicurus was simple and abstemious. Barley-bread and water are said to have been their ordinary food and drink. But in time this form of philosophy became identified with the coarsest sensuality and the most wicked lust. This was especially true after it was transplanted from Greece to Italy. The doctrines of this school met with a ready response from the pleasure-seeking, luxury-loving Roman people who were now enriched by the spoils and treasures of a conquered world. "This philosophy therefore became at Rome a mere school of self-indulgence, and lost the refinement which, in Greece, had led it to recognize in virtue that which gave zest to pleasure and in temperance that which prolonged it. It called simply for a continuous round of physical delights; it taught the grossest sensuality; it proclaimed the inanity of goodness and the lawfulness of lust. It was the road—sure, steep and swift, to awful demoralization."

Stoicism, on the other hand, furnished spiritual and intellectual food to that nobler class of Romans who were at once the support and ornament of a magnificent but decadent civilization. This form of philosophy was peculiarly consonant with early Roman instincts and habits. In its teachings were perfectly reflected that vigor, austerity, and manly self-reliance which had made the Roman race undisputed masters of the world. Many of its precepts were not only moral and ennobling, but deeply religious and sustaining. A striking kinship between them and certain Christian precepts has been frequently pointed out. Justice, fortitude, prudence, and temperance were the four cardinal virtues of Stoicism. Freedom from all passions and complete simplicity of life, resulting in perfect purity of manners, was its chief aim. But the fundamental principles of both Epicureanism and Stoicism were destructive of those spiritual elements which furnish complete and permanent nourishment to the soul. Stoicism was pantheism, and Epicureanism was materialism. The Stoic believed that the human soul was corporeal, but that it was animated and illuminated by the universal soul. The Epicurean taught that the soul was composed of material atoms, which would perish when its component parts separated or dissolved. Epicureanism was materialistic in its tendency, and its inevitable result, in perverted form, was sensualism. Stoicism was pervaded throughout by a melancholy and desolating fatalism. It was peculiarly the philosophy of suicide; or, as a great French writer once described it, "an apprenticeship for death."[152] To take one's life was not only allowable but commendable in certain cases. Zeno, the founder of the sect, taught that incurable disease was a sufficient excuse for suicide. Marcus Aurelius considered it an obligation of nature and of reason to make an end of life when it became an intolerable burden. "Kill thyself and die erect in the consciousness of thy own strength," would have been a suitable inscription over the doorway of every Stoic temple. Seneca furnished to his countrymen this Stoic panacea for all the ills of life:

Seest thou yon steep height, that is the descent to freedom. Seest thou yon sea, yon river, yon well; freedom sits there in the depths. Seest thou yon low withered tree; there freedom hangs. Seest thou thy neck, thy throat, thy heart; they are the ways of escape from bondage.

And the Roman philosopher was not only conscientious but consistent in his teachings. He was heroic enough to take the medicine himself which he had prescribed for others. Indeed, he took a double dose; for he not only swallowed poison, but also opened his veins, and thus committed suicide, as other Stoics—such as Zeno, Cleanthes and Cato—had done before him.

It was not a problem of the Stoic philosophy,

Whether 'tis nobler in the mind to suffer
The slings and arrows of outrageous fortune,
Or to take arms against a sea of troubles,
And by opposing end them?[153]

A familiar illustration of the advocates of suicide among the Roman writers was that a human body afflicted with incurable disease, or a human mind weighed down with intolerable grief, was like a house filled with smoke. As it was the duty of the occupant of the house to escape from the smoke by flight, so it was the duty of the soul to leave the body by suicide.

But neither Epicureanism nor Stoicism could satisfy the natural longing of the soul for that which is above the earth and beyond the grave. It was impossible that philosophy should completely displace religion. The spiritual nature of the Roman people was still intact and vigorous after belief in myths was dead. As a substitute for their ancient faith and as a supplement to philosophy, they began to deify their illustrious men and women. The apotheosis of the emperors was the natural result of the progressive degradation of the Roman religion. The deification of Julius Cæsar was the beginning of this servile form of worship; and the apotheosis of Diocletian was the fifty-third of these solemn canonizations. Of this number, fifteen were those of princesses belonging to the imperial family.

Divine honors began to be paid to Cæsar before he was dead. The anniversary of his birth became a national holiday; his bust was placed in the temple, and a month of the year was named for him. After his assassination, he was worshiped as a god under the name of Divus Julius; and sacrifices were offered upon his altar. After Julius Cæsar, followed the deification of Augustus Cæsar. Even before his death, Octavian had consented to be worshiped in the provinces, especially in Nicomedia and Pergamus. After his death, his worship was introduced into Rome and Italy.

The act of canonizing a dead emperor was accomplished by a vote of the senate, followed by a solemn ceremony, in which an eagle was released at the funeral pile, and soaring upward, became a symbol of the ascent of the deceased to the skies. A Roman senator, Numerius Atticus, swore that he had seen Augustus ascending to heaven at the time of his consecration; and received from Livia a valuable gift of money as a token of her appreciation of his kindness.

Not only were grand and gifted men like Julius and Augustus Cæsar, but despicable and contemptible tyrants like Nero and Commodus, raised to the rank of immortals. And, not content with making gods of emperors, the Romans made goddesses of their royal women. Caligula had lived in incestuous intercourse with his sister Drusilla; nevertheless, he had her immortalized and worshiped as a divine being. This same Caligula who was a monster of depravity, insisted on being worshiped as a god in the flesh throughout the Roman empire, although the custom had been not to deify emperors until after they were dead. The cowardly and obsequious Roman senate decreed him a temple in Rome. The royal rascal erected another to himself, and appointed his own private priests and priestesses, among whom were his uncle Claudius, and the Cæsonia who afterwards became his wife. This temple and its ministry were maintained at an enormous expense. Only the rarest and most costly birds like peacocks and pheasants, were allowed to be sacrificed to him. Such was the impious conceit of Caligula that he requested the Asiatics of Miletus to convert a temple of Apollo into a shrine sacred to himself. Some of the noblest statuary of antiquity was mutilated in displacing the heads of gods to make places for the head of this wicked monster. A mighty descent this, indeed, from the Olympian Zeus of Phidias to a bust of Caligula!

Domitian, after his deification, had himself styled "Lord and God," in all documents, and required all his subjects to so address him. Pliny tells us that the roads leading into Rome were constantly filled with flocks and herds being driven to the Capital to be sacrificed upon his altar.[154]

The natural and inevitable result of the decay of the Roman religion was the corruption and demoralization of Roman social life. All experience teaches that an assault upon a people's religious system is an assault upon the entire social and moral organization. Every student of history knows that a nation will be prosperous and happy to the extent that it is religiously intelligent, and in proportion to its loyalty to the laws of social virtue, to the laws of good government, and the laws of God; and that an abandonment of its gods means the wreck and dissolution of its entire social structure. The annals of Rome furnish a striking confirmation of this fact.

The closing pages of this chapter will be devoted to a short topical review of Roman society at the time of Christ. Only a few phases of the subject can be presented in a work of this character.

II.—GRÆCO-ROMAN SOCIAL LIFE

Marriage and Divorce.—The family is the unit of the social system; and at the hearthstone all civilization begins. The loosening of the domestic ties is the beginning of the dissolution of the state; and whatever weakens the nuptial bonds, tends to destroy the moral fiber of society. The degradation of women and the destruction of domestic purity were the first signs of decay in Roman life. In the early ages of the republic, marriage was regarded not only as a contract, but as a sacrament as well. Connubial fidelity was sacredly maintained. Matrons of the type of Cornelia, the mother of the Gracchi, were objects of national pride and affection. The spirit of desperation which caused the father of Virginia to plunge a butcher's knife into the chaste and innocent heart of his child to save her from the lust of Appius Claudius, was a tragic illustration of the almost universal Roman respect for virtue in the age of the Tarquins. To such an extent were the marital relations venerated by the early Romans that we are assured by Dionysius that five hundred and twenty years had passed before a single divorce was granted. Carvilius Ruga, the name of the first Roman to procure a divorce, has been handed down to us.[155]

If we are to believe Döllinger, the abandonment of the policy of lifelong devotion to the marriage relation and the inauguration of the system of divorce were due not to the faults of the men but to the dangerous and licentious qualities of the Roman women. In connection with the divorce of Carvilius Ruga, he discusses a widespread conspiracy of Roman wives to poison their husbands. Several of these husbands fell victims to this plot; and, as punishment for the crime, twenty married women were forced to take the poison which they had themselves prepared, and were thus put to death. And, about a half century after this divorce, several wives of distinguished Romans were discovered to be participants in the bacchanalian orgies. From all these things, Döllinger infers that the Roman men began to tire of their wives and to seek legal separation from them.[156]

But, whatever the cause, the marriage tie was so easily severed during the latter years of the republic, that divorce was granted on the slightest pretext. Q. Antistius Vetus divorced his wife because she was talking familiarly and confidentially to one of his freedmen. The wife of C. Sulpicius imprudently entered the street without a veil, and her husband secured a divorce on that ground. P. Sempronius Sophus put away his wife for going to the theater without his knowledge.

Cicero divorced his first wife that he might marry a younger and wealthier woman; and because this second one did not exhibit sufficient sorrow at the death of his daughter, Tullia, he repudiated her.

Cato, the stern Stoic moralist, was several times divorced. To accommodate his friend Hortensius he gave him his second wife Marcia, with her father's consent; and, after the death of the orator, he remarried her.

After being several times previously divorced, Pompey put away Mucia in order that he might wed Julia, Cæsar's daughter, who was young enough to be the child of Pompey.

Cæsar himself was five times married. He divorced his wife, Pompeia, because of her relationship to Clodius, a dashing and dissolute young Roman, who entered Cæsar's house on the occasion of the celebration of the feast of the Bona Dea in a woman's dress, in order that he might pay clandestine suit to the object of his lust. Cæsar professed to believe that the charges against Pompeia were not true, but he divorced her nevertheless, with the remark that "Cæsar's wife must be above suspicion." We are reminded by this that, in ancient as in modern times, society placed greater restrictions upon women than upon men; for Cæsar, who uttered this virtuous and heroic sentiment, was a most notorious rake and profligate. Suetonius tells us that he debauched many Roman ladies of the first rank; among them "Lollia, the wife of Aulus Gabinius; Tertulla, the wife of Marcus Crassus; and Mucia, the wife of Cneius Pompey." It was frequently made a reproach to Pompey, "that to gratify his ambition, he married the daughter of a man upon whose account he had divorced his wife, after having had three children by her; and whom he used, with a deep sigh, to call Ægisthus." But the favorite mistress of Cæsar was Servilia, the mother of Marcus Brutus. To consummate an intrigue with her, he gave Servilia a pearl which cost him six millions of sesterces. And at the time of the civil war he had deeded to her for a trifling consideration, several valuable farms. When people expressed surprise at the lowness of the price, Cicero humorously remarked: "To let you know the real value of the purchase, between ourselves, Tertia was deducted." It was generally suspected at Rome that Servilia had prostituted her daughter Tertia to Cæsar; and the witticism of the orator was a *double entendre*, Tertia signifying the third (of the value of the farm), as well as being the name of the girl, whose virtue had paid the price of the deduction. Cæsar's lewdness was so flagrant and notorious that his soldiers marching behind his chariot, on the occasion of his Gallic triumph, shouted in ribald jest, to the multitude along the way:

Watch well your wives, ye cits, we bring a blade,
A bald-pate master of the wenching trade.[157]

If this was the private life of the greatest Roman of the world, who, at the time of his death, was Pontifex Maximus, the supreme head of the Roman religion, what must have been the social life of the average citizen who delighted to style Cæsar the demigod while living and to worship him as divine, when dead?

A thorough knowledge of the details of the most corrupt and abandoned state of society recorded in history may be had by a perusal of the Annals of Tacitus and the Satires of Juvenal. The Sixth Satire is a withering arraignment of Roman profligacy and wickedness. "To see the world in its worst estate," says Professor Jowett, "we turn to the age of the satirists and of Tacitus, when all the different streams of evil, coming from east, west, north, south, the vices of barbarism and the vices of civilization, remnants of ancient cults, and the latest refinements of luxury and impurity, met and mingled on the banks of the Tiber." Rome was the heart of the empire that pumped its filthy blood from the center to the extremities, and received from the provinces a return current of immorality and corruption. Juvenal complains that

Long since the stream that wanton Syria laves,
Has disembogued its filth in Tiber's waves.

Grecian literature and manners were the main cause of Roman dissoluteness.

The grandfather of Cicero is said to have made this declaration: "A Roman's wickedness increases in proportion to his acquaintance with Greek authors." It is undeniably true that the domestic immorality of the Greeks exercised a most baneful influence upon the social life of the Romans. Both at Athens and in Sparta marriage was regarded as the means to an end, the procreation of children as worshipers of the gods and citizens of the state. In this fundamental purpose were involved, the Greeks believed, the mission and the destiny of woman. Marriage was not so much a sacred institution, as it was a convenient arrangement whereby property rights were regulated and soldiers were provided for the army and the navy. This view was entertained by both the Athenians and the Spartans. The code of Lycurgus regulated the family relations to the end that healthy, vigorous children might be born to a military commonwealth. The Spartan maidens were required to exercise in the palestra, almost naked, in the presence of men and strangers. And so loose and extravagant were the ideas of conjugal fidelity among the Spartans that it was not regarded as an improper thing to borrow another man's wife for the purpose of procreating children, if there had already been born to the legitimate husband all the children that he desired. This we learn from

Xenophon[158] and from Polybius,[159] who assure us that it often happened that as many as four Spartans had one woman, in common, for a wife. "Already in the time of Socrates, the wives of Sparta had reached the height of disrepute for their wantonness throughout the whole of Greece; Aristotle says that they lived in unbridled licentiousness; and, indeed, it is a distinctive feature in the female character there, that publicly and shamelessly they would speed a well-known seducer of a woman of rank by wishing him success, and charging him to think only of endowing Sparta with brave boys."[160]

AVE CÆSAR! IO SATURNALIA (ALMA-TADEMA)

At Athens the principle was the same, even if the gratification of lust was surrounded with a halo of poetry and sentiment which the Spartan imagination was incapable of creating. The Athenians were guilty of a strange perversion of the social instincts by placing a higher appreciation upon the charms of a certain class of lewd women that they did upon the virtuous merits of their own wives and mothers. These latter were kept in retirement and denied the highest educational advantages; while the former, the Hetairai, beautiful and brilliant courtesans, destined for the pleasure and entertainment of illustrious men, were accorded the utmost freedom, as well as all the advantages of culture in the arts and sciences. Demosthenes has classified the women of ancient Athens in this sentence: "We have Hetairai for our pleasure, concubines for the ordinary requirements of the body, and wives for the procreation of lawful issue and as confidential domestic guardians." The most renowned of the Hetairai was Aspasia, the mistress of Pericles. She was exceedingly beautiful and brilliantly accomplished. At her house in Athens, poets, philosophers, statesmen, and sculptors frequently gathered to do her honor. Pericles is said to have wept only three times in life; and one of these was when he defended Aspasia before the dicastery of Athens against the charge of impiety.

Another of the Hetairai scarcely less famous than Aspasia was the celebrated Athenian courtesan, Phryne. Praxiteles, the sculptor, was one of her adorers. She, too, was tried for impiety before the dicastery. Hiperides, the Attic orator, defended her. To create a favorable impression upon the court, he bade her reveal her bosom to the judges. She did so, and was acquitted. So great was the veneration in which Phryne was held that it was considered no profanation to place her image in the sacred temple at Delphi. And so overwhelming was her beauty, that her statues were identified with the Aphrodite of Apelles and the Cnidian goddess of Praxiteles. At Eleusis, on the occasion of a national festival, she impersonated Venus by entering naked into the waves, in the presence of spectators from all the cities of Greece. She is said to have amassed such a fortune that she felt justified in offering to build the walls of Thebes.

Such was the esteem in which these elegant harlots were held, that we find recorded among their patrons on the pages of Greek history the names of Pericles, Demades, Lysias, Demosthenes, Isocrates, Aristotle, Aristippus, and Epicurus. So little odium attached to the occupation of this class of women that we read that Socrates frequently paid visits to one of them named Theodota and advised her as to the best method of gaining "friends" and keeping them.[161]

As the sculptors did not hesitate to carve the images of the Hetairai in marble and give them the names of the goddesses of Olympus, so the poets, orators, and historians did not fail to immortalize them in their poems, orations, and annals. Greek statuary and literature were then transported to Italy to corrupt Roman manners. It was not long before adultery and seduction had completely poisoned and polluted every fountain of Roman private life. "Liaisons in the first houses," says Mommsen, "had become so frequent, that only a scandal altogether exceptional could make them the subject of special talk; a judicial interference seems now almost ridiculous."

Roman women of patrician rank, not content with noblemen as lovers, sought out "lewd fellows of the baser sort" among slaves and gladiators, as companions of corrupt intrigues. Juvenal, in his Sixth Satire, paints a horrible picture of social depravity when he describes the lewdness of Messalina, the wife of Claudius I. This woman, the wife of an emperor, and the mother of the princely Britannicus, descends from the imperial bed, in the company of a single female slave, at the dead of night, to a common Roman brothel, assumes the name Lycisca, and submits to the embraces of the coarsest Roman debauchees.

The degradation of women was not peculiar to the Capital of the empire, but extended to every province. Social impurity was rankest in the East, but it was present everywhere. Virtue seemed to have left the earth, and Vice had taken her place as the supreme mistress of the world.

Luxury and Extravagance.—At the birth of Christ, the frontiers of the Roman empire comprised all the territory of the then civilized world. In extending her conquests, Rome laid heavy tribute upon conquered nations. All the wealth of the earth flowed into her coffers. The result was unexampled luxury and extravagance. A single illustration will serve to show the mode of life of the wealthy Roman citizen of the time of which we write. Lucullus, the lieutenant of Sulla, and the friend of Cicero and Pompey, had amassed enormous wealth in the Mithradatic wars. This fortune he employed to inaugurate and maintain a style of social life whose splendor and extravagance were the astonishment and scandal of his age and race. The meals served upon his table, even when no guests were present, were marked by all the taste, elegance, and completeness of a banquet. On one occasion, when he happened to dine alone, the table was not arranged with the ordinary fullness and splendor; whereupon he made complaint to the servants, who replied that they did not think it necessary to prepare so completely when he was alone. "What! did you not know that Lucullus would dine with Lucullus?" was his answer. At another time, Cicero and Pompey met him in the Forum and requested that he take them with him to dine, as they desired to learn how his table was spread when no visitors were expected. Lucullus was embarrassed for a moment; but soon regained his composure, and replied that he would be delighted to have such distinguished Romans dine with him, but that he would like to have a day for preparation. They refused this request, however; nor would they consent that he send directions to his servants, as they desired to see how meals were served in his home when no guests were there. Lucullus then requested Cicero and Pompey to permit him to tell his servants, in their presence, in what room the repast should be served. They consented to this; and Lucullus then directed that the Hall of Apollo should be arranged for the dinner. Now the dining rooms in the home of Lucullus were graded in price; and it was only necessary to designate the room in order to notify the servants of the style and costliness of the entertainment desired. The Hall of Apollo called for an expenditure, at each meal, of fifty thousand drachmas, the equivalent of $10,000 in our money. And when Cicero and Pompey sat down at the table of Lucullus a few hours later, the decorations of the room and the feast spread before them, offered a spectacle of indescribable beauty and luxury. The epicure had outwitted the orator and the general.

Other anecdotes related by Plutarch also illustrate the luxurious life of Lucullus. Once when Pompey was sick, his physician prescribed a thrush for his meal; whereupon Pompey's servants notified him that a thrush could not be secured in Italy during the summer time, except in the fattening coops of Lucullus.

Cato despised the luxurious habits of Lucullus; and, on one occasion, when a young man was extolling the beauties of frugality and temperance in a speech before the senate, the Stoic interrupted him by asking: "How long do you mean to go on making money like Crassus, living like Lucullus and talking like Cato?"[162]

Lucullus was not the only Roman of his day who spent fabulous sums of money in luxurious living and in building palatial residences. M. Lepidus, who was elected Consul in 87 B.C., erected the most magnificent private edifice ever seen in Rome.

But the culmination of magnificence in Roman architecture was the Golden House of Nero. Its walls were covered with gold and studded with precious stones. The banquet rooms were decorated with gorgeous ceilings, and were so constructed that from them flowers and perfumes could be showered from above on the guests below.

Concerning the luxurious life of the later days of the republic, Mommsen says: "Extravagant prices, as much as one hundred thousand sesterces (£1,000) were paid for an exquisite cook. Houses were constructed with special reference to this subject.... A dinner was already described as poor at which the fowls were served up to the guests entire, and not merely the choice portions.... At banquets, above all, the Romans displayed their hosts of slaves ministering to luxury, their bands of musicians, their dancing-girls, their elegant furniture, their carpets glittering with gold, or pictorially embroidered, their rich silver plate."[163]

But the luxury and extravagance of the Romans were nowhere so manifest as in their public bathing establishments. "The magnificence of many of the thermæ and their luxurious arrangements were such that some writers, as Seneca, are quite lost in their descriptions of them. The piscinæ were often of immense size—that of Diocletian being 200 feet long—and were adorned with beautiful marbles. The halls were crowded with magnificent columns, and were ornamented with the finest pieces of statuary. The walls, it has been said, were covered with exquisite mosaics that imitated the art of the painter in their elegance of design and variety of color. The Egyptian syenite was encrusted with the precious green marbles of Numidia. The rooms contained the works of Phidias and Praxiteles. A perpetual stream of water was poured into capacious basins through the wide mouths of lions of bright and polished silver. 'To such a pitch of luxury have we reached,' says Seneca, 'that we are dissatisfied if we do not tread on gems in our baths.'"[164]

The circuses were scarcely inferior to the baths in magnificence. Caligula is said to have strewn them with gold dust.

The result of Roman luxury in the matter of food and drink was a coarse and loathsome gluttony which finds no parallel in modern life. Epicureanism had degenerated from barley-bread and water to the costliest diet ever known. Wealthy Romans of the age of Augustus did not hesitate to pay two hundred and fifty dollars for a single fish—the mullet. And that they might indulge their appetite to the fullest extent, and prolong the pleasures of eating beyond the requirements and even the capacity of nature, they were in the habit of taking an emetic at meal times. We learn from the letters of Cicero that Julius Cæsar did this on one occasion when he went to visit the orator at his country villa. And the degeneracy of Roman life is nowhere more clearly indicated than in the Fourth Satire of Juvenal where he describes the gathering of the great men of the state, at the call of Domitian, to determine how a turbot should be cooked.

But the reader must not infer that all Romans were rich and that luxury was indulged in every home. In the Roman capital the extremes of wealth and poverty met. The city was filled with idlers, vagabonds and paupers from all quarters of the globe. In the early days of the Republic, sturdy farmers had tilled the soil of Italy and had filled the legions with brave and hardy warriors. The beginning of the empire witnessed a radical change. Hundreds of thousands of these farmers had been driven from their lands to furnish homes to the disbanded soldiers of conquerors like Sulla, Marius, and Cæsar. Homeless and poverty-stricken, they wandered away to Rome to swell the ranks of mendicants and adventurers that crowded the streets of the imperial city. The soldiers themselves, finding agriculture distasteful and unprofitable, sold their lands to Roman speculators, and returned to the scene of the triumphs of their military masters. The inevitable consequence of this influx of strangers and foreigners, without wealth and without employment, was the degradation and demoralization of Roman social and industrial life. Augustus was compelled to make annual donations of money and provisions to 200,000 persons who wandered helpless about the streets. This state of things—fabulous wealth in the hands of a few, and abject poverty as the lot of millions—was the harbinger sure and swift of the destruction of the state.

Slavery.—At the beginning of the Christian era, slavery existed in every province of the Roman empire. Nearly everywhere the number of slaves was much greater than that of the free citizens. In Attica, according to the census of Demetrius Phalereus, about the beginning of the fourth century B.C., there were 400,000 slaves, 10,000 foreign settlers, and 20,000 free citizens. Zumpt estimates that there were two slaves to every freeman in Rome in the year 5 B.C. It frequently happened that a wealthy Roman possessed as many as 20,000 slaves. Slaves who gained their freedom might themselves become masters and own slaves. During the reign of Augustus, a freedman died, leaving 4,116 slaves. Crassus possessed so many that his company of architects and carpenters alone exceeded 500 in number.

The principal slave markets of Greece were those at Athens, Ephesus, Cyprus, and Samos. In the market place of each of these cities, slaves were exposed for sale upon wooden scaffolds. From the neck of each was hung a tablet or placard containing a description of his or her meritorious qualities, such as parentage, educational advantages, health and freedom from physical defects. They were required to strip themselves at the request of purchasers. In this way, the qualifications of slaves for certain purposes could be accurately judged. The vigorous, large-limbed Cappadocians, for instance, like our modern draft horses, were selected for their strength and their ability to lift heavy loads and endure long-continued work.

The property of the master in the slave was absolute. The owner might kill or torture his slave at will. Neither the government nor any individual could bring him to account for it. Roman law compelled female slaves to surrender themselves, against their will, to their master's lust. All the coarseness and brutality of the haughty, arrogant, and merciless Roman disposition were manifested in the treatment of their slaves. Nowhere do we find any mercy or humanity shown them. On the farms they worked with chains about their limbs during the day; and at night they were lodged in the *ergastula*—subterranean apartments, badly lighted and poorly ventilated. The most cruel punishment awaited the slave who attempted to escape. The *fugitavarii*—professional slave chasers—ran him down, branded him on the forehead, and brought him back to his master. If the master was very rich, or cared little for the life of the slave, he usually commanded him to be thrown, as a punishment for his attempt to flee, to the wild beasts in the amphitheater. This cruel treatment was not exceptional, but was ordinary. Cato, the paragon among the Stoics, was so merciless in his dealings with his slaves that one of them committed suicide rather than await the hour of punishment for some transgression of which he was guilty.[165] It frequently happened that the slaves had knowledge of crimes committed by their masters. In such cases they were fortunate if they escaped death, as the probability of their becoming witnesses against their masters offered every inducement to put them out of the way. In his defense of Cluentius, Cicero speaks of a slave who had his tongue cut out to prevent his betraying his mistress.[166] If a slave murdered his master, all his fellow-slaves under the same roof were held responsible for the deed. Thus four hundred slaves were put to death for the act of one who assassinated Pedanius Secundus, during the reign of Nero.[167] Augustus had his steward, Eros, crucified on the mast of his ship because the slave had roasted and eaten a quail that had been trained for the royal quail-pit. Once a slave was flung to the fishes because he had broken a crystal goblet.[168] On another occasion, a slave was compelled to march around a banquet table, in the presence of the guests, with his hands, which had been cut off, hanging from his neck, because he had stolen some trifling article of silverware. Cicero, in his prosecution of Verres, recites an instance of mean and cowardly cruelty toward a slave. "At the time," he says, "in which L. Domitius was prætor in Sicily, a slave killed a wild boar of extraordinary size. The prætor, struck by the dexterity and courage of the man, desired to see him. The poor wretch, highly gratified with the distinction, came to present himself before the prætor, in hopes, no doubt, of praise and reward; but Domitius, on learning that he had only a javelin to attack and kill the boar, ordered him to be instantly crucified, under the barbarous pretext that the law prohibited the use of this weapon, as of all others, to slaves."

The natural consequence of this cruel treatment was unbounded hatred of the master by the slave. "We have as many enemies," says Seneca, "as we have slaves." And what rendered the situation perilous was the numerical superiority of the slave over the free population. "They multiply at an immense rate," says Tacitus, "whilst freemen diminish in equal proportion." Pliny the Younger gave expression to the universal apprehension when he wrote: "By what dangers we are beset! No one is safe; not even the most indulgent, gentlest master." Precautionary measures were adopted from time to time both by individuals and by the government to prevent concerted action among the slaves and to conceal from them all evidences of their own strength. To keep down mutiny among his slaves, Cato is said to have constantly excited dissension and enmity among them. "It was once proposed," says Gibbon, "to discriminate the slaves by a peculiar habit; but it was justly apprehended that there might be some danger in acquainting them with their own numbers."[169]

If the Roman masters maltreated and destroyed the bodies of their slaves, the slaves retaliated by corrupting and destroying the morals of their masters. The institution of slavery was one of the most potent agencies in the demoralization of ancient Roman manners. The education of children was generally confided to the slaves, who did not fail to poison their minds and hearts in many ways. In debauching their female slaves, the Roman masters polluted their own morals and corrupted their own manhood. The result teaches us that the law of physics is the law of morals: that action and reaction are equal, but in opposite directions.

Destruction of New-Born Infants.—The destruction of new-born children was the deepest stain upon the civilization of the ancient Greeks and Romans. In obedience to a provision of the code of Lycurgus, every Spartan child was exhibited immediately after birth to public view; and, if it was found to be deformed and weakly, so that it was unfit to grow into a strong and healthy citizen of the Spartan military commonwealth, it was exposed to perish on Mount Taygetus. The practice of exposing infants was even more arbitrary and cruel in Rome than in Greece. The Roman father was bound by no limitations; but could cast his offspring away to die, through pure caprice. Paulus, the celebrated jurist of the imperial period, admitted that this was a paternal privilege. Suetonius tells us that the day of the death of Germanicus, which took place A.D. 19, was signalized by the exposition of children who were born on that day.[170] This was done as a manifestation of general sorrow. The emperor Augustus banished his granddaughter Julia on account of her lewdness and licentiousness, as he had done in the case of his daughter, Julia. In exile, she gave birth to a child which Augustus caused to be exposed. It often happened that new-born babes that had been cast away to die of cold and hunger or to be devoured by dogs or wild beasts were rescued by miscreants who brought them up to devote them to evil purposes. The male children were destined to become gladiators, and the females were sold to houses of prostitution. Often such children were picked up by those who disfigured and deformed them for the purpose of associating them with themselves as beggars.

The custom of exposing infants was born of the spirit of fierceness and barbarity that characterized many ancient races. Its direct tendency was to make savages of men by destroying those tender and humane feelings for the weak and helpless which have been the most marked attributes of modern civilizations. Occasionally in our day one hears or reads of a proposition by some pseudo-philanthropist that the good of the race demands the destruction of certain persons—deformed infants, imbecile adults and the like. But the humanity of the age invariably frowns upon such proposals. The benign and merciful features of our Christian creed would be outraged by such a practice.

Gladiatorial Games.—The combats of gladiators were the culmination of Roman barbarity and brutality. All the devotees of vice and crime met and mingled at the arena, and derived strength and inspiration from its bloody scenes. The gatherings in the amphitheater were miniatures of Roman life. There, political matters were discussed and questions of state determined, as was once the case in the public assemblies of the people. Now that the gates of Janus were closed for the third time in Roman history, the combats of the arena took the place, on a diminutive scale, of those battles by which Romans had conquered the world. The processions of the gladiators reminded the enthusiastic populace of the triumphal entries of their conquerors into the Roman capital. Nothing so glutted the appetite and quenched the thirst of a cruel and licentious race as the gorgeous ceremonials and bloody butchery of the gladiatorial shows.

These contests, strange to say, first took place at funerals, and were intended to honor the dead. In 264 B.C., at the burial of D. Junius Brutus, we are told, three pairs of gladiators fought in the cattle market. Again, in 216 B.C., at the obsequies of M. Æmilius Lepidus, twenty-two pairs engaged in combat in the Forum. And, in 174 B.C., on the death of his father, Titus Flaminius caused seventy-four pairs to fight for three days.[171] It will thus be seen that the death of one Roman generally called for that of several others.

In time, the fondness of these contests had grown so great that generals and statesmen arranged them on a gigantic scale as a means of winning the favor and support of the multitude. The Roman proletariat demanded not only bread to satisfy their hunger, but games to amuse them in their hours of idleness. Augustus not only gave money and rations to 200,000 idlers, but inaugurated gladiatorial shows in which 10,000 combatants fought. Not only men but wild beasts were brought into the arena. Pompey arranged a fight of 500 lions, 18 elephants and 410 other ferocious animals, brought from Africa. In a chase arranged by Augustus, A.D. 5, 36 crocodiles were killed in the Flaminian circus, which was flooded for the purpose. Caligula brought 400 bears into the arena to fight with an equal number of African wild animals. But all previous shows were surpassed in the magnificent games instituted by Trajan, A.D. 106, to celebrate his victories on the Danube. These games lasted four months; and, in them, 10,000 gladiators fought, and 11,000 beasts were slain.

Such was the thirst for blood, and to such a pitch had the fury of the passions reached at the beginning of the empire that Romans were no longer satisfied with small fights by single pairs. They began to demand regular battles and a larger flow of blood. And to please the populace, Julius Cæsar celebrated his triumph by a real battle in the circus. On each side were arrayed 500 foot soldiers, 300 cavalrymen, and 20 elephants bearing soldiers in towers upon their backs. This was no mimic fray, but an actual battle in which blood was shed and men were killed. To vary the entertainment, Cæsar also arranged a sea fight. He caused a lake to be dug out on Mars Field, and placed battleships upon it which represented Tyrian and Egyptian fleets. These he caused to be manned by a thousand soldiers and 2,000 oarsmen. A bloody fight then ensued between men who had no other motive in killing each other than to furnish a Roman holiday. Augustus also arranged a sea fight upon an artificial lake where 3,000 men were engaged. But both these battles were eclipsed by the great sea fight which the emperor Claudius caused to be fought on Lake Fucinus, in the presence of a great multitude that lined the shore. Nineteen thousand men engaged in the bloody struggle. On an eminence overlooking the lake, the Empress Agrippina, in gorgeous costume, sat by the side of the emperor and watched the battle.

Announcement of gladiatorial fights in the amphitheater was made by posters on the walls of the city. In these advertisements, the number and names of the fighters were announced. On the day of the performance a solemn procession of gladiators, walking in couples, passed through the streets to the arena. The arrangements of the building and the manner of the fights were so ordered as to arouse to the highest pitch of excitement the passions and expectations of the spectators. The citizens were required to wear the white toga. The lower rows of seats were occupied by senators, in whose midst were the boxes occupied by the imperial family. The equestrian order occupied places immediately above the senators. The citizens were seated next after the equestrians, and in the top-most rows, on benches, were gathered the Roman rabble. An immense party-colored awning, stretched above the multitude, reflected into the arena its variegated hues. Strains of music filled the air while preparations for the combat were being made. The atmosphere of the amphitheater was kept cool and fragrant by frequent sprays of perfume. The regular combat was preceded by a mock fight with blunt weapons. Then followed arrangements for the life-and-death struggle. The manager of the games finally gave the command, and the fight was on. When one of the gladiators was wounded, the words "hoc habet" were shouted. The wounded man fell to the earth, dropped his weapon, and, holding up his forefinger, begged his life from the people. If mercy was refused him, he was compelled to renew the combat or to submit to the death stroke of his antagonist. Attendants were at hand with hot irons to apply to the victim to see that death was not simulated. If life was not extinct, the fallen gladiator was dragged out to the dead room, and there dispatched. Servants then ran into the arena and scattered sand over the blood-drenched ground. Other fighters standing in readiness, immediately rushed in to renew the contest. Thus the fight went on until the Roman populace was glutted with butchery and blood.

Gladiators were chosen from the strongest and most athletic among slaves and condemned criminals. Thracians, Gauls, and Germans were captured and enslaved for the purpose of being sacrificed in the arena. They were trained with the greatest care in gladiatorial schools. The most famous of these institutions was at Capua in Italy. It was here that Spartacus, a young Thracian, of noble ancestry, excited an insurrection that soon spread throughout all Italy and threatened the destruction of Rome. Addressing himself to seventy of his fellow-gladiators, Spartacus is said to have made a bitter and impassioned speech in which he proposed that, if they must die, they should die fighting their enemies and not themselves; that, if they were to engage in bloody battles, these battles should be fought under the open sky in behalf of life and liberty, and not in the amphitheater to furnish pastime and entertainment to their masters and oppressors. The speech had its effect. The band of fighters broke out of Capua, and took refuge in the crater of Mount Vesuvius (73 B.C.). Spartacus became the leader, with Crixus and œnomaus, two Celtic gladiators, as lieutenants. Their ranks soon swelled to the proportions of an army, through accessions of slaves and desperadoes from the neighborhood of the volcano. During two years, they terrorized all Italy, defeated two consuls, and burned many cities. Crixus was defeated and killed at Mount Gargarus in Apulia by the prætor Arrius. Spartacus compelled three hundred Roman prisoners, whom he had captured, to fight as gladiators, following Roman custom, at the grave of his fallen comrade and lieutenant. Finally, he himself was slain, sword in hand, having killed two centurions before he fell. With the death of their leaders, the insurgents either surrendered or fled. Those who were captured were crucified. It is said that the entire way from Capua to Rome was marked by crosses on which their bodies were suspended, to the number of ten thousand.[172]

Throughout Italy were amphitheaters for gladiatorial games. But the largest and most celebrated of all was the Coliseum at Rome. Its ruins are still standing. It was originally called the Flavian Amphitheater. This vast building was begun A.D. 72, upon the site of the reservoir of Nero, by the emperor Vespasian, who built as far as the third row of arches, the last two rows being finished by Titus after his return from the conquest of Jerusalem. It is said that twelve thousand captive Jews were employed in this work, as the Hebrews were employed in building the Pyramids of Egypt, and that the external walls alone cost nearly four millions of dollars. It consists of four stories: the first, Doric; the second, Ionic; the third and fourth, Corinthian. Its circumference is nearly two thousand feet; its length, six hundred and twenty feet; and its width, five hundred and thirteen. The entrance for the emperor was between two arches facing the Esquiline, where there was no cornice. The arena was surrounded by a wall sufficiently high to protect the spectators from the wild beasts, which were introduced by subterranean passages, closed by huge gates from the side. The Amphitheater is said to have been capable of seating eighty-seven thousand people, and was inaugurated by gladiatorial games that lasted one hundred days, and in which five thousand beasts were slain. The emperor Commodus himself fought in the Coliseum, and killed both gladiators and wild beasts. He insisted on calling himself Hercules, was dressed in a lion's skin, and had his hair sprinkled with gold dust.

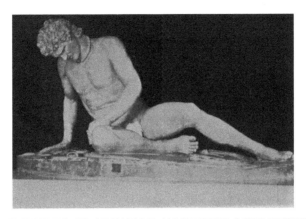

THE DYING GLADIATOR (ANTIQUE SCULPTURE)

An oriental monk, Talemachus, was so horrified at the sight of the gladiatorial games, that he rushed into the midst of the arena, and besought the spectators to have them stopped. Instead of listening to him, they put him to death.

The first martyrdom in the Coliseum was that of St. Ignatius, said to have been the child especially blessed by our Savior, the disciple of John, and the companion of Polycarp, who was sent to Rome from Antioch when he was bishop. When brought into the arena, St. Ignatius knelt down and exclaimed: "Romans who are here present, know that I have not been brought into this place for any crime, but in order that by this means I may merit the fruition of the glory of God, for love of whom I have been made a prisoner. I am as the grain of the field and must be ground by the teeth of the lions that I may become bread fit for His table." The lions were then let loose, and devoured him, except the larger bones which the Christians collected during the night.

The spot where the Christian martyrs suffered was for a long time marked by a tall cross devoutly kissed by the faithful. The Pulpit of the Coliseum was used for the stormy sermons of Gavazzi, who called the people to arms from thence in the Revolution of March, 1848.

Græco-Roman Social Depravity, Born of Religion and Traceable to the Gods.—The modern mind identifies true religion with perfect purity of heart and with boundless love. "Do unto others as you would have others do unto you" is the leading aphorism of both the Hebrew and Christian faiths. The Sermon on the Mount is the chart of the soul on the sea of life; and its beatitudes are the glorifications of the virtues of meekness, mercy, and peace. To the mind imbued with the divine precepts of the Savior, it seems incredible that religion should have ever been the direct source of crime and sin. It is, nevertheless, a well-established fact that the Roman and Greek mythologies were the potent causes of political corruption and social impurity in both Italy and Greece. Nothing better illustrates this truth than the abominable practice that found its inspiration and excuse in the myth of the rape of Ganymede. The guilty passion of Zeus for the beautiful boy whom he, himself, in the form of an eagle, had snatched up from earth and carried away to Olympus to devote to shameful and unnatural uses, was the foundation, in Greece, of the most loathsome habit that ever disgraced the conduct of men. Passionate fondness for beautiful boys, called paiderastia in Greek, termed sodomy in modern criminal law, was the curse and infamy of both Roman and Grecian life. This unnatural vice was not confined to the vulgar and degenerate. Men of letters, poets, statesmen and philosophers, debased themselves with this form of pollution. It was even legalized by the laws of Crete and Sparta. Polybius tells us that many Romans paid as much as a talent ($1,000) for a beautifully formed youth. This strange perversion of the sexual instincts was marked by all the tenderness and sweetness of a modern courtship or a honeymoon. The victim of this degrading and disgusting passion treated the beautiful boy with all the delicacy and feeling generally paid a newly wedded wife. Kisses and caresses were at times showered upon him. At other times, he became an object of insane jealousy.

An obscene couplet in Suetonius attributes this filthy habit to Julius Cæsar in the matter of an abominable relationship with the King of Bithynia.[173] "So strong was the influence of the prevalent epidemic on Plato, that he had lost all sense of the love of women, and in his descriptions of Eros, divine as well as human, his thoughts were centered only in his boy passion. The result in Greece confessedly was that the inclination for a woman was looked upon as low and dishonorable, while that for a youth was the only one worthy of a man of education."[174]

A moment's reflection will convince the most skeptical of the progress of morality and the advance of civilization. That which philosophers and emperors not only approved but practiced in the palmiest days of the commonwealths of Greece and Rome, is to-day penalized; and the person guilty of the offense is socially ostracized and branded with infamy and contempt.

The above is only one of many illustrations of the demoralizing influence of the myths. The Greeks looked to the gods as models of behavior, and could see nothing wrong in paiderastia, since both Zeus and Apollo had practiced it. Nearly every crime committed by the Greeks and Romans was sought to be excused on the ground that the gods had done the same thing. Euthyphro justified mistreatment of his own father on the ground that Zeus had chased Cronos, his father, from the skies.

Homer was not only the Bible, but the schoolbook of Grecian boys and girls throughout the world; and their minds were saturated at an early age with the escapades of the gods and goddesses as told by the immortal bard. Plato, in the "Republic," deprecates the influence of the Homeric myths upon the youth of Greece, when he says: "They are likely to have a bad effect on those who hear them; for everybody will begin to excuse his own vices when he is convinced that similar wickednesses are always being perpetrated by the kindred of the gods." And Seneca thus condemns the moral effect of the myth of Zeus and Alcmene: "What else is this appeal to the precedent of the gods for, but to inflame our lusts, and to furnish a free license and excuse for the corrupt act under shelter of its divine prototype?" "This," says the same author in another treatise, "has led to no other result than to deprive sin of its shame in man's eyes, when he saw that the gods were no better than himself."

We have seen that, in the matter of the multiplicity of the gods, there were deities of the baser as well as of the better passions, and of criminal as well as virtuous propensities. Pausanias tells us that in his day, on the road to Pellene, there were statues of Hermes Dolios (the cheat), and that the worshipers of this god believed that he was always ready to help them in their intrigues and adventures. The same writer also tells us that young maidens of Trœzene dedicated their girdles to Athene Apaturia, the deceiver, for having cunningly betrayed Æthra into the hands of Neptune. The festivals of Bacchus were far-famed in ancient times for the drunken debauches and degrading ceremonies that accompanied them. The Attic feasts of Pan were celebrated with every circumstance of low buffoonery. The solemnities of the Aphrodisia were akin to the bacchanalian orgies in all the features of inebriety and lust. The name of the goddess of love and beauty was blazoned across the portal of more than one Greek and Roman brothel. The Aphrodite-Lamia at Athens and the Aphrodite-Stratonikis at Smyrna were the favorite resorts of the most famous courtesans of antiquity. Venus was the recognized goddess of the harlots. A thousand of them guarded her temple at Corinth; and, when an altar was erected to her at the Colline gate in Rome, in the year 183 A.U.C., they celebrated a great feast in her honor, and dedicated chaplets of myrtle and roses, as a means of obtaining her favor as the guardian divinity of their calling.

What more could be expected, then, of the morality of the Greeks and Romans, when we consider the nature of their religion and the character of their gods? Jupiter and Apollo were notorious rakes and libertines; Venus and Flora were brazen-faced courtesans; Harmonia was a Phrygian dancer, who had been seduced by Cadmus; Hercules was a gladiator; Pan was a buffoon; Bacchus was a drunkard, and Mercury was a highway robber. And not only in the poems of Homer and Hesiod did the Greek and Roman youth learn these things, but from the plays of the theaters and from plastic art as well. If we except the gladiatorial fights in the amphitheaters, nothing was more cruel and unchaste than Greek and Roman tragedy and comedy. At the time of Christ, the tastes and appetites of the multitude had grown so fierce and depraved that ordinary spectacles were regarded as commonplace and insipid. Lifelike realities were demanded from the actors on the stage; and accordingly, the hero who played the rôle of the robber chief, Laureolus, was actually crucified before the spectators, and was then torn to pieces by a hungry bear. The burning of Hercules on Mount Œta and the emasculation of Atys were sought to be realized on the stage by the actual burning and emasculation of condemned criminals. Lustful as well as cruel appetites were inflamed and fed by theatrical representations of the intrigues and adventures of the gods and goddesses. Pantomimes and mimic dances, with flute accompaniment, were employed to reproduce the amours and passionate devotions of the inhabitants of Olympus. The guilty loves of Aphrodite with Mars and Adonis, the adventures of Jupiter and Apollo with the wives and daughters of mortals, were the plays most frequently presented and most wildly applauded. And the ignorant rabble were not the only witnesses of these spectacles. "The sacerdotal colleges and authorities," says Arnobius, "flamens, and augurs, and chaste vestals, all have seats at these public amusements. There are seated the collective people and senate, consuls and consulars, while Venus, the mother of the Roman race, is danced to the life, and in shameless mimicry is represented as reveling through all the phases of meretricious lust. The great mother, too, is danced; the Dindymene of Pessinus, in spite of her age, surrendering herself to disgusting passion in the embraces of a cowherd. The supreme ruler of the world is himself brought in, without respect to his name or majesty, to play the part of an adulterer, masking himself in order to deceive chaste wives, and take the place of their husbands in the nuptial bed."[175]

Not only gladiatorial games and theatrical shows, but painting and sculpture as well, served to corrupt and demoralize Roman and Greek manners. Nor is there any prudery in this statement. The masterpieces of the Greek artists have been the astonishment and despair of all succeeding ages; and the triumphs of modern art have been but poor imitations of the models of the first masters. But it is, nevertheless, true that the embodiment in marble of certain obscene myths was destructive of ancient morals. The paintings in the temples and houses of the cities of Greece and Italy were a constant menace to the mental purity of those who gazed upon them. The statue of Ganymede at the side of Zeus was a perpetual reminder to the youth of Athens of the originator of the loathsome custom of paiderastia. The paintings of Leda and the swan, of the courtship of Dionysus and Ariadne, of the naked Aphrodite ensnared and caught in the net with Ares that adorned the walls and ceilings of Greek and Roman homes, were not too well calculated to inspire pure and virtuous thoughts in the minds and hearts of tender youths and modest maidens who looked upon and contemplated them. At Athens, especially, was the corrupting influence of painting and plastic art most deeply felt. "At every step," says Döllinger, "which a Greek or Roman took, he was surrounded by images of his gods and memorials of their mythic history. Not the temples only, but streets and public squares, house walls, domestic implements and drinking vessels, were all covered and incrusted with ornaments of the kind. His eye could rest nowhere, not a piece of money could he take into his hand without confronting a god. And in this way, through the magical omnipresence of plastic art, the memory of his gods had sunk into his soul indelibly, grown up with every operation of his intellect, and inseparably blended with every picture of his imagination."[176]

It can thus be easily imagined how close the connection between the social depravity and the religion of the Greeks and Romans. What was right in the conduct of the gods, men could not deem sinful in their own behavior. Indeed, lewd and lascivious acts were frequently proclaimed not only right, but sacred, because they had been both sanctioned and committed by the gods themselves. "As impurity," says Döllinger, "formed a part of religion, people had no scruples in using the temple and its adjoining buildings for the satisfaction of their lust. The construction of many of the temples and the prevalent gloom favored this. 'It is a matter of general notoriety,' Tertullian says, 'that the temples are the very places where adulteries were arranged, and procuresses pursue their victims between the altars.' In the chambers of the priests and ministers of the temple, impurity was committed amid clouds of incense; and this, Minucius adds, more frequently than in the privileged haunts of this sin. The sanctuaries and priests of Isis at Rome were specially notorious in this respect. 'As this Isis was the concubine of Jove herself, she also makes prostitutes of others,' Ovid said. Still more shameful sin was practiced in the temples of the Pessinuntine mother of the gods, where men prostituted themselves and made a boast of their shame afterwards."[177]

The Bacchanalian Orgies.—The most interesting passage of ancient literature dealing with social life in its relation to religious observances, is an extract from Livy, the most elegant of Roman historians. This passage describes the bacchanalian orgies, and gives exquisite touches to certain phases of ancient Roman social life. Its insertion here entire is excused on the ground of its direct bearing upon the subject matter of this chapter:

A Greek of mean condition came, first, into Etruria; not with one of the many trades which his nation, of all others the most skilful in the cultivation of the mind and body, has introduced among us, but a low operator in sacrifices, and a soothsayer; nor was he one who, by open religious rites, and by publicly professing his calling and teaching, imbued the minds of his followers with terror, but a priest of secret and nocturnal rites. These mysterious rites were, at first, imparted to a few, but afterwards communicated to great numbers, both men and women. To their religious performances were added the pleasures of wine and feasting, to allure a greater number of proselytes. When wine, lascivious discourse, night, and the intercourse of the sexes had extinguished every sentiment of modesty, then debaucheries of every kind began to be practiced, as every person found at hand that sort of enjoyment to which he was disposed by the passion predominant in his nature. Nor were they confined to one species of vice—the promiscuous intercourse of free-born men and women, but from this store-house of villany proceeded false witnesses, counterfeit seals, false evidences, and pretended discoveries. From the same place, too, proceeded poison and secret murders, so that in some cases, even the bodies could not be found for burial. Many of their audacious deeds were brought about by treachery, but most of them by force; it served to conceal the violence, that on account of the loud shouting, and the noise of drums and cymbals, none of the cries uttered by the persons suffering violation or murder could be heard abroad.

READING FROM HOMER (ALMA-TADEMA)

The infection of this mischief, like that from the contagion of disease, spread from Etruria to Rome; where, the size of the city affording greater room for such evils, and more means of concealment, cloaked it at first; but information of it was at length brought to the consul, Postumius, principally in the following manner. Publius Æbutius, whose father had held equestrian rank in the army, was left an orphan, and his guardians dying, he was educated under the eye of his mother Duronia, and his stepfather Titus Sempronius Rutilus. Duronia was entirely devoted to her husband; and Sempronius, having managed the guardianship in such a manner that he could not give an account of the property, wished that his ward should be either made away with, or bound to compliance with his will by some strong tie. The Bacchanalian rites were the only way to effect the ruin of the youth. His mother told him, that, "During his sickness, she had made a vow for him, that if he should recover, she would initiate him among the Bacchanalians; that being, through the kindness of the gods, bound by this vow, she wished now to fulfil it; that it was necessary he should preserve chastity for ten days, and on the tenth, after he should have supped and washed himself, she would conduct him into the place of worship." There was a freedwoman called Hispala Fecenia, a noted courtesan, but deserving of a better lot than the mode of life to which she had been accustomed when very young, and a slave, and by which she had maintained herself since her manumission. As they lived in the same neighborhood, an intimacy subsisted between her and Æbutius, which was far from being injurious either to the young man's character or property; for he had been loved and wooed by her unsolicited; and as his friends supplied his wants illiberally, he was supported by the generosity of this woman; nay, to such a length did she go under the influence of her affection, that, on the death of her patron, because she was under the protection of no one, having petitioned the tribunes and prætors for a guardian, when she was making her will, she constituted Æbutius her sole heir.

As such pledges of mutual love subsisted, and as neither kept anything secret from the other, the young man jokingly bid her not be surprised if he separated himself from her for a few nights, as, "on account of a religious duty, to discharge a vow made for his health, he intended to be initiated among the Bacchanalians." On hearing this, the woman, greatly alarmed, cried out, "May the gods will more favorably!" affirming that "It would be better, both for him and her, to lose their lives than that he should do such a thing:" she then imprecated curses, vengeance, and destruction on the head of those who advised him to such a step. The young man, surprised both at her expressions and at the violence of her alarm, bid her refrain from curses, for "it was his mother who ordered him to do so, with the approbation of his stepfather." "Then," said she, "your stepfather (for perhaps it is not allowable to censure your mother), is in haste to destroy, by that act, your chastity, your character, your hopes and your life." To him, now surprised by such language, and inquiring what was the matter, she said, (after imploring the favor and pardon of the gods and goddesses, if, compelled by her regard for him, she disclosed what ought not to be revealed), that "when in service, she had gone into that place of worship, as an attendant on her mistress, but that, since she had obtained her liberty, she had never once gone near it: that she knew it to be the receptacle of all kinds of debaucheries; that it was well known that, for two years past, no one older than twenty had been initiated there. When any person was introduced he was delivered as a victim to the priests, who led him away to a place resounding with shouts, the sound of music, and the beating of cymbals and drums, lest his cries while suffering violation, should be heard abroad." She then entreated and besought him to put an end to that matter in some way or other, and not to plunge himself into a situation, where he must first suffer, and afterwards commit, everything that was abominable. Nor did she quit him until the young man gave her his promise to keep himself clear of those rites.

When he came home, and his mother made mention of such things pertaining to the ceremony as were to be performed on that day, and on the several following days, he told her that he would not perform any of them, nor did he intend to be initiated. His stepfather was present at this discourse. Immediately the woman observed that "he could not deprive himself of the company of Hispala for ten nights; that he was so fascinated by the caresses and baneful influence of that serpent, that he retained no respect for his mother or stepfather, or even the gods themselves." His mother on one side and his stepfather on the other loading him with reproaches, drove him out of the house, assisted by four slaves. The youth on this repaired to his aunt Æbutia, told her the reason of his being turned out by his mother, and the next day, by her advice, gave information of the affair to the consul Postumius, without any witnesses of the interview. The consul dismissed him, with an order to come again on the third day following. In the meantime, he inquired of his mother-in-law, Sulpicia, a woman of respectable character, "whether she knew an old matron called Æbutia, who lived on the Aventine hill?" When she had answered that "she knew her well, and that Æbutia was a woman of virtue, and of the ancient purity of morals;" he said that he required a conference with her, and that a messenger should be sent for her to come. Æbutia, on receiving the message, came to Sulpicia's house, and the consul, soon after, coming in, as if by accident, introduced a conversation about Æbutius, her brother's son. The tears of the woman burst forth, and she began to lament the unhappy lot of the youth: who after being robbed of his property by persons whom it least of all became, was then residing with her, being driven out of doors by his mother, because, being a good youth (may the gods be propitious to him), he refused to be initiated in ceremonies devoted to lewdness, as report goes.

The consul thinking that he had made sufficient inquiries concerning Æbutius, and that his testimony was unquestionable, having dismissed Æbutia, requested his mother-in-law to send again to the Aventine, and bring from that quarter Hispala, a freedwoman, not unknown in that neighborhood; for there were some queries which he wished to make of her. Hispala being alarmed because she was being sent for by a woman of such high rank and respectable character, and being ignorant of the cause, after she saw the lictors in the porch, the multitude attending to the consul and the consul himself, was very near fainting. The consul led her into the retired part of the house, and, in the presence of his mother-in-law, told her, that she need not be uneasy, if she could resolve to speak the truth. She might receive a promise of protection either from Sulpicia, a matron of such dignified character, or from himself. That she ought to tell him, what was accustomed to be done at the Bacchanalia, in the nocturnal orgies in the grove of Stimula. When the woman heard this, such terror and trembling of all her limbs seized her, that for a long time she was unable to speak; but recovering at length she said, that "when she was very young, and a slave, she had been initiated, together with her mistress; but for several years past, since she had obtained her liberty, she knew nothing of what was done there." The consul commended her so far, as not having denied that she was initiated, but charged her to explain all the rest with the same sincerity; and told her, affirming that she knew nothing further, that "there would not be the same tenderness or pardon extended to her, if she should be convicted by another person, and one who had made a voluntary confession; that there was such a person, who had heard the whole from her, and had given him a full account of it."

The woman, now thinking without a doubt that it must certainly be Æbutius who had discovered the secret, threw herself at Sulpicia's feet, and at first began to beseech her, "not to let the private conversation of a freedwoman with her lover be turned not only into a serious business, but even capital charge;" declaring that "she had spoken of such things merely to frighten him, and not because she knew anything of the kind." On this Postumius, growing angry, said "she seemed to imagine that then too she was wrangling with her gallant Æbutius, and not that she was speaking in the house of a most respectable matron, and to a consul." Sulpicia raised her, terrified, from the ground, and while she encouraged her to speak out, at the same time pacified her son-in-law's anger. At length she took courage, and, having censured severely the perfidy of Æbutius, because he had made such a return for the extraordinary kindness shown to him in that very instance, she declared that "she stood in great dread of the gods, whose secret mysteries she was to divulge; and in much greater dread of the men implicated, who would tear her asunder with their hands if she became an informer. Therefore she entreated this favor of Sulpicia, and likewise of the consul, that they would send her away some place out of Italy, where she might pass the remainder of her life in safety." The consul desired her to be of good spirits, and said that it should be his care that she might live securely in Rome.

Hispala then gave a full account of the origin of the mysteries. "At first," she said, "those rites were performed by women. No man used to be admitted. They had three stated days in the year on which such persons were initiated among the Bacchanalians, in the daytime. The matrons used to be appointed priestesses, in rotation. Paculla Minia, a Campanian, when priestess, made an alteration in every particular as if by the direction of the gods. For she first introduced men, who were her own sons, Minucius and Herrenius, both surnamed Cerrinius; changed the time of celebration, from day to night; and, instead of three days in the year, appointed five days of initiation in each month. From the time that the rites were thus made common, and men were intermixed with women, and the licentious freedom of the night was added, there was nothing wicked, nothing flagitious, that had not been practiced among them. There were more frequent pollution of men, with each other, than with women. If any were less patient in submitting to dishonor, or more averse to the commission of vice, they were sacrificed as victims. To think nothing unlawful, was the grand maxim of their religion. The men, as if bereft of reason, uttered predictions, with frantic contortions of their bodies; the women, in the habit of Bacchantes, with their hair dishevelled, and carrying blazing torches, ran down to the Tiber; where, dipping their torches in the water, they drew them up again with the flame unextinguished, being composed of native sulphur and charcoal. They said that those men were carried off by the gods, whom the machines laid hold of and dragged from their view into secret caves. These were such as refused to take the oath of the society or to associate in their crimes, or to submit to defilement. Their number was exceedingly great now, almost a second state in themselves and among them were many men and women of noble families. During the last two years it had been a rule, that no person above the age of twenty should be initiated, for they sought for people of such age as made them more liable to suffer deception and personal abuse." When she had completed her information, she again fell at the consul's knees, and repeated the same entreaties, that he might send her out of the country. The consul requested his mother-in-law to clear some part of the house, into which Hispala might remove; accordingly an apartment was assigned her in the upper part of it, of which the stairs, opening into the street, were stopped up, and the entrance made from the inner court. Thither all Fecenia's effects were immediately removed, and her domestics sent for. Æbutius, also, was ordered to remove to the house of one of the consul's clients.

When both the informers were by these means in his power, Postumius represented the affair to the senate, laying before them the whole circumstance, in due order; the information given to him at first, and the discoveries gained by his inquiries afterwards. Great consternation seized on the senators; not only on the public account, lest such conspiracies and nightly meetings might be productive of secret treachery and mischief, but, likewise, on account of their own particular families, lest some of their relations might be involved in this infamous affair. The senate voted, however, that thanks should be given to the consul because he had investigated the matter with singular diligence, and without exciting any alarm. They then commit to the consuls the holding an inquiry, out of the common course, concerning the Bacchanals and their nocturnal orgies. They ordered them to take care that the informers, Æbutius and Fecenia, might suffer no injury on that account; and to invite other informers in the matter, by offering rewards. They ordered that the officials in those rites, whether men or women, should be sought for, not only at Rome, but also throughout all the market towns and places of assembly, and be delivered over to the power of the consuls; and also that proclamation should be made in the city of Rome, and published through all Italy, that "no persons initiated in the Bacchanalian rites should presume to come together or assemble on account of those rites, or to perform any such kind of worship;" and above all, that search should be made for those who had assembled or conspired for personal abuse, or for any other flagitious practices. The senate passed these decrees. The consuls directed the curule ædiles to make strict inquiry after all the priests of those mysteries, and to keep such as they could apprehend in custody until their trial; they at the same time charged the plebeian ædiles to take care that no religious ceremonies should be performed in private. To the capital triumvirs the task was assigned to post watches in proper places in the city, and to use vigilance in preventing any meetings by night. In order likewise to guard against fires, five assistants were joined to the triumvirs, so that each might have the charge of the buildings in his own separate district, on this side the Tiber.

After despatching these officers to their several employments, the consuls mounted the rostrum; and, having summoned an assembly of the people, one of the consuls, when he had finished the solemn form of prayer which the magistrates are accustomed to pronounce before they address the people, proceeded thus: "Romans, to no former assembly was this solemn supplication to the gods more suitable or even more necessary: as it serves to remind you, that these are the deities whom your forefathers pointed out as the objects of your worship, veneration and prayers: and not those which infatuated men's minds with corrupt and foreign modes of religion, and drove them, as if goaded by the furies, to every lust and every vice. I am at a loss to know what I should conceal, or how far I ought to speak out; for I dread lest, if I leave you ignorant of any particular, I should give room for carelessness, or if I disclose the whole, that I should too much awaken your fears. Whatever I shall say, be assured that it is less than the magnitude and atrociousness of the affair would justify: exertions will be used by us that it may be sufficient to set us properly on our guard. That the Bacchanalian rites have subsisted for some time past in every country in Italy, and are at present performed in many parts of this city also, I am sure you must have been informed, not only by report, but by the nightly noises and the horrid yells that resound through the whole city; but still you are ignorant of the nature of that business. Part of you think it is some kind of worship of the gods; others, some excusable sport and amusement, and that whatever it may be, it concerns but a few. As regards the number if I tell you that there are many thousands, that you would be immediately terrified to excess is a necessary consequence; unless I further acquaint you who and what sort of persons they are. First, then, a great part of them are women, and this was the source of the evil; the rest are males, but nearly resembling women; actors and pathics in the vilest lewdness; night revellers, driven frantic by wine, noise of instruments, and clamors. The conspiracy, as yet, has no strength; but it has abundant means of acquiring strength, for they are becoming more numerous every day. Your ancestors would not allow that you should ever assemble casually without some good reason; that is, either when the standard was erected on the Janiculum, and the army led out on occasion of elections; or when the tribunes proclaimed a meeting of the commons, or some of the magistrates summoned you to it. And they judged it necessary, that wherever a multitude was, there should be a lawful governor of that multitude present. Of what kind do you suppose are the meetings of these people? In the first place, held in the night, and in the next, composed promiscuously of men and women. If you knew at what ages the males are initiated, you would feel not only pity, but also shame for them. Romans, can you think youths initiated, under such oaths as theirs, are fit to be made soldiers? That arms should be intrusted with wretches brought out of that temple of obscenity? Shall these, contaminated with their own foul debaucheries and those of others, be champions for the chastity of your wives and children?

"But the mischief were less, if they were only effeminated by their practices; or that the disgrace would chiefly affect themselves; if they refrained their hands from outrage, and their thoughts from fraud. But never was there in the state an evil of so great magnitude, or one that extended to so many persons or so many acts of wickedness. Whatever deeds of villany have, during late years been committed through lust; whatever through fraud; whatever through violence; they have all, be assured, proceeded from that association alone. They have not yet perpetrated all the crimes for which they combine. The impious assembly at present confines itself to outrages on private citizens; because it has not yet acquired force sufficient to crush the commonwealth: but the evil increases and spreads daily; it is already too great for the private ranks of life to contain it, and aims its views at the body of the state. Unless you take timely precautions, Romans, their nightly assembly may become as large as this, held in open day and legally summoned by a consul. Now they one by one dread you collected together in the assembly; presently, when you shall have separated and retired to your several dwellings, in town and country, they will again come together, and will hold a consultation on the means of their own safety, and, at the same time, of your destruction. Thus united, they will cause terror to every one of you. Each of you therefore, ought to pray that his kindred may have behaved with wisdom and prudence; and if lust, if madness, has dragged any of them into that abyss, to consider such a person as the relation of those with whom he has conspired for every disgraceful and reckless act, and not as one of your own. I am not secure, lest some even of yourselves may have erred through mistake; for nothing is more deceptive in appearance than false religion. When the authority of the gods is held out as a pretext to cover vice, fear enters our minds, lest in punishing the crimes of men, we may violate some divine right connected therewith. Numberless decisions of the pontiffs, decrees of the senate, and even answers of the aruspices, free you from religious scruples of this character. How often in the ages of our fathers was it given in charge to the magistrates, to prohibit the performances of any foreign religious rites; to banish strolling sacrificers and soothsayers from the Forum, the circus and the city; to search for and burn books of divination; and to abolish every mode of sacrificing that was not conformable to the Roman practice! For they, completely versed in every divine and human law, maintained that nothing tended so strongly to the subversion of religion as sacrifice, when we offered it not after the institutions of our forefathers, but after foreign customs. Thus much I thought necessary to mention to you beforehand, that no vain scruple might disturb your minds when you should see us demolishing the places resorted to by the Bacchanalians, and dispersing their impious assemblies. We shall do all these things with the favor and approbation of the gods; who, because they were indignant that their divinity was dishonored by those people's lust and crimes, have drawn forth their proceedings from hidden darkness into the open light; and who have directed them to be exposed, not that they may escape with impunity, but in order that they may be punished and suppressed. The senate have committed to me and my colleague, an inquisition extraordinary concerning that affair. What is requisite to be done by ourselves, in person, we will do with energy. The charge of posting watches through the city, during the night, we have committed to the inferior magistrates; and, for your parts, it is incumbent on you to execute vigorously whatever duties are assigned you, and in the several places where each will be placed, to perform whatever orders you shall receive, and to use your best endeavors that no danger or tumult may arise from the treachery of the party involved in the guilt."

They then ordered the decrees of the senate to be read, and published a reward for any discoverer who should bring any of the guilty before them, or give information against any of the absent, adding, that "if any person accused should fly, they would limit a certain day upon which, if he did not answer when summoned, he would be condemned in his absence; and if anyone should be charged who was out of Italy, they would not allow him any longer time, if he should wish to come and make his defence." They then issued an edict, that "no person whatever should presume to buy or sell anything for the purpose of leaving the country; or to receive or conceal, or by any means aid the fugitives." On the assembly being dismissed, great terror spread throughout the city; nor was it confined merely within the walls, or to the Roman territory, for everywhere throughout the whole of Italy alarm began to be felt—when the letters from the guest-friends were received—concerning the decree of the senate, and what passed in the assembly and the edict of the consuls. During the night, which succeeded the day in which the affair was made public, great numbers attempting to fly, were seized and bought back by the triumvirs, who had posted guards at all the gates; and informations were lodged against many, some of whom, both men and women, put themselves to death. Above seven thousand men and women are said to have taken the oath of the association. But it appeared that the heads of the conspiracy were the two Catinii, Marcus and Caius, Roman plebeians; Lucius Opiturnius, a Faliscian; and Minius Cerrinius, a Campanian: that from these proceeded all their criminal practices, and that these were the chief priests and founders of the sect. Care was taken that they should be apprehended as soon as possible. They were brought before the consuls, and confessing their guilt, caused no delay to the ends of justice.

But so great were the numbers that fled from the city, that because the lawsuits and property of many persons were going to ruin, the prætors, Titius Mænius and Marcus Licinius were obliged, under the direction of the senate, to adjourn their courts for thirty days until the inquiries should be finished by the consuls. The same deserted state of the law courts, since the persons against whom charges were brought did not appear to answer, nor could be found in Rome, necessitated the consuls to make a circuit of the country towns, and there to make their inquisitions and hold the trials. Those who, as it appeared, had been only initiated, and had made after the priest, and in the most solemn form, the prescribed imprecations, in which the accursed conspiracy for the perpetration of every crime and lust was contained, but who had not themselves committed, or compelled others to commit, any of those acts to which they were bound by the oath—all such they left in prison. But those who had forcibly committed personal defilements or murders, or were stained with the guilt of false evidence, counterfeit seals, forged wills, or other frauds, all these they punished with death. A greater number were executed than thrown into prison; indeed the multitude of men and women who suffered in both ways, was very considerable. The consuls delivered the women who were condemned to their relations, or to those under whose guardianship they were, that they might inflict the punishment in private; but if there did not appear any proper person of the kind to execute the sentence, the punishment was inflicted in public. A charge was then given to demolish all the places where the Bacchanalians had held their meetings; first, in Rome, and then throughout all Italy; excepting those wherein should be found some ancient altar, or consecrated statue. With regard to the future, the senate passed a decree, "that no Bacchanalian rites should be celebrated in Rome or in Italy:" and ordering that, "in case any person should believe some such kind of worship incumbent upon him, and necessary; and that he could not, without offence to religion, and incurring guilt, omit it, he should represent this to the city prætor, and the prætor should lay the business before the senate. If permission were granted by the senate, when not less than one hundred members were present, then he might perform those rites, provided that no more than five persons should be present at the sacrifice, and that they should have no common stock of money, nor any president of the ceremonies, nor priest."

Another decree connected with this was then made, on a motion of the consul, Quintus Marcius, that "the business respecting the persons who had served the consuls as informers should be proposed to the senate in its original form, when Spurius Postumius should have finished his inquiries, and returned to Rome." They voted that Minus Cerrinius, the Campanian, should be sent to Ardea, to be kept in custody there; and that a caution should be given to the magistrates of that city, to guard him with more than ordinary care, so as to prevent not only his escaping, but his having an opportunity of committing suicide.

Spurius Postumius some time after came to Rome and on his proposing the question, concerning the reward to be given to Publius Æbutius and Hispala Fecenia, because the Bacchanalian ceremonies were discovered by their exertions, the senate passed a vote, that "the city quæstors should give to each of them, out of the public treasury, one hundred thousand asses; and that the consuls should desire the plebeian tribunes to propose to the commons as soon as convenient, that the campaigns of Publius Æbutius should be considered as served, that he should not become a soldier against his wishes, nor should any censor assign him a horse at the public charge." They voted also, that "Hispala Fecenia should enjoy the privileges of alienating her property by gift or deed; of marrying out of her rank, and of choosing a guardian, as if a husband had conferred them by will; that she should be at liberty to wed a man of honorable birth, and that there should be no disgrace or ignominy to him who should marry her; and that the consuls and prætors then in office, and their successors, should take care that no injury should be offered to that woman, and that she might live in safety. That the senate wishes, and thought proper, that all these things should be so ordered."—All these particulars were proposed to the commons, and executed, according to the vote of the senate; and full permission was given to the consuls to determine respecting the impunity and rewards of the other informers.[178]

The bacchanalian orgies were first suppressed nearly two hundred years before Christ. The above extract from Livy reminds us that at that time the Romans were still strong and virtuous, and that a proposal of their Consul to eradicate a vicious evil that threatened the existence of both domestic life and the State, met with warm approval and hearty support from both the Senate and the people. But the insidious infection was never completely eradicated; and the work of the "Greek from Etruria" bore bitter fruit in the centuries that followed. And when we consider that not only bacchanalian orgies, but Greek literature, painting, sculpture, tragedy and comedy, were the chief causes of the pollution of Roman morals and the destruction of the Roman State, should we be surprised that Juvenal, in an outburst of patriotic wrath, should have declaimed against "a Grecian capital in Italy";[179] and that he should have hurled withering scorn at

The flattering, cringing, treacherous, artful race,
Of fluent tongue and never-blushing face,
A Protean tribe, one knows not what to call,
That shifts to every form, and shines in all.

And, when we consider the state of the Roman world at the time of Christ, should we be surprised that St. Paul should have described Romans as "Being filled with all unrighteousness, fornication, wickedness, covetousness, maliciousness; full of envy, murder, debate, deceit, malignity; whisperers, backbiters, haters of God, despiteful, proud, boasters, inventors of evil things, disobedient to parents, without understanding, covenant-breakers, without natural affection, implacable, unmerciful"?[180]

Suffice it to say, in closing the chapter on Græco-Roman paganism, that, at the beginning of the Christian era, the Roman empire had reached the limit of physical expansion. Roman military glory had culminated in the sublime achievements of Pompey and of Cæsar. Mountains, seas, and deserts, beyond which all was barbarous and desolate, were the natural barriers of Roman dominion. Roman arms could go no farther; and Roman ambition could be no longer gratified by conquest. The Roman religion had fallen into decay and contempt; and the Roman conscience was paralyzed and benumbed. Disgusted with this world, the average Roman did not believe in any other, and was utterly without hope of future happiness. A gloomy despondency filled the hearts of men and drove them into black despair. When approaching death, they wore no look of triumph, expressed no belief in immortality, but simply requested of those whom they were leaving behind, to scatter flowers on their graves, or to bewail their early end. An epigram of the Anthology is this: "Let us drink and be merry; for we shall have no more of kissing and dancing in the kingdom of Proserpine: soon shall we fall asleep to wake no more." The same sentiments are expressed in epitaphs on Roman sepulchral monuments of the period. One of them reads thus: "What I have eaten and drunk, that I take with me; what I have left behind me, that have I forfeited." This is the language of another: "Reader, enjoy thy life; for after death there is neither laughter nor play, nor any kind of enjoyment." Still another: "Friend, I advise, mix thee a goblet of wine, and drink, crowning thy head with flowers. Earth and fire consume all that remains after death." And, finally, one of them assures us that Greek mythology is false: "Pilgrim, stay thee, listen and learn. In Hades there is no ferryboat, nor ferryman Charon; no Æacus or Cerberus;—once dead, and we are all alike."[181]

Matthew Arnold has very graphically described the disgusting, sickening, overwhelming despair of the Roman people at the birth of Christ.

Ah! carry back thy ken,
What, some two thousand years! Survey
The world as it was then.

Like ours it looked, in outward air,
Its head was clear and true;
Sumptuous its clothing, rich its fare;
No pause its action knew.

Stout was its arm, each thew and bone
Seem'd puissant and alive—
But ah! its heart, its heart was stone
And so it could not thrive.

On that hard pagan world disgust
And secret loathing fell;
Deep weariness and sated lust
Made human life a hell.

In his goodly hall with haggard eyes,
The Roman noble lay;
He drove abroad in furious guise
Along the Appian Way.

He made a feast, drank fierce and fast,
And crowned his hair with flowers;

> No easier, nor no quicker passed
> The impracticable hours.[182]

But the "darkest hour is just before the dawn," and "the fulness of the time was come." Already the first faint glimmers of the breaking of a grander and better day were perceptible to the senses of the noblest and finest of Roman intellects. Already Cicero had pictured a glorious millennium that would follow if perfect virtue should ever enter into the flesh and come to dwell among men.[183] Already Virgil, deriving inspiration from the Erythræan Sibylline prophecies, had sung of the advent of a heaven-born child, whose coming would restore the Golden Age, and establish enduring peace and happiness on the earth.[184] Already a debauched, degraded and degenerate world was crying in the anguish of its soul: "I know that my Redeemer liveth!" And, even before the Baptist began to preach in the wilderness, the ways had been made straight for the coming of the Nazarene.

APPENDICES

APPENDIX I

CHARACTERS OF THE SANHEDRISTS WHO TRIED JESUS

THE following short biographical sketches of about forty of the members of the Sanhedrin who tried Jesus are from a work entitled "Valeur de l'assemblée qui prononça la peine de mort contre Jésus Christ"—Lémann. The English translation, under the title "Jesus Before the Sanhedrin," is by Julius Magath, Oxford, Georgia.

Professor Magath's translation is used in this work by special permission.—THE AUTHOR.

THE MORAL CHARACTERS OF THE PERSONAGES WHO SAT AT THE TRIAL OF CHRIST

The members of the Sanhedrin that judged Christ were seventy-one in number, and were divided into three chambers; but we must know the names, acts, and moral characters of these judges. That such a knowledge would throw a great light on this celebrated trial can be easily understood. The characters of Caiaphas, Ananos, and Pilate are already well known to us. These stand out as the three leading figures in the drama of the Passion. But others have appeared in it; would it not be possible to produce them also before history? This task, we believe, has never yet been undertaken. It was thought that documents were wanting. But this is an error; such documents exist. We have consulted them; and in this century of historical study and research we shall draw forth from the places where they have been hidden for centuries, the majority of the judges of Christ.

Three kinds of documents have, in a particular manner, enabled us to discover the characters of these men: the books of the Evangelists, the valuable writings of Josephus the historian, and the hitherto unexplored pages of the Talmud. We shall bring to light forty of the judges, so that more than half of the Sanhedrin will appear before us; and this large majority will be sufficient to enable us to form an opinion of the moral tone of the whole assembly.

To proceed with due order, we will begin with the most important chamber—viz., the chamber of the priests.

I. THE CHAMBER OF THE PRIESTS

We use the expression "chamber of the *priests*." In the Gospel narrative, however, this division of the Sanhedrin bears a more imposing title.

Matthew, Mark, and the other Evangelists, designate it by the following names: the council *of the high priests*, and the council *of the princes of the priests*.[185]

But we may ask, Why is this pompous name given to this chamber by the Evangelists? Is this not an error on their part? An assembly of priests seems natural, but how can there be an assembly of high priests, since according to the Mosaic institution there could be only one high priest, whose office was tenable for life. There is, however, neither an error nor an undue amplification on the part of the Gospel narrators; and we may also add here that both Talmuds positively speak of an assembly of high priests.[186] But how, then, can we account for the presence of several high priests at the same time in the Sanhedrin? Here is the explanation, to the shame of the Jewish assembly:

For nearly a century a detestable abuse prevailed, which consisted in the arbitrary nomination and deposition of the high priest. The high priesthood, which for fifteen centuries had been preserved in the same family, being hereditary according to the divine command,[187] had at the time of Christ's advent become an object of commercial speculation. Herod commenced these arbitrary changes,[188] and after Judea became one of the Roman conquests the election of the high priest took place almost every year at Jerusalem, the procurators appointing and deposing them in the same manner as the prætorians later on made and unmade emperors.[189] The Talmud speaks sorrowfully of this venality and the yearly changes of the high priest.

This sacred office was given to the one that offered the most money for it, and mothers were particularly anxious that their sons should be nominated to this dignity.[190]

The expression, "*the council of the high priests*," used by the Evangelists to designate this section of the Sanhedrin, is therefore rigorously correct; for at the time of the trial of Christ there were about twelve ex-high priests, who still retained the honorable title of their charge, and were, by the right of that title, members of the high tribunal. Several ordinary priests were also included in this chamber, but they were in most cases related to the high priests; for in the midst of the intrigues by which the sovereign pontificate was surrounded in those days, it was customary for the more influential of the chief priests to bring in their sons and allies as members of their chamber. The spirit of caste was very powerful, and as M. Dérembourg, a modern Jewish savant, has remarked: "*A few priestly, aristocratic, powerful, and vain families, who cared for neither the dignity nor the interests of the altar, quarreled with each other respecting appointments, influence, and wealth.*"[191]

To sum up, we have, then, in this first chamber a double element—high priests and ordinary priests. We shall now make them known by their names and characters, and indicate the sources whence the information has been obtained.

CAIAPHAS, high priest then in office. He was the son-in-law of Ananos, and exercised his office for eleven years—during the whole term of Pilate's administration (25-36 A.D.). It is he who presided over the Sanhedrin during this trial, and the history of the Passion as given by the Evangelists is sufficient to make him known to us. (See Matt. xxvi. 3; Luke iii. 2, etc.; Jos., "Ant.," B. XVIII. C. II. 2.)

ANANOS held the office of high priest for seven years under Coponius, Ambivus, and Rufus (7-11 A.D.). This personage was the father-in-law of Caiaphas, and although out of office was nevertheless consulted on matters of importance. It may be said, indeed, that in the midst of the instability of the sacerdotal office he alone preserved in reality its authority. For fifty years this high office remained without interruption in his family. Five of his sons successively assumed its dignity. This family was even known as the "sacerdotal family," as if this office had become hereditary in it. Ananos had charge also of the more important duties of the Temple, and Josephus says that he was considered the most fortunate man of his time. He adds, however, that the spirit of this family was haughty, audacious, and cruel. (Luke iii. 2; John xviii. 13, 24; Acts iv. 6; Jos., "Ant.," B. XV. C. III 1; XX. IX. 1, 3; "Jewish Wars," B. IV. V. 2, 6, 7.)

ELEAZAR was high priest during one year, under Valerius Grattus (23-24 A.D.). He was the eldest son of Ananos. (Jos., "Ant.," B. XVIII. II. 2.)

JONATHAN, son of Ananos, simple priest at that time, but afterwards made high priest for one year in the place of Caiaphas when the latter was deposed, after the disgrace of Pilate, by Vitellius, Governor-general of Syria (37 A.D.). (Jos., "Ant.," B. XVIII. IV. 3.)

THEOPHILUS, son of Ananos, simple priest at that time, but afterwards made high priest in the place of his brother Jonathan, who was deposed by Vitellius. Theophilus was in office five years (38-42 A.D.). (Jos., "Ant.," B. XIX. VI. 2; Munk, "Hist. de la Palestine," p. 568.)

MATTHIAS, son of Ananos. Simple priest; afterwards high priest for two years (42-44 A.D.). He succeeded Simon Cantharus, who was deposed by King Herod Agrippa. (Jos., "Ant.," XIX. VI. 4.)

ANANUS, son of Ananos. Simple priest at the time; afterwards made high priest by Herod Agrippa after the death of the Roman governor, Portius Festus (63 A.D.). Being a Sadducee of extravagant zeal, he was deposed at the end of three months by Albanus, successor of Portius Festus, for having illegally condemned the apostle James to be stoned. (Acts xxiii. 2, xxiv. 1; Jos., "Ant.," B. XX. IX. 1.)

JOAZAR, high priest for six years during the latter days of Herod the Great and the first years of Archelaus (4 B.C.-2 A.D.). He was the son of Simon Boethus, who owed his dignity and fortune to the following dishonorable circumstance, as related by Josephus the historian: "There was one Simon, a citizen of Jerusalem, the son of Boethus, a citizen of Alexandria and a priest of great note there. This man had a daughter, who was esteemed the most beautiful woman of that time. And when the people of Jerusalem began to speak much in her commendation, it happened that Herod was much affected by what was said of her; and when he saw the damsel he was smitten with her beauty. Yet did he entirely reject the thought of using his authority to abuse her ... so he thought it best to take the damsel to wife. And while Simon was of a dignity too inferior to be allied to him, but still too considerable to be despised, he governed his inclinations after the most prudent manner by augmenting the dignity of the family and making them more honorable. Accordingly he forthwith deprived Jesus, the son of Phabet, of the high priesthood, and conferred that dignity on Simon." Such, according to Josephus, is the origin—not at all of a supernatural nature—of the call to the high priesthood of Simon Boethus and his whole family. Simon, at the time of this trial, was already dead; but Joazar figured in it with two of his brothers, one of whom was, like himself, an ex-high priest. (Jos., "Ant.," B. XV. IX. 3; XVII. VI. 4; XVIII. I. 1; XIX. VI. 2.)

ELEAZAR, second son of Simon Boethus. He succeeded his brother Joazar when the latter was deprived of that function by King Archelaus (2 A.D.). Eleazar was high priest for a short time only, the same king deposing him three months after his installation. (Jos., "Ant.," B. XVII. XIII. 1; XIX. VI. 2.)

SIMON CANTHARUS, third son of Simon Boethus. Simple priest at the time; was afterwards made high priest by King Herod Agrippa (42 A.D.), who, however, deposed him after a few months. (Jos., "Ant.," B. XIX. VI. 2, 4.)

JESUS *ben* SIE succeeded Eleazar to the high priesthood, and held the office for five or six years (1-6 A.D.) under the reign of Archelaus. (Jos., "Ant.," XVII. XIII. 1.)

ISMAEL *ben* PHABI. High priest for nine years under procurator Valerius Grattus, predecessor of Pontius Pilate. He was considered, according to the rabbins, the handsomest man of his time. The effeminate love of luxury of this chief priest was carried to such an extent that his mother, having made him a tunic of great price, he deigned to wear it once, and then consigned it to the public wardrobe, as a grand lady might dispose of a robe which no longer pleased her caprices. ("Talmud," "Pesachim," or "of the Passover," fol. 57, verso; "Yoma," or "the Day of Atonement," fol. 9, verso; 35, recto; Jos., "Ant.," XVIII. II. 2; XX. VIII. 11; Bartolocci, "Grand Bibliothèque Rabbinique," T. III. p. 297; Munk, "Palestine," pp. 563, 575.)

SIMON *ben* CAMITHUS, high priest during one year under procurator Valerius Grattus (24-25 A.D.). This personage was celebrated for the enormous size of his hand, and the Talmud relates of him the following incident: On the eve of the day of atonement it happened, in the course of a conversation which he had with Arathus, King of Arabia—whose daughter Herod Antipas had just married—that some saliva, coming out of the mouth of the king, fell on the robe of Simon. As soon as the king left him, he hastened to divest himself of it, considering it desecrated by the circumstance, and hence unworthy to be worn during the services of the following day. What a remarkable instance of Pharisaical purity and charity! ("Talmud," "Yoma," or "the Day of Atonement," fol. 47, verso; Jos., "Ant.," XVIII. II. 2; Dérembourg, "Essai sur l'histoire," p. 197, n. 2.)

JOHN, simple priest. He is made known to us through the Acts of the Apostles. "And Annas the high priest, and Caiaphas, and John, and Alexander, and as many as were of the kindred of the high priest, were gathered together in Jerusalem." (Acts iv. 6.)

ALEXANDER, simple priest; also mentioned in the Acts of the Apostles in the passage above quoted. Josephus also makes mention of him, and says that he afterwards became an *Alabarch*—that is to say, first magistrate of the Jews in Alexandria. That he was very rich is to be learned from the fact that King Herod Agrippa asked and obtained from him the loan of two hundred thousand pieces of silver. (Acts iv. 6; Jos., "Ant.," XVIII. VI. 3; XX. V. 2; Petri Wesselingii, "Diatribe de Judæorum Archontibus," Trajecti ad Rhenum, pp. 69-71.)

ANANIAS *ben* NEBEDEUS, simple priest at that time; was elected to the high priesthood under procurators Ventideus, Cumanus, and Felix (48-54 A.D.). He is mentioned in the Acts of the Apostles and by Josephus. It was this high priest who delivered the apostle Paul to procurator Felix. "Ananias the high priest descended with the elders, and with a certain orator named Tertullus, who informed the governor against Paul." (Acts xxiv. 1.) According to Jewish tradition, this high priest is chiefly known for his excessive gluttony. What the Talmud says of his voracity is quite phenomenal. It mentions three hundred calves, as many casks of wine, and forty pairs of young pigeons as having been brought together for his repast. ("Talmud," Bab., "Pesachim," or "of the Passover," fol. 57, verso; "Kerihoth," or "Sins which Close the Entrance to Eternal Life," fol. 28, verso; Jos., "Ant.," XX. V. 2; Dérembourg, work quoted above, pp. 230, 234; Munk, "Palestine," p. 573, n. 1.)

HELCIAS, simple priest, and keeper of the treasury of the Temple. It is probably from him that Judas Iscariot received the thirty pieces of silver, the price of his treason. (Jos., "Ant.," XX. VIII. 11.)

SCEVA, one of the principal priests. He is spoken of in the Acts apropos of his seven sons, who gave themselves up to witchcraft. (Acts xix. 13, 14.)

Such are the chief priests that constituted the first chamber of the Sanhedrin at the time of the trial of Christ.

From the documents which we have consulted and the résumé which we have just given, we gather:

1. That several of the high priests were personally dishonorable.

2. That all these high priests, who succeeded each other annually in the Aaronic office in utter disregard of the order established by God, were but miserable intruders. We trust that these expressions will not offend our dear Israelitish readers, for they are based on the statements of eminent and zealous Jewish writers.

To begin with Josephus the historian. Although endeavoring to conceal as much as possible the shameful acts committed by the priests composing this council, yet he was unable, in a moment of disgust, to refrain from stigmatizing them. "About this time," he says, "there arose a sedition between the high priests and the principal men of the multitude of Jerusalem, each of which assembled a company of the boldest sort of men, and of those that loved innovations, and became leaders to them. And when they struggled together they did it by casting reproachful words against one another, and by throwing stones also. And there was nobody to reprove them; but these disorders were done after a licentious manner in the city, as if it had no government over it. And such was the impudence and boldness that had seized on the high priests that they had the hardness to send their servants into the threshing-floors, to take away those tithes that were due the [simple] priests. Insomuch that the poorest priests died of want."[192] Such are the acts, the spirit of equity and kindness, that characterized the chief judges of Christ! But the Talmud goes farther still. This book, which ordinarily is not sparing of eulogies on the people of our nation, yet, considering separately and by name, as we have done, the high priests of that time, it exclaims: "What a plague is the family of Simon Boethus; cursed be their lances! What a plague is the family of Ananos; cursed be their hissing of vipers! What a plague is the family of Cantharus; cursed be their pens! What a plague is the family of Ismael ben Phabi; cursed be their fists! They are high priests themselves, their sons are treasurers, their sons-in-law are commanders, and their servants strike the people with staves."[193] The Talmud continues: "The porch of the sanctuary cried out four times. The first time, Depart from here, descendants of Eli;[194] ye pollute the Temple of the Eternal! The second time, Let Issachar ben Keifar Barchi depart from here, who polluteth himself and profaneth the victims consecrated to God![195] The third time, Widen yourselves, ye gates of the sanctuary, and let Israel ben Phabi the willful enter, that he may discharge the functions of the priesthood! Yet another cry was heard, Widen yourselves, ye gates, and let Ananias ben Nebedeus the gourmand enter, that he may glut himself on the victims!" In the face of such low morality, avowed by the least to be suspected of our own nation, is it possible to restrain one's indignation against those who sat at the trial of Christ as members of the chamber of priests? This indignation becomes yet more intense when one remembers that an ambitious hypocrisy, having for its aim the domineering over the people, had perverted the law of Moses in these men. The majority of the priests belonged, in fact, to the Pharisaic order, the members of which sect made religion subservient to their personal ambition; and in order to rule over the people with more ease, they used religion as a tool to effect this purpose, encumbering the law of Moses with exaggerated precepts and insupportable burdens which they strenuously imposed upon others, but failed to observe themselves. Can we, then, be astonished at the murderous hatred which these false and ambitious men conceived for Christ? When his words, sharper than a sword, exposed their hypocrisy and displayed the corrupt interior of these whitened sepulchers wearing the semblance of justice, the hatred they already cherished for him grew to a frenzied intensity. They never forgave him for having publicly unmasked them. Hypocrisy never forgives that.

Such were the men composing the council of priests, when the Sanhedrin assembled to judge Christ. Were we not justified in forming of them an unfavorable opinion?... But let us pass on to the second chamber, viz., the chamber of the scribes.

II. CHAMBER OF THE SCRIBES

Let us recall in a few words who the scribes were. Chosen indiscriminately among the Levites and laity, they formed the *corps savant* of the nation; they were doctors in Israel, and were held in high esteem and veneration. It is well known what respect the Jews, and the Eastern nations generally, have always had for their *wise men*.

Next to the chamber of the priests, that of the scribes was the most important. But from information gathered from the documents to which we have already referred, we are constrained to affirm that, with a few individual exceptions, this chamber was no better than that of the priests.

The following is a list of the names and histories of the *wise men* who composed the chamber of the scribes at the trial of Christ:

GAMALIEL, surnamed the ancient. He was a very worthy Israelite, and his name is spoken of with honor in the Talmud as well as in the Acts of the Apostles. He belonged to a noble family, being a grandson of the famous Hillel, who, coming from Babylon forty years before Christ, taught with such brilliant success in Jerusalem. Gamaliel acquired so great a reputation among his people for his scientific acquirements that the Talmud could say of him: "*With the death of Rabbi Gamaliel the glory of the law has departed.*" It was at the feet of this doctor that Saul, afterwards Paul the apostle, studied the law and Jewish traditions, and we know how he gloried in this fact. Gamaliel had also among his disciples Barnabas and Stephen, the first martyr for the cause of Christ. When the members of the Sanhedrin discussed the expediency of putting the apostles to death, this worthy Israelite prevented the passing of the sentence by pronouncing these celebrated words: "Ye men of Israel, take heed to yourselves what ye intend to do as touching these men.... And now I say unto you, refrain from these men, and let them alone; for if this counsel be of men it will come to naught; but if it be of God ye cannot overthrow it; lest haply ye be found even to fight against God." Gamaliel died nineteen years after Christ (52 A.D.). (Acts v. 34-39; xxii. 3; Mishna, "Sotah," or "the Woman Suspected of Adultery," C. IX.; "Sepher Juchasin," or "the Book of the Ancestors," p. 53; David Ganz, "Germe de David ou Chronologie" to 4768; Bartolocci, "Bibliotheca magna Rabbinica," T. i. pp. 727-732.)

SIMON, son of Gamaliel, like his father, had a seat in the assembly. The rabbinical books speak of him in the highest terms of eulogy. The Mishna, for instance, attributes to him this sentence: "Brought up from my infancy among learned men, I have found nothing that is of greater value to man than silence. Doctrines are not the chief things, but work. He who is in the habit of much talking falls easily into error." This Simon became afterwards the intimate friend of the too celebrated bandit, John of Giscala, whose excesses and cruelty toward the Romans, and even the Jews, caused Titus to order the pillaging of Jerusalem. Simon was killed in the last assault in 70 A.D. (David Ganz, "Chronologie" to 4810; Mishna, "Aboth," or "of the Fathers," C. I.; "Talmud," Jerusalem, "Berachoth," or "of Blessings," fol. 6, verso; "Historia Docorium Misnicorum," J. H. Otthonis, pp. 110-113; De Champagny, "Rome et la Judée," T. ii. 86-171.)

ONKELOS was born of heathen parents, but embraced Judaism, and became one of the most eminent disciples of Gamaliel. He is the author of the famous Chaldaic paraphrase of the Pentateuch. Although the rabbinical books do not mention him as a member of the Sanhedrin, yet it is highly probable that he belonged to that body, his writings and memory having always been held in great esteem by the Jews; even at the present day every Jew is enjoined to read weekly a portion of his version of the books of Moses. Onkelos carried the Pharisaical intolerance to the last degree.

Converted from idolatry to Judaism, he hated the Gentiles to such an extent that he cast into the Dead Sea, as an object of impurity, the sum of money that he had inherited from his parents. We can easily understand how that, with such a disposition, he would not be favorably inclined toward Jesus, who received Gentiles and Jews alike. ("Talmud," "Megilla," or "Festival of Esther," fol. 3, verso; "Baba-bathra," or "the Last Gate," fol. 134, verso; "Succa," or "the Festival of Tabernacles," fol. 28, verso; "Thosephthoth," or "Supplements to the Mishna," C. v.; Rabbi Gedalia, "Tzaltzeleth Hakkabalah," or "the Chain of the Kabalah," p. 28; "Histor. Doct. Misnic.," p. 110; De Rossi, "Dizionario degli Autori Ebrei," p. 81.)

JONATHAN *ben* UZIEL, author of a very remarkable paraphrase of the Pentateuch and the Prophets. There is a difference of opinion regarding the precise time at which he lived. Some place it several years before Christ; others at the time of Christ. We believe, however, that not only was he contemporary with Christ, but that he was also one of his judges. In support of our assertion we give the two following proofs, which we think indisputable: 1. Jonathan, the translator of the Prophets, has purposely omitted Daniel, which omission the Talmud explains as due to the special intervention of an angel who informed him that the manner in which the prophet speaks of the death of the Messiah coincided too exactly with that of Jesus of Nazareth. Now, since Jonathan has intentionally left out the prophecies of Daniel on account of their coincidence with the death of Christ, it proves that he could not have lived before Christ, but must have been contemporary with him. 2. In comparing the paraphrase of Onkelos with that of Jonathan, we find that the latter had made use of the work of the former, who lived in the time of Christ. Examples may be found in Deut. xxii. 5, Judges v. 26, Num. xxi. 28, 29. If, then, Jonathan utilized the work of Onkelos, who lived in the time of Christ, the fact proves beyond question that he could not have lived before Christ. The Talmudists, in order to reward this person for having, through his hatred of Christ, erased the name of Daniel from the roll of prophets, eulogize him in the most absurd manner. They relate that while engaged in the study of the law of God, the atmosphere which surrounded him, and came in contact with the light of his understanding, so caught fire from his fervor that the birds, silly enough to be attracted toward it, were consumed immediately. ("Talmud," "Succa," or "the Festival of Tabernacles," fol. 28, verso; David Ganz, "Chronol." 4728; Gesenius, "Comm. on Isaiah," Part I. p. 65; Zunz, "Culte divin des Juifs," Berlin, 1832, p. 61; Dérembourg, work quoted above, p. 276; Hanneburg, "Révelat Bibliq.," ii. 163, 432.)

SAMUEL HAKATON, or *the Less*. Surnamed to distinguish him from Samuel the prophet. It was he who, some time after the resurrection of Christ, composed the famous imprecation against the Christians, called "Birchath

Hamminim" (Benedictions of Infidels). The "Birchath Hamminim," says the Talmud, and the commentary of R. Jarchi, "was composed by R. Samuel Hakaton at Jabneh, where the Sanhedrin had removed after the misconduct of the Nazarene, who taught a doctrine contrary to the words of the living God." The following is the singular benediction: "*Let there be no hope for the apostates of religion, and let all heretics, whosoever they may be, perish suddenly. May the kingdom of pride be rooted out; let it be annihilated quickly, even in our days! Be blessed, O Lord, who destroyest the impious, and humblest the proud!*" As soon as Samuel Hakaton had composed this malediction, it was inserted as an additional blessing in the celebrated prayer of the synagogue, the "Shemonah-Essara" (the eighteen blessings). These blessings belonged to the time of Ezra—that is to say, five centuries before the Christian era; and every Jew has to recite it daily. St. Jerome was not ignorant of this strange prayer. He says: "*The Jews anathematize three times daily in their synagogue the name of the Christian, disguising it under the name of Nazarene.*" According to R. Gedalia, Samuel died before the destruction of Jerusalem, about fifteen or twenty years after Christ. ("Talmud," "Berachoth," or "of Prayers," fol. 28, verso; "Megilla," or "the Festival of Esther," fol. 28, verso; St. Jerome, "Comment. on Isaiam," B. II. C. V. 18, 19; Tom. iv. p. 81 of the "Valarsius," quarto edition; Vitringa, "de Synagoga vetr.," T. ii. p. 1036, 1047, 1051; Castellus, "Lexicon heptaglotton," art. Min.)

CHANANIA *ben* CHISKIA. He was a great conciliator in the midst of the doctrinal quarrels so common at that time; and it happened that the rival schools of Shammai and Hillel, which were not abolished with the death of their founders, often employed him as their arbitrator. This skillful umpire did not always succeed, however, in calming the disputants; for we read in the ancient books that in the transition from force of argument to argument of force, the members of the schools of Shammai and Hillel frequently came to blows. Hence the French expression *se chammailler*. It happened, however, according to the Talmud, that Chanania once departed from his usual system of equilibrium in favor of the prophet Ezekiel. It appears that on one occasion the most influential members of the Sanhedrin proposed to censure, and even reject, the book of this prophet, because, according to their opinion, it contained several passages in contradiction of the law of Moses; but Chanania defended it with so much eloquence that they were obliged to desist from their project. This fact alone, reported fully as it is in the Talmud, would be sufficient to show the laxity of the study of the prophecies at that time. Although the exact date of his death is uncertain, it is, nevertheless, sure that it took place before the destruction of the Temple. ("Talmud," "Chagiga," or "the obligations of the males to present themselves three times a year at Jerusalem," 2, 13; "Shabbath," or "of the Sabbath," C. I.; "Sepher Juchasin," or "the Book of Ancestors," p. 57.)

ISMAEL *ben* ELIZA, renowned for the depth of his mind and the beauty of his face. The rabbins record that he was learned in the most mysterious things; for example, he could command the angels to descend from heaven and ascend thither. We have it also from the same authority that his mother held him in such high admiration that one day on his return from school she washed his feet, and, through respect for him, drank the water she had used for that purpose. His death was of a no less romantic nature. It appears that after the capture of Jerusalem, the daughter of Titus was so struck with his beauty that she obtained permission of her father to have the skin of his face taken off after his death, which skin she had embalmed, and, having perfumed it, she sent it to Rome to figure among the spoils as a trophy. ("Talmud," "Aboda Zarah," or "of Idolatry," C. I.; Rabbi Gedalia, "Tzaltzeleth Hakkabalah," or "the Chain of the Kabalah," p. 29; "Sepher Juchasin," or "the Book of Ancestors," p. 25; "Tosephoth Kiddushin," C. IV.)

Rabbi ZADOK. He was about forty years old at the trial of Christ, and died after the burning of the Temple, aged over seventy. The Talmud relates that for forty years he ceased not from fasting, that God might so order it that the Temple should not be destroyed by fire. Upon this the question is propounded in the same book, but no answer given, as to how this rabbin could have known that the Temple was threatened with so great a calamity. We believe that Rabbi Zadok could have obtained information of this terrible event in one of the two ways—either from the prophetic voice of Daniel which proclaimed more than forty years previous to the occurrence that abomination and desolation should crush the Temple of Jerusalem when the Messiah should have been put to death; or by the voice of Jesus himself, who said forty years before the destruction of the Temple: "See ye not all these things?" (i.e., the buildings of the Temple) "verily, verily I say unto you, There shall not be left here one stone upon another that shall not be thrown down." (Mishna, "Shabbath," or "of the Sabbath," C. XXIV. 5 to end; "Eduth," or "of Testimony," C. VII. 1; "Aboth," or "of the Fathers of Tradition," IV. 5; David Ganz, "Chronol." 4785; Seph. Juchasin," fol. 21, 26; Schikardi, "Jus Regium Hebræorum," p. 468; Dan. ix. 25-27; Luke xxi. 6; Matt. xxvi. 2.)

JOCHANAN *ben* ZAKAI. The rabbinical books accord to this rabbi an extraordinary longevity. From their writings it would appear that, like Moses, he lived a hundred and twenty years, forty years of which he consecrated to manual labor; another forty to the study of the law; and the last forty years of his life he devoted to imparting his knowledge to others. His reputation as a savant was so well established that he was surnamed the *Splendor of Wisdom*. After the destruction of the Temple, he rallied together the remaining members of the Sanhedrin to Jabneh, where he presided over this remnant for the last four or five years of his life. He died in the year 73 A.D. When he breathed his last, says the Mishna, a cry of anguish was heard, saying: "With the death of Jochanan ben Zakai the splendor of wisdom has been quenched!" We have, however, other information regarding this rabbi which is, so to speak, like the reverse side of a medal. The Bereshith Rabba says that Rabbi Jochanan was in the habit of eulogizing himself in the most extravagant manner, and gives the following as a specimen of the praises he bestowed upon himself: "If the skies were parchment, all the inhabitants of the world writers, and all the trees of the forest pens, all these would not suffice to transcribe the doctrines which he had learned from the masters." What humility of language! One day his disciples asked him to what he attributed his long life. "To my wisdom and piety," was his reply in his tone of habitual modesty. Besides, if we were to judge of his moral character by an ordinance of which he is the author, his morality might be equal to the standard of his humility. He abolished the Mosaical command of the ordeal of bitter waters, immorally isolating a passage in Isaiah from its context. Finally, to fill up the measure of his honesty, he became one of the lewdest courtiers of Titus, and the destroyer of his country. But while obsequious to human grandeur, he was obdurate to the warnings of God, and died proud and impenitent. ("Talmud," "Rosh Hashanah," or "of the New Year," fol. 20, recto; 31, recto; "Sotah," or "of the Woman Suspected," etc., IX. 9; "Yoma," or "the Day of Atonement," fol. 39, recto, and 43; "Gittin," or "of Divorce," fol. 56, verso and recto; "Succa," or "of the Festival of Tabernacles," fol. 28, verso; Mishna, Chapter, "Egla arupha"; "Sepher Juchasin," or "the Book of Ancestors," fol. 20, recto; "Seph. Hakkabalah"; Otthonis, "Hist. Doct. Misn.," pp. 93-103; Hosea iv. 14; Jos., "Wars," VI. V. 3; De Champagny, "Rome et la Judée," T. i. p. 158.)

ABBA SAUL. He was of prodigious height, and had the charge of superintending the burials of the dead, that everything might be done according to the law. The rabbins, who delight in the marvelous, affirm that in the exercise of his duties he found the thigh bone of Og, the King of Bashan, and the right eye of Absalom. By virtue of the marrow extracted from the thigh of Og, he was enabled to chase a young buck for three leagues; as for the eye of Absalom, it was so deep that he could have hidden himself in it as if in a cavern. These stories, no doubt, appear very puerile; and yet, according to a Talmudical book (Menorath-Hammoer, "the lighted candlestick"), which is considered of great authority even in the modern [orthodox] synagogue, we must judge of these matters in the following manner: "Everything which our doctors have taught in the Medrashim (allegoric or historical commentaries) we are bound to consider and believe in as the law of Moses our master; and if we find anything in it which appears exaggerated and incredible, we must attribute it to the weakness of our understandings, rather than to their teachings; and whoever turns into ridicule whatever they have said will be punished." According to Maimonides, Abba Saul died before the destruction of the Temple. (Mishna, "Middoth," or "of the Dimensions of the Temple," Chapter, "Har habbaith"; "Talmud," "Nidda," or "the Purification of Women," C. III. fol. 24, recto; Maimonides, "Proef ad zeraim"; Drach, "Harmonies entre l'Eglise et la Synagogue," T. ii. p. 375.)

R. CHANANIA, surnamed the Vicar of the Priests. The Mishna attributes to him a saying which brings clearly before us the social position of the Jewish people in the last days of Jerusalem. "Pray," said he, "for the Roman Empire; for should the terror of its power disappear in Palestine, neighbor will devour neighbor alive." This avowal shows the deplorable state of Judea, and the divisions to which she had become a prey. The Romans seem, however, to have cared very little for the sympathy of R. Chanania, for, having possessed themselves of the city, they put him to death. (Mishna, "Aboth," or "of the Fathers of Tradition," C. III. 2; "Zevachim," or "of Sacrifices," C. IX. 3; "Eduth," or "of Testimony," C. II. 1; David Ganz, "Chronologie," 4826; "Sepher Juchasin," or "the Book of Ancestors," p. 57.)

Rabbi ELEAZAR *ben* PARTAH, one of the most esteemed scribes of the Sanhedrin, on account of his scientific knowledge. Already very aged at the destruction of the Temple, he yet lived several years after that national calamity. ("Talmud," "Gittin," or "of Divorces," C. III. 4; "Sepher Juchasin," p. 31.)

Rabbi NACHUM HALBALAR. He is mentioned in the rabbinical books as belonging to the Sanhedrin in the year 28 A.D., but nothing particular is mentioned of his history. ("Talmud," "Peah," or "of the Angle," C. II. 6, "Sanhedrin.")

Rabbi SIMON HAMIZPAH. He also is said to have belonged to the Sanhedrin in the year 28 A.D. Beyond this but little is known. ("Talmud," "Peah," C. II. 6.)

These are, according to Jewish tradition, the principal scribes, or doctors, that composed the second chamber of the Sanhedrin at the time of the trial of Christ. The ancient books which speak of them are, of course, filled with their praises. Nevertheless, blended with these praises are some remarks which point to the predominant vice of these men—namely, pride. We read in Rabbi Nathan's book, "Aruch" (a Talmudical dictionary of great authority[196]): "*In the past and more honorable times the titles of rabbin, rabbi, or rav,[197] to designate the learned men of Babylon and Palestine, were unknown; thus when Hillel came from Babylon the title of rabbi was not added to his name. It was the same with the prophets, who were styled simply Isaiah, Haggai, etc., and not Rabbi Isaiah, Rabbi Haggai, etc. Neither did Ezra bring the title of rabbi with him from Babylon. It was not until the time of Gamaliel, Simon, and Jochanan ben Zackai that this imposing title was first introduced among the worthies of the Sanhedrin."*

This pompous appellation appears, indeed, for the first time among the Jews contemporary with Christ. "They love the uppermost rooms at feasts, and the chief seats in the synagogues, and greetings in the market-places, and to be called of men, Rabbi, Rabbi." Proud of their titles and learning, they laid claim to the foremost rank in society. *A wise man,* say they, *should be preferred to a king; the king takes the precedence of the high priest; the priest of the Levite; the Levite of the ordinary Israelite. The wise man should be preferred to the king, for if the wise man should die he could not easily be replaced; while the king could be succeeded by an Israelite of any order.*[198] Basing the social status on this maxim we are not astonished to find in the Talmud[199] that at a certain time twenty-four persons were excommunicated for having failed to render to the rabbi the reverence due his position. Indeed, a very small offense was often sufficient to call forth maledictions from this haughty and intolerant dignitary. Punishment was mercilessly inflicted wherever there was open violation of any one of the following rules established by the rabbis themselves:

If any one opposes his rabbi, he is guilty in the same degree as if he opposed God himself.[200]

If any one quarrels with his rabbi, it is as if he contended with the living God.[201]

If any one thinks evil of his rabbi, it is as if he thought evil of the Eternal.[202]

This self-sufficiency was carried to such an enormous extent that when Jerusalem fell into the hands of Titus, who came against it armed with the sword of vengeance of Jehovah, Rabbi Jehudah wrote with an unflinching pen: "*If Jerusalem was destroyed, we need look for no other cause than the people's want of respect for the rabbis.*"[203]

We ask now of every sincere Israelite, What opinion can be formed of the members of the second chamber who are about to assist in pronouncing judgment upon Christ? Could impartiality be expected of those proud and selfish men, whose lips delighted in nothing so much as sounding their own praises? What apprehensions must one not have of an unjust and cruel verdict when he remembers it was of these very men that Christ had said: "Beware of the scribes, which desire to walk in long robes; they make broad their phylacteries and enlarge the borders of their garments; they love greetings in the market, and to be called Rabbi, Rabbi; which devour widows' houses; and for show make long prayers."[204] The remembrance of this rebuke, so galling to their pride, continually rankled in their minds; and when the opportunity came, with what remorseless hate did they wreak upon him their vengeance! We may, then, conclude from the foregoing facts that the members of the chamber of the scribes were no better than those composing the chamber of the priests. To this assertion, however, there is one exception to be made; for, as we have already seen, there was among those arrogant and unscrupulous men[205] one whose sense of justice was not surpassed by his great learning. That man was Gamaliel.

III. Chamber of the Elders

This chamber was the least influential of the three; hence, but few names of the persons composing it at the period to which we refer have been preserved.

JOSEPH OF ARIMATHEA. The Gospel makes of him the following eulogy: Rich man; honorable counselor; good and just man; the same had not consented to the counsel and deed of the others. Joseph of Arimathea is called in the Vulgate, or the Latin version of the Bible, "noble centurion," because he was one of the ten magistrates or senators who had the principal authority in Jerusalem under the Romans. His noble position is more clearly marked in the Greek version. That he was one of the seventy may be concluded, first, because it was common to admit senators who were considered the ancients of the people in this assembly; they were indeed the chiefs and the princes of the nation—*seniores populi, principes nostri*; second, because these words, "he had not consented to the counsel and deed of the others," proves that he had a right to be in the grand assembly and take part in the discussions. (Matt. xxvii. 57-59; Mark xv. 43-46; Luke xxiii. 50; John xix. 38; Jacobi Alting, "Schilo seu de Vaticinio patriarchæ Jacobi," p. 310; Goschler, *Diction. Encyclopediq.*; word, "Arimathea"; Cornelius Lapidus, "Comment. in Script. sac.," edition Vivés, T. xv. p. 638, second col.)

NICODEMUS. St. John the Evangelist says that he was by profession a Pharisee, a prince of the Jews, a master in Israel, and a member of the Sanhedrin, where he one day attempted to oppose his colleagues by speaking in defense of Jesus. This act brought down upon him the disdainful retort from the others, "Art thou also a Galilean?" He was one, it is true, but in secret. We know from the Gospel account of him that he possessed great riches, and that he used nearly a hundred pounds of myrrh and spices for the burial of Christ. The name of Nicodemus is mentioned in the Talmud also; and, although it was known that his attachment to Christ was great, he is, nevertheless, spoken of with honor. But this fact may be due to his great wealth. There were, says the Hebrew book, three eminent men in Jerusalem—Nicodemus ben Gurien, ben Tzitzith Hacksab, ben Kalba Shevuah—each of whom could have supported the whole city for ten years. (John iii. 1-10; vii. 50-52; xix. 39; "Talmud" "Gittin," or "of Divorces," C. V. fol. 56, verso; "Abodah Zarah," or "of Idolatry," C. II. fol. 25, verso;

"Taanith," or "of the Fast Days," III. fol. 19, recto; fol. 20, verso; Midrash Rabbah on "Koheleth," VII. II; David Ganz, "Chron." 4757; Knappius, "Comment. in Colloquium Christi cum Nicodemo"; Cornelius Lapidus, "Comment. in Joann." Cap. III. *et seq.*)

BEN KALBA SHEVUAH. After stating that he was one of the three rich men of Jerusalem, the Talmud adds: "His name was given to him because whosoever entered his house as hungry as a dog came out filled." There is no doubt that his high financial position secured for him one of the first places in the chamber of the ancients. His memory, according to Ritter, is still preserved among the Jews in Jerusalem. ("Talmud," "Gittin," or "of Divorces," C. V. fol. 56, verso; David Ganz, "Chronol." 4757; Ritter, "Erdkunde," XVI. 478.)

BEN TZITZITH HACKSAB. The effeminacy of this third rich man is made known to us by the Talmud, where it is stated that the border of his pallium trained itself always on the softest carpets. Like Nicodemus and Kalba Shevuah, he no doubt belonged to the Sanhedrin. ("Talmud," "Gittin," C. V. fol. 56, verso; David Ganz, "Chron." 4757.)

SIMON. From Josephus the historian we learn that he was of Jewish parentage, and was highly esteemed in Jerusalem on account of the accurate knowledge of the law which he possessed. He had the boldness, one day, to convoke an assembly of the people and to bring an accusation against King Herod Agrippa, who, he said, deserved, on account of his bad conduct, that the entrance into the sacred portals should be forbidden him. This took place eight or nine years after Christ—that is to say, in the year 42 or 43 A.D. We may safely conclude that a man who had power enough to convoke an assembly and sufficient reputation and knowledge to dare accuse a king, must undoubtedly have belonged to the council of the Sanhedrin. Besides, his birth alone at a time when nobility of origin constituted, as we have already said, a right to honors, would have thrown wide open to him the doors of the assembly. (Jos., "Ant.," XIX. VII. 4; Dérembourg, "Essai sur l'histoire et la géographie de la Palestine," p. 207, n. 1; Frankel, *Monatsschrift.*, III. 440.)

DORAS was a very influential citizen of Jerusalem, and is thus spoken of by Josephus. He was, however, a man of cruel and immoral character, not hesitating, for the sake of ingratiating himself with Governor Felix, to cause the assassination of Jonathan, the high priest who had made himself obnoxious to that ruler by some just remonstrances respecting his administration. Doras effected the assassination in cold blood by means of murderers hired at the expense of Felix (52 or 53 A.D.). The prominence which this man for a long time maintained in Jerusalem warrants the presumption that he was a member of the Sanhedrin. (Jos., "Ant.," XX. VIII. 5.)

- JOHN, son of JOHN.
- DOROTHEAS, son of NATHANAEL.
- TRYPHON, son of THEUDION.
- CORNELIUS, son of CERON.

These four personages were sent as ambassadors by the Jews of Jerusalem to Emperor Claudius in the year 44, when Cuspius Fadus was governor of Judea. Claudius mentions this fact in a letter sent by him to Cuspius Fadus, and which Josephus has preserved. It is very probable that either they themselves or their fathers were members of the chamber of the ancients; for the Jews appointed as their ambassadors only such members of the Sanhedrin as were distinguished for superior learning. (Jos., "Ant.," XX. I. 1, 2.)

The rabbinical books limit their information concerning the members of this chamber to the names we have just mentioned. To be guided, then, by the documents quoted, one would suppose that although this chamber was the least important of the three, yet its members were perhaps more just than those composing the other two, and consequently manifested less vehemence against Christ during His trial. But a statement made by Josephus the historian proves beyond doubt that this third chamber was made up of men no better than were to be found in the others. It was from among the wealthy element of Jewish society, says Josephus, that Sadduceeism received most of its disciples.[206] Since, then, the chamber of ancients was composed principally of the rich men of Jerusalem, we may safely conclude that the majority of its members were infected with the errors of Sadduceeism—that is to say, with a creed that taught that the soul dies before the body.[207] We are, then, in the presence of real materialists, who consider the destiny of man to consist in the enjoyment of material and worldly things,[208] and who are so carnally minded that it would seem as if the prophetic indignation of David had stigmatized them beforehand when he says: "They have so debased themselves as to become like the beasts that have no understanding."[209] Let not our readers imagine that in thus speaking we at all mean to do injustice to the memory of these men. A fact of great importance proves indisputably that Sadducees or Epicureans were numerous among the Sanhedrin. When, several years after the trial of Christ, the apostle Paul had in his turn to appear before that body, he succeeded by the skill of his oratory in turning the doctrinal differences of that assembly to his benefit. "Men and brethren," he exclaimed, "I am a Pharisee, the son of a Pharisee; of the hope and the resurrection of the dead I am called in question."[210] Hardly had the apostle pronounced these words when a hot discussion arose between the Sadducees and the Pharisees, all of them rising and speaking in great confusion—some for the resurrection, others against it—and it was in the tumult of recrimination and general uproar that the apostle was able peacefully to withdraw. Such was the state of things in the supreme council of the Hebrews; and men of notorious heresy, and even impiety, were appointed as judges to decide on questions of doctrine. Among these materialists there were, however, two just men; and, like Lot among the wicked inhabitants of Sodom, there were in this assembly Nicodemus and Joseph of Arimathea.

We shall now briefly sum up the contents of the preceding chapter. We possess certain information respecting more than one half of the seventy-one members of the Sanhedrin. We know almost all the high priests, who, as we have already said, formed the principal element of this council. This majority, as we have intimated, is sufficient for the forming of an estimate of the moral tone of all the judges; and before the debates begin, it is easy to foresee the issue of the trial of Christ.

What, indeed, could have been the issue of a trial before the first chamber, composed as it was of demoralized, ambitious, and scheming priests? of priests who were mostly Pharisees—that is to say, men of narrow minds, careful only of the external, haughty, overbearing, and self-satisfied, believing themselves to be both infallible and impeccable?[211] It is true they expected a Messiah; but their Messiah was to subdue unto them all their enemies, impose for their benefit a tax on all the nations of the earth, and uphold them in all the absurdities with which they have loaded the law of Moses.

But this man who is about to be brought before them has exposed their hypocritical semblance of piety, and justly stripped them of the undeserved esteem in which they were held by the people. He has absolutely denounced the precepts which they invented and placed above the law. He even desired to abolish the illegal taxes which they had imposed upon the people. Are not all these more than sufficient to condemn Him in their eyes and prove Him worthy of death?

Can a more favorable verdict be expected of the members of the second chamber, composed as it was of men so conceited and arrogant? These doctors expected a Messiah who would be another Solomon, under whose reign and with whose aid they would establish at Jerusalem an academy of learning that would attract all the kings, even as the Queen of Sheba was attracted to the court of the wisest king of Israel. But this Jesus, who claims to be the Messiah, has the boldness to declare blessed those who are humble in spirit. His disciples are but ignorant fishermen, chosen from the least of the tribes; his speech of a provoking simplicity, condemning before the multitude the haughty and pretentious language of the doctors. Are not these things sufficient to bring down upon him their condemnation?

And what justice can we expect, in fine, from the third chamber, when we remember that most of its members were depraved Sadducees, caring only for the enjoyment of the things of this world, heedless of the welfare of the soul, almost denying the existence of God, and disbelieving in the resurrection of the dead? According to their views, the mission of the Messiah was not to consist in the regenerating of Israel as well as of the whole human race, but in the making of Jerusalem the center of riches and worldly goods, which would be brought hither by the conquered and humbled Gentiles, who were to become the slaves of the Israelites. But the man upon whom they are called to pass judgment, far from attaching great importance to wealth and dignity, as did they, prescribes to his disciples the renunciation of riches and honors. He even despises those things which the Sadducees esteem most—viz., pedigree, silk attire, cups of gold, and sumptuous repast. What could have rendered his condemnation surer than such manifestations of contempt for the pride and voluptuousness of these men?

To limit our inquiry to the moral characters of the judges alone, the issue of the trial can be but fatal to the accused; and so, when the three chambers constituting the Sanhedrin council had entered into session, we can well imagine that there was no hope for the acquittal of Jesus; for are not all the high priests, as well as the majority of the scribes and ancients, against him?[212]

APPENDIX II

ACTS OF PILATE

THE apocryphal Acts of Pilate are herewith given under Appendix II. The authenticity of these writings has never been finally settled by the scholarship of the world. It is safe to say, however, that the current of modern criticism is decidedly against their genuineness. Nevertheless, the following facts seem to be very generally conceded by the critics: That there are now in existence certain ancient documents called the "Acts of Pilate"; that they were probably discovered at Turin, in northern Italy, and were first used by the noted New Testament palæographer, Dr. Constantine Tischendorf, who studied them in company with the celebrated orientalist, Victor Amadee Peyron, professor of oriental languages in the University of Turin; and, furthermore, that these documents that we now have are approximately accurate copies of the document mentioned by Justin Martyr about the year 138 A.D., and by Tertullian about the year 200 A.D.

But, admitting all these things, the question of *genuineness* and *authenticity* still remains to be settled. Was the document referred to by Justin as the "Acts of Pilate," and again as the "Acts recorded under Pontius Pilate," a genuine manuscript, written by or composed under the direction of Pilate, or was it a "pious fraud of some Christian," who gathered his prophecies from the Old, and his facts from the New Testament, and then embellished both with his imagination?

The subject is too vast and the space at our disposal is too limited to permit a discussion of the authenticity of the Acts of Pilate. We have deemed it sufficient to insert under Appendix II lengthy extracts from the writings of Tischendorf and Lardner, two of the most celebrated biblical critics, relating to the genuineness of these Acts. The reader would do well to peruse these extracts carefully before reading the Acts of Pilate.

LARDNER'S REMARKS ON THE ACTS OF PILATE

The Acts of Pontius Pilate, and his letter to Tiberius

"Justin Martyr, in his first Apology, which was presented to the emperor Antoninus Pius, and the Senate of Rome, about the year 140, having mentioned our Savior's crucifixion and some of the circumstances of it, adds: 'And that these things were so done you may know from the Acts made in the time of Pontius Pilate.'

"Afterwards in the same Apology, having mentioned some of our Lord's miracles, such as healing diseases and raising the dead, he adds: 'And that these things were done by him you may know from the Acts made in the time of Pontius Pilate.'

"Tertullian, in his Apology, about the year 200, having spoken of our Savior's crucifixion and resurrection, and his appearance to his disciples, who were ordained by him to preach the gospel over the world, goes on: 'Of all these things, relating to Christ, Pilate, in his conscience a Christian, sent an account to Tiberius, then emperor.'

"In another chapter or section of his Apology, nearer the beginning, he speaks to this purpose: 'There was an ancient decree that no one should be received for a deity unless he was first approved by the senate. Tiberius, in whose time the Christian religion had its rise, having received from Palestine in Syria an account of such things as manifested our Savior's divinity, proposed to the senate, and giving his own vote as first in his favor, that he should be placed among the gods. The senate refused, because he himself had declined that honor.'

"'Nevertheless the emperor persisted in his own opinion, and ordered that if any accused the Christians they should be punished.' And then adds: 'Search,' says he, 'your own writings, and you will there find that Nero was the first emperor who exercised any acts of severity toward the Christians, because they were then very numerous at Rome.'

"It is fit that we should now observe what notice Eusebius takes of these things in his Ecclesiastical History. It is to this effect: 'When the wonderful resurrection of our Savior, and his ascension to heaven, were in the mouths of all men, it being an ancient custom for the governors of provinces to write the emperor, and give him an account of new and remarkable occurrences, that he might not be ignorant of anything; our Savior's resurrection being much talked of throughout all of Palestine, Pilate informed the emperor of it, as likewise of his miracles, which he had heard of, and that being raised up after he had been put to death, he was already believed by many to be a god. And it is said that Tiberius referred the matter to the senate, but that they refused their consent, under a pretence that it had not been first approved of by them; there being an ancient law that no one should be deified among the Romans without an order of the senate; but, indeed, because the saving and divine doctrine of the gospel needed not to be confirmed by human judgment and authority. However, Tiberius persisted in his former sentiment, and allowed not anything to be done that was prejudicial to the doctrine of Christ. These things are related by Tertullian, a man famous on other accounts, and particularly for his skill in the Roman laws. I say he speaks thus in his Apology for the Christians, written by him in the Roman tongue, but since (in the days of Eusebius) translated into the Greek.' His words are these: 'There was an ancient decree that no one should be consecrated as a deity by the emperor, unless he was first approved of by the senate. Marcus Aemilius knows this by his god Alburnus. This is to our purpose, forasmuch as among you divinity is bestowed by human judgment.'

"And if God does not please man, he shall not be God. And, according to this way of thinking, man must be propitious to God. Tiberius, therefore, in whose time the Christian name was first known in the world, having received an account of this doctrine out of Palestine, where it began, communicated that account to the senate; giving his own suffrage at the same time in favor of it. But the senate rejected it, because it had not been approved by themselves. 'Nevertheless the emperor persisted in his judgment, and threatened death to such as should accuse the Christians.' 'Which,' adds Eusebius, 'could not be other than the disposal of Divine Providence, that the doctrine of the gospel, which was then in its beginning, might be preached all over the world without molestation.' So Eusebius.

"Divers exceptions have been made by learned moderns to the original testimonies of Justin Martyr and Tertullian. 'Is there any likelihood,' say they, 'that Pilate should write such things to Tiberius concerning a man whom he had condemned to death? And if he had written them, is it probable that Tiberius should propose to the senate to have a man put among the gods upon the bare relation of a governor of a province? And if he had proposed it, who can make a doubt that the senate would not have immediately complied? So that though we dare not say that this narration is absolutely false, yet it must be reckoned as doubtful.' So says Du Pin.

"These and other difficulties shall now be considered.

"Now, therefore, I shall mention some observations:

"In the first place, I shall observe that Justin Martyr and Tertullian are early writers of good repute. That is an observation of Bishop Pearson. These testimonies are taken from the most public writings, Apologies for the Christian religion, presented, or at least proposed and recommended to the emperor and senate of Rome, or to magistrates of high authority and great distinction in the Roman empire.

Secondly: It certainly was the custom of governors of provinces to compose Acts or memoirs or commentaries of the remarkable occurrences in the places where they presided.

In the time of the first Roman emperors there were Acts of the Senate, Acts of the City, or People of Rome, Acts of other cities, and Acts of governors of provinces. Of all these we can discern clear proofs and frequent mention in ancient writers of the best credit. Julius Cæsar ordered that Acts of the Senate, as well as daily Acts of the People, should be published. See Sueton. Jul. Cæs. c. xx.

"Augustus forbade publishing Acts of the Senate.

"There was an officer, himself a senator, whose province it was to compose those Acts.

"The Acts of the Senate must have been large and voluminous, containing not only the question proposed, or referred to the senate by the consul, or the emperor, but also the debates and speeches of the senators.

"The Acts of the People, or City, were journals or registers of remarkable births, marriages, divorces, deaths, proceedings in courts of judicature, and other interesting affairs, and some other things below the dignity of history.

"To these Acts of each kind Roman authors frequently had recourse for information.

"There were such Acts or registers at other places besides Rome, particularly at Antium. From them Suetonius learned the day and place of the birth of Caligula, about which were other uncertain reports. And he speaks of those Acts as public authorities, and therefore more decisive and satisfactory than some other accounts.

"There were also Acts of the governors of provinces, registering all remarkable transactions and occurrences.

"Justin Martyr and Tertullian could not be mistaken about this; and the learned bishop of Cæsarea admits the truth of what they say. And in the time of the persecuting emperor Maximin, about the year of Christ 307, the heathen people forged Acts of Pilate, derogatory to the honor of our Savior, which were diligently spread abroad, to unsettle Christians, or discourage them in the profession of their faith. Of this we are informed by Eusebius in his Ecclesiastical History.

Thirdly: It was customary for the governors of provinces to send to the emperor an account of remarkable transactions in places where they presided.

"So thought the learned Eusebius, as we have seen.

"And Pliny's letters to Trajan, still extant, are a proof of it. Philo speaks of the Acts or Memoirs of Alexandria sent to Caligula, which that emperor read with more eagerness and satisfaction than anything else.

"Fourthly: It has been said to be very unlikely that Pilate should write such things to Tiberius, concerning a man whom he [Pilate] had condemned to death.

"To which it is easy to reply, that if he wrote to Tiberius at all, it is very likely that he should speak favorably and honorably of the Savior.

"That Pilate passed sentence of condemnation upon our Lord very unwillingly, and not without a sort of compulsion, appears from the history of the Evangelist: Matt. xxvii.; Mark xv.; Luke xxiii.; John xviii. Pilate was hard pressed. The rulers of the Jews vehemently accused our Lord to him. They said they had found him perverting the nation, and forbidding to give tribute to Cæsar, saying that himself is Christ, a king, and the like; and all without effect for a while.

"Pilate still sought for expedients to set Jesus at liberty.

"As his reluctance had been very manifest and public in a court of judicature, in the chief city of the nation at the time of one of their great festivals, it is highly probable that when he sent to Rome he should make some apology for his conduct. Nor could anything be more proper than to allege some of our Savior's miracles which he had heard of, and to give an account to the zeal of those who professed faith in him after his ignominious crucifixion, and openly asserted that he had risen from the dead and ascended to heaven.

"Pilate would not dare in such a report to write falsehood, nor to conceal the most material circumstances of the case about which he was writing. At the trial he publicly declared his innocence: and told the Jews several times 'that he found no fault in him at all.'

"And when he was going to pronounce the sentence of condemnation, he took water and washed his hands before the multitude, saying: I am innocent of the blood of this just person: 'See ye to it.' Matt. xxvii. 24.

"When he wrote to Tiberius he would very naturally say something of our Lord's wonderful resurrection and ascension, which were much talked of and believed by many, with which he could not be possibly unacquainted. The mention of these things would be the best vindication of his inward persuasion, and his repeated declarations of our Lord's innocence upon trial notwithstanding the loud clamors and united accusations of the Jewish people and their rulers.

"Pilate, as has been said several times, passed condemnation upon Jesus very unwillingly, and not until after long trial.

"When he passed sentence upon him he gave orders that this title or inscription should be put upon the cross: 'Jesus of Nazareth, the king of the Jews.'

"When he had expired, application was made to Pilate, by Joseph of Arimathea, an honorable counsellor, that the body might be taken down and buried. To which he consented; but not till assurance from the centurion that he had been sometime dead. The next day some of the priests and pharisees came to him, saying: 'Sir, we remember that that deceiver said while he was yet alive, After three days I will rise again. Command, therefore, that the sepulchre be made sure, until the third day, lest his disciples come by night and steal him away, and say unto the people, He is risen from the dead.' 'So the last error shall be worse than the first.'

"Pilate said unto them: 'Ye have a watch; go your way, make it sure as you can.' So they went and made the sepulchre sure, sealing the stone and setting a watch.

"Whilst they were at the sepulchre there was a 'great earthquake,' the stone was rolled away by an Angel, 'whose countenance was like lightning, and for fear of whom the guards did shake and become as dead men.' Some of the guards went down into the City, and showed unto the chief priests all the things that were done.

"Nor can there be any doubt that these things came also to the governor's ears. Pilate, therefore, was furnished with materials of great importance relating to this case, very proper to be sent to the emperor. And very probably he did send them, for he could do no otherwise.

"Fifthly: it is said, 'That if Pilate had sent such things to Tiberius, it is nevertheless very unlikely that Tiberius should propose to the senate that our Savior might be put among the gods, because that emperor had little or no regard for things of religion.'

"But it is easy to answer that such observations are of little or no importance. Few princes are able to preserve uniformity in the whole of their conduct, and it is certain that Tiberius varied from himself upon many occasions and in different parts of his life.

"Sixthly: it is further urged, that if Tiberius had proposed the thing to the senate, there can be no doubt that the senate would have immediately complied.

"But neither is this difficulty insuperable; for we are assured by Suetonius that Tiberius let several things be decided by the senate contrary to his own opinion, without showing much uneasiness.

(It must be observed here that Dr. Lardner is very copious in quotations from the best authorities in proof of all his statements. The reader is referred to Vol. VI of his great works, pages 605-620, where will be found these quotations in foot-notes too lengthy to be transcribed here.)

"Seventhly: The right interpretation of the words of Tertullian will be of use to remove difficulties and to confirm the truth of the account.

"I have translated them in this manner: 'When Tiberius referred the matter to the senate, that our Lord should be placed in the number of gods, the senate refused, because he had himself declined that honor.'

"The words are understood to the like purpose by Pearson.

"There is another sense, which is that of the Greek translation of Tertullian's Apology, made use of by Eusebius: 'The senate refused because it had not itself approved of it.' But that sense, if it be any sense at all, is absurd, and therefore unlikely. If none beside the senate had a right to consecrate any for the deity, yet certainly the consul or the emperor might *refer* such a thing to that venerable body. According to Tertullian's account, the whole is in a fair way of legal proceeding." [And it may be remarked here that Tertullian, being well versed in Roman law, would hardly have passed by a blunder here or committed one in anything wherein he may have had to do with the statement.]

"By virtue of an ancient law, no one might be reckoned a god (at least by the Romans) without the approbation of the senate. Tiberius having been informed of some extraordinary things concerning Jesus, referred it to the senate, that he also might be placed in the number of deities. Was it possible after this that the senate should refuse it, under a pretense that Tiberius had bestowed divinity upon Jesus without their consent, when he had done no such thing, and at the very time was referring it to their judgment in the old legal way?

"Le Clerc objects that the true reading in Tertullian is not—*Non quia in se non probaverat*, but *quia non ipse probaverat*.

"Be it so. The meaning is the same. *Ipse* must intend the emperor, not the senate. The other sense is absurd, and next to a contradiction, and therefore not likely to be right, and at the same time it is a rude and needless affront. The other interpretation represents a handsome compliment, not without foundation. For it is very true that Tiberius had himself declined receiving divine honors.

"Eighthly: It has been objected that Tiberius was unfriendly to the Jewish people, and therefore it must be reckoned very improbable that he should be willing to put a man who was a Jew among the gods.

"But there is little or no ground for this objection. It was obviated long ago in the first part of this work, where beside other things it is said: In the reign of Tiberius the Jewish people were well used. They were indeed banished out of Italy by an edict; but it was for a misdemeanor committed by some villains of that nation. The great hardship was that many innocent persons suffered beside the guilty.

"Upon other occasions Tiberius showed the Jews all the favor that could be desired, especially after the death of Sejanus; and is much applauded for it by Philo.

"Ninthly: Still it is urged, 'Nothing can be more absurd than to suppose that Tiberius would receive for a deity a man who taught the worship of one God only, and whose religion decried all other deities as mere fiction.'

"Upon which I must say, nothing can be more absurd than this objection. Tertullian does not suppose Tiberius to be well acquainted with the Christian religion, our Savior's doctrine.

"All he says is, that, having heard of some extraordinary things concerning him, he had a desire to put him among the Roman deities.

"Tenthly: Tertullian proceeds: 'Nevertheless the emperor persisted in his opinion, and ordered that if any accused the Christians they should be punished.' This was very natural. Though the senate would not put Jesus in the number of deities, the emperor was still of opinion that it might have been done.

"And he determined to provide by an edict for the safety of those who professed a high regard for Jesus Christ. Which edict, as Eusebius reasonably supposes, was of use for securing the free preaching of the gospel in many places.

"But the authority of that edict would cease at the emperor's demise, if not sooner. Unfortunately, it could not be in force, or have any great effect, for a long season.

"Nor need we consider the ordering such an edict as in favor of the Christians as an incredible thing, if we observe what Philo says, who assures us that 'Tiberius gave orders to all the governors of provinces, to protect the Jews in the cities where they lived in the observation of their own rights and customs; and that they should bear hard on none of them, but such as were unpeaceable and transgressed the laws of the State.'

"Nor is it impossible that the Christians should partake of the like civilities, they being considered as a sect of the Jews. And it is allowed that the Roman empire did not openly persecute the Christians, till they became so numerous that the heathen people were apprehensive of the total overthrow of their religion.

"In the eleventh place, says a learned and judicious writer, 'It is probable that Pilate, who had no enmity toward Christ, and accounted him a man unjustly accused and an extraordinary person, might be moved by the wonderful circumstances attending and following his death, to hold him in veneration, and perhaps to think him a hero and the son of some deity. It is possible that he might send a narrative, such as he thought most convenient, of these transactions to Tiberius: but it is not at all likely that Tiberius proposed to the senate that Christ should be deified, and that the senate rejected it, and that Tiberius continued favorably disposed toward Christ, and that he threatened to punish those who should molest and accuse the Christians.' 'Observe also,' says the same learned writer, 'that the Jews persecuted the apostles, and slew Stephen, and that Saul made havoc of the church, entering into every house, and hailing men and women, committing them to prison, and that Pilate connived at all this violence, and was not afraid of the resentment of Tiberius on that account.'

"Admitting the truth of all these particulars just mentioned, it does not follow that no orders were given by Tiberius for the protection of the followers of Jesus.

"For no commands of princes are obeyed by all men everywhere. They are oftentimes transgressed.

"Nor was any place more likely than Judea, where the enmity of many against the disciples of Jesus was so great. Nor need it be supposed that Tiberius was very intent to have this order strictly regarded. For he was upon many occasions very indolent and dilatory; and he was well known to be so. Moreover, the death of Stephen was tumultuous, and not an act of the Jewish council. And further, the influence of Pilate in that country was not now at its full height. We perceive from the history of our Lord's trial before him, as recorded in the gospels, that he stood in fear of the Jews.

"He was apprehensive that, if he did not gratify them in that point, they might draw up a long list of maladministrations for the emperor's view. His condemnation of Jesus at the importunity of the Jews, contrary to his own judgment and inclination, declared to them more than once, was a point gained; and his government must have been ever after much weakened by so mean a condescension. And that Pilate's influence in the province continued to decline is manifest, in that the people of it prevailed at last to have him removed in a very ignominious manner by Vitellius, president of Syria.

"Pilate was removed from his government before the Passover in the year of Christ 36. After which there was no procurator or other person with the power of life and death, in Judea, before the ascension of Herod Agrippa, in the year 41.

"In that space of time the Jews would take an unusual license, and gratify their own malicious dispositions, beyond what they could otherwise have done, without control.

"Twelfth: Some have objected that Tertullian is so absurd as to speak of Christians in the time of Tiberius; though it be certain that the followers of Jesus were not known by that denomination till some time afterwards.

"But this is a trifling objection. Tertullian intends no more by Christians than followers of Jesus, by whatever name they were known or distinguished; whether that of Nazarenes, or Galileans, or disciples.

"And it is undoubted, that the Christian religion had its rise in the reign of Tiberius; though they who professed to believe in Jesus, as risen from the dead and ascended to heaven, were not called Christians till some time afterwards.

"So at the beginning of the paragraph he says, 'There was an ancient law that no god should be consecrated by the emperor, unless it was first approved by the senate.' Nevertheless, Tertullian was not so ignorant as not to know that there were not any emperors when the ancient decree was passed.

"His meaning is, that no one should be deified by any man, no, not by a consul or emperor, without the approbation of the senate.

"Finally: We do not suppose that Tiberius understood the doctrine of the Savior, or that he was at all inclined to be a Christian.

"Nor did Tertullian intend to say any such thing, for immediately after the passage first cited from him, he adds: 'But the Cæsars themselves would have believed in Jesus Christ, if they had not been necessary for the world, or if Christians could have been Cæsars.'

"Grotius appears to have rightly understood the importance of these passages of Tertullian; whose note upon Matthew xxiv. 2, I have transcribed below." The reader is referred to Vol. VI. of Lardner's Works, where he will find the notes of this learned writer, as quoted from various ancients and moderns, in proof of all he has brought forward in these lengthy arguments, and which cannot be transcribed here.

"Admit, then, the right interpretation of Tertullian, and it may be allowed that what he says is not incredible or improbable. The Romans had almost innumerable deities, and yet they frequently added to that number and adopted new. As deifications were very frequent, Tiberius might have indulged a thought of placing Jesus among the established deities without intending to derogate from the worship or honor of those who were already received.

"But the senate was not in a humor to gratify him.

"And the reason assigned is, because the emperor himself had declined that honor, which is so plausible a pretense, and so fine a compliment, that we cannot easily suppose it to be Tertullian's own invention; which, therefore, gives credibility to his account.

"Eusebius, though he acknowledged the overruling providence of God in the favorable disposition of Tiberius toward the first followers of Jesus, by which means the Christian religion in its infancy was propagated over the world with less molestation, does also say, at the beginning of the chapter quoted, 'The senate refused their consent to the emperor's proposal, under a pretence that they had not been first asked, there being an ancient law, that no one should be deified without the approbation of the senate, but, indeed,' adds he, 'because the saving and divine doctrine of the gospel needed not to be ratified by human judgment and authority.'

Chrysostom's observation is to like purpose, but with some inaccuracies. It is likely that he was not at all acquainted with Tertullian; and he was no admirer of Eusebius. Perhaps he builds upon general tradition only. 'The Roman senate,' says he, 'had the power of nominating and decreeing who should be gods. When, therefore, all things concerning Christ had been published, he who was the governor of the Jewish nation sent to them to know if they would be pleased to appoint him also to be a god. But they refused, being offended and provoked, that before their decree and judgment had been obtained, the power of the crucified one had shined out and had attracted all the world to the worship of him. But, by the overruling providence of God, this was brought to pass against their will, that the divinity of Christ might not be established by human appointment and that he might not be reckoned one of the many who were deified by them.'

"Some of which, as he proceeds to show, had been of infamous characters.

"I shall now transcribe below in his own words what Orosius, in the fifth century, says of this matter, that all my readers may have it at once before them without looking farther for it." This quotation from Orosius will be found in the "Testimony of the Fathers," under the title, "Testimony of Orosius."

"And I refer to Zonoras and Nicephoras. The former only quotes Eusebius, and transcribes into his Annals the chapter of his Ecclesiastical History quoted by me. Nor has Nicephoras done much more."[213]

TISCHENDORF'S COMMENTS ON THE ACTS OF PILATE

"It is the same with the second apocryphal work brought under review above, the so-called Acts of Pilate, only with the difference that they refer as much to John as to the synoptical Gospels. Justin, in like manner as before, is the most ancient voucher for this work, which is said to have been written under Pilate's jurisdiction, and by reason of its specification of wonderful occurrences before, during, and after the crucifixion, to have borne strong evidence to the divinity of Christ. Justin saw as little reason as Tertullian and others for believing that it was a work of pious deception from a Christian hand." [As has been alleged by opponents.] "On the contrary, Justin appeals to it twice in his first Apology in order to confirm the accounts of the occurrences which took place at the crucifixion in accordance with prophecy, and of the miraculous healings effected by Christ, also the subject of prophetic announcement. He cites specifically (chap. 35) from Isaiah lxv. 2, and lviii. 2: 'I have spread out my hands all the day unto a rebellious people which walketh in a way that was not good. They ask of me the ordinances of justice, they take delight in approaching to God.' Further, from the 22nd Psalm: 'They pierced my hands and my feet; they parted my garments upon them and cast lots upon my vesture.' With reference to this he remarks that Christ fulfilled this; that he did stretch forth his hands when the Jews crucified him—the men who contended against him and denied that he was Christ. 'Then,' he says further, 'as the prophet foretold, they dragged him to the judgment seat, set him upon it and said, Judge us.' The expression, however, 'they pierced,' etc., refers to the nails with which they fastened his feet and hands to the cross. And after they had crucified him they threw lots for his clothing, and they who had taken part in the act of crucifixion divided it among themselves. To this he adds: And you can learn from the Acts, composed during the governorship of Pontius Pilate, that these things really happened.

"Still more explicit is the testimony of Tertullian. It may be found in Apologeticus (chap. 2) where he says that out of envy Jesus was surrendered to Pilate by the Jewish ceremonial lawyers, and by him, after he had yielded to the cries of the people, given over for crucifixion; that while hanging on the cross he gave up the ghost with a loud cry, and so anticipated the executioner's duty; that at that same hour the day was interrupted by a sudden darkness; that a guard of soldiers was set at the grave for the purpose of preventing his disciples stealing his body, since he had predicted his resurrection, but that on the third day the ground was suddenly shaken and the stone rolled away from before the sepulchre; that in the grave nothing was found but the articles used in his burial; that the report was spread abroad by those who stood outside that the disciples had taken the body away; that Jesus spent forty days with them in Galilee, teaching them what their mission should be, and that after giving them their instructions as to what they should preach, he was raised in a cloud to heaven. Tertullian closes this account with the words, 'All this was reported to the Emperor at that time, Tiberius, by Pilate, his conscience having compelled even him to become a Christian.'

"The document now in our possession corresponds with this evidence of Justin and Tertullian. Even in the title it agrees with the account of Justin, although instead of the word *acta*, which he used, and which is manifestly much more Latin than Greek, a Greek expression is employed which can be shown to have been used to indicate genuine Acts. The details recounted by Justin and Tertullian are all found in our text of the Acts of Pilate, with this variation, that nothing corresponds to what is joined to the declaration of the prophet, 'They dragged him to the seat of judgment and set him upon it and said,' etc. Besides this, the casting lots for the vesture is expressed simply by the allusion to the division of the clothes. We must give even closer scrutiny to one point. Justin alludes to the miracles which were performed in fulfillment of Old Testament prophecy, on the lame, the dumb, the blind, the dead, and on lepers. In fact, in our Acts of Pilate there are made to appear before the Roman governor a palsied man who had suffered for thirty-eight years, and was brought in a bed by young men, and healed on the Sabbath day; a blind man cured by the laying on of hands; a cripple who had been restored; a leper who had been cleansed; the woman whose issue of blood had been stanched, and a witness of the raising of Lazarus from the dead. Of that which Tertullian cites we will adduce merely the passage found in no one of our gospels, that Jesus passed forty days after his resurrection in company with his disciples in Galilee.

"This is indicated in our Acts of Pilate at the end of the fifteenth chapter, where the risen man is represented as saying to Joseph: 'For forty days go not out of thy house, for behold I go to my brethren in Galilee.'

"Every one will perceive how strongly the argument that our Acts of Pilate are the same which Justin and Tertullian read is buttressed by these unexpected coincidences. The assertion recently made requires, consequently, no labored contradiction that the allusions to both men have grown out of their mere suspicion that there was such a record as the Acts of Pilate, or out of the circulation of a mere story about such a record, while the real work was written as the consequence of these allusions at the close of the third century. What an uncommon fancy it requires in the two men to coincide so perfectly in a single production, as is the case in the Acts to which I am now referring. And are we to imagine that they referred with such emphasis as they employed to the mere creations of their fancy?

"The question has been raised with more justice, whether the production in our possession may not have been a copy or a free revision of the old and primitive one. The modern change in the title has given support to this conjecture, for it has occasioned the work to be commonly spoken of as the Gospel of Nicodemus. But this title is borne neither by any Greek manuscript, the Coptic-Sahidian papyrus, nor the Latin manuscripts with the exception of a few of the most recent. It may be traced only subsequently to the twelfth century, although at a very early period, in one of the two prefaces attached to the work, Nicodemus is mentioned in one place as a Hebrew author and in another as a Greek translator. But aside from the title, the handwriting displays great variation, and the two prefaces alluded to above show clearly the work of two hands. Notwithstanding this, however, there are decisive grounds for holding that our Acts of Pilate contains in its main substance the document drawn from Justin and Tertullian. The first of these to be noticed is, that the Greek text, as given in the version most widely circulated in the manuscripts, is surprisingly corroborated by two documents of the rarest character, and first used by myself—a Coptic-Sahidian papyrus manuscript and a Latin palimpsest—both probably dating from the fifth century. Such a documentary confirmation of their text is possessed by scarcely ten works of the collective Greek classic literature. Both of these ancient writings make it in the highest degree probable that the Egyptian and Latin translations which they contain were executed still earlier.

"But could a work which was held in great consideration in Justin's and Tertullian's time and down to the commencement of the fourth century, and which strenuously insists that the Emperor Maximin caused other blasphemous Acts of Pilate to be published and zealously circulated, manifestly for the purpose of displacing and discrediting the older Christian Acts—could such a work suddenly change its whole form, and from the fifth century, to which in so extraordinary a manner translators, wholly different in character, point back with such wonderful concurrence, continue in the new form? Contrary as this is to all historical criticism, there is in the contents of the work, in the singular manner in which isolated and independent details are shown to be related to the canonical books, no less than in the accordance with the earliest quotations found in Justin and Tertullian, a guaranty of the greatest antiquity.

"There are in the contents, also, matters of such a nature that we must confess that they are to be traced back to the primitive edition, as, for example the narrative in the first chapter of the bringing forward of the accused.

"It is incorrect, moreover, to draw a conclusion from Justin's designation of the Acta which is not warranted by the whole character of the work. The Acta, the ὑπομνήματα, are specified in Justin's account not less than in the manuscripts which we possess, as being written *under* Pontius Pilate, and that can signify nothing else than that they were an official production composed under the direct sanction of the Roman governor. Their transmission to the emperor must be imagined as accompanied by a letter of the same character with that which has been brought down to us in the Greek and Latin edition, and yet not at all similar in purport to the notable Acts of Pilate."[214]

The Acts of Pilate

(First Greek Form)

I, Ananias, of the proprætor's bodyguard, being learned in the law, knowing our Lord Jesus Christ from the Holy Scriptures, coming to Him by faith, and counted worthy of the holy baptism, searching also the memorials written at that time of what was done in the case of our Lord Jesus Christ, which the Jews had laid up in the time of Pontius Pilate, found these memorials written in Hebrew, and, by the favor of God, have translated them into Greek for the information of all who call upon the name of our Master Jesus Christ, in the seventeenth year of the reign of our lord Flavius Theodosius, and the sixth of Flavius Valentianus, in the ninth indiction.

All ye, therefore, who read and transfer into other books, remember me and pray for me, and pardon my sins which I have sinned against Him.

Peace be to those who read and those who hear, and to their households. Amen.

CHAPTER 1.—Having called a council, the high priests and the scribes Annas and Caiaphas and Semes and Dathaes, and Gamaliel, Judas, Levi and Nepthalim, Alexander and Jaïrus, and the rest of the Jews, came to Pilate accusing Jesus about many things, saying: We know this man to be the son of Joseph the carpenter, born of Mary; and he says that he is the Son of God, and a king; moreover, profanes the Sabbath, and wishes to do away with the law of our fathers. Pilate says: And what are the things which he does, to show that he wishes to do away with it? The Jews say: We have a law not to cure anyone on the Sabbath; but this man has, on the Sabbath, cured the lame and the crooked, the withered and the blind and the paralytic, the dumb and the demoniac, by evil practices. Pilate says to them: What evil practices? They say to him: He is a magician, and by Beelzebub, prince of the demons, he casts out the demons, and all are subject to him. Pilate says to them: This is not casting out the demons by an unclean spirit, but by the god Esculapius.

The Jews say to Pilate: We entreat your highness that he stand at the tribunal and be heard. And Pilate, having called them, says: Tell me how I, being a procurator, can try a king? They say to him: We do not say that he is a king, but he himself says that he is. And Pilate, having called the runner, says to him: Let Jesus be brought in with respect. And the runner, going out and recognizing him, adored him, and took his cloak into his hand and spread it on the ground, and says to him: My Lord, walk on this and come in, for the procurator calls thee. And the Jews, seeing what the runner had done, cried out against Pilate, saying: Why hast thou ordered him to come in by a runner, and not by a crier? for assuredly the runner, when he saw him, adored him, and spread his doublet on the ground and made him walk like a king.

And Pilate, having called the runner, says to him: Why hast thou done this, and spread out thy cloak upon the earth and made Jesus walk upon it? The runner says to him: My Lord procurator, when thou didst send me to Jerusalem to Alexander, I saw him sitting upon an ass, and the sons of the Hebrews held branches in their hands and shouted; and others spread their clothes under him saying: Save now, thou who art in the highest; blessed is he that cometh in the name of the Lord.

The Jews cry out and say to the runner: The sons of the Hebrews shouted in Hebrew; whence, then, hast thou the Greek? The runner says to them: I asked one of the Jews, and said: What is it they are shouting in Hebrew? And he interpreted it for me. Pilate says to them: And what did they shout in Hebrew? The Jews say to him: *Hosanna membrome baruchamma adonai.* Pilate says to them: And this hosanna, etc., how is it interpreted? The Jews say to him: Save now in the highest; blessed is he that cometh in the name of the Lord. Pilate says to them: If you bear witness to the words spoken by the children, in what has the runner done wrong? And they were silent. And the procurator says to the runner: Go out and bring him in what way thou wilt. And the runner, going out, did in the same manner as before, and says to Jesus: My Lord, come in; the procurator calleth thee.

And Jesus, going in, and the standard bearers holding their standards, the tops of the standards bent down, and adored Jesus. And the Jews, seeing the bearing of the standards how they were bent down and adored Jesus, cried out vehemently against the standard bearers. And Pilate says to the Jews: Do you not wonder how the tops of the standards were bent down and adored Jesus? The Jews say to Pilate: We saw how the standard bearers bent them down and adored him. And the procurator, having called the standard bearers, says to them: Why have you done this? They say to Pilate: We are Greeks and temple slaves, and how could we adore him? and assuredly, as we were holding them up, the tops bent down of their own accord and adored him.

Pilate says to the rulers of the synagogue and the elders of the people: Do you choose for yourselves men strong and powerful, and let them hold up the standards, and let us see whether they will bend down with them. And the elders of the Jews picked out twelve men powerful and strong, and made them hold up the standards six by six; and they were placed in front of the procurator's tribunal. And Pilate says to the runner: Take him outside of the Pretorium, and bring him in again in whatever way may please thee. And Jesus and the runner went out of the Pretorium. And Pilate, summoning those who had formerly held up the standards, says to them: I have sworn by the health of Cæsar, that if the standards do not bend down when Jesus comes in, I will cut off your heads. And the procurator ordered Jesus to come in the second time. And the runner did in the same manner as before, and made many entreaties to Jesus to walk on his cloak. And he walked on it and went in. And as he went in the standards were again bent down and adored Jesus.

CHAP. 2.—And Pilate, seeing this, was afraid, and sought to go away from the tribunal, but when he was still thinking of going away, his wife sent to him saying: Have nothing to do with this just man, for many things have I suffered on his account this night. And Pilate, summoning the Jews, says to them: You know that my wife is a worshiper of God, and prefers to adhere to the Jewish religion along with you. They say to him: Yes, we know. Pilate says to them: Behold, my wife has sent to me, saying, Have nothing to do with this just man, for many things have I suffered on account of him this night. And the Jews answering, say unto Pilate: Did we not tell thee that he was a sorcerer? Behold, he has sent a dream to thy wife.

And Pilate, having summoned Jesus, says to him: What do these witness against thee? Sayest thou nothing? And Jesus said: Unless they had the power, they would say nothing; for every one has the power of his own mouth to speak both good and evil. They shall see to it.

And the elders of the Jews answered, and said to Jesus: What shall we see? First, that thou wast born of fornication; secondly, that thy birth in Bethlehem was the cause of the murder of the infants; thirdly, that thy father Joseph and thy mother Mary fled into Egypt because they had no confidence in the people.

Some of the bystanders, pious men of the Jews, say: We deny that he was born of fornication; for we know that Joseph espoused Mary, and he was not born of fornication. Pilate says to the Jews who said he was of fornication: This story of yours is not true, because they were betrothed, as also these fellow-countrymen of yours say. Annas and Caiaphas say to Pilate: All the multitude of us cry out that he was born of fornication, and are not believed; these are proselytes and his disciples. And Pilate, calling Annas and Caiaphas, says to them: What are proselytes? They say to him: They are by birth children of the Greeks, and have now become Jews. And those that said that he was not born of fornication, viz.: Lazarus, Asterius, Antonius, James, Amnes, Zeras, Samuel, Isaac, Phinees, Crispus, Agrippas and Judas, say: We are not proselytes, but are children of the Jews, and speak the truth; for we were present at the betrothal of Joseph and Mary.

And Pilate, calling these twelve men who said that he was not born of fornication, says to them: I adjure you, by the health of Cæsar, to tell me whether it be true that you say, that he was not born of fornication. They say to Pilate: We have a law against taking oaths, because it is a sin; but they will swear by the health of Cæsar that it is not as we have said, and we are liable to death. Pilate says to Annas and Caiaphas: Have you nothing to answer to this? Annas and Caiaphas say to Pilate: These twelve are believed when they say that he was not born of fornication; all the multitude of us cry out that he was born of fornication, and that he is a sorcerer; and he says that he is the Son of God and a king, and we are not believed.

And Pilate orders all the multitude to go out, except the twelve men who said that he was not born of fornication, and he ordered Jesus to be separated from them. And Pilate says to them: For what reason do they wish to put him to death? They say to him: They are angry because he cures on the Sabbath. Pilate says: For a good work do they wish to put him to death? They say to him: Yes.

CHAP. 3.—And Pilate, filled with rage, went outside of the Pretorium and said to them: I take the sun to witness that I find no fault in this man. The Jews answered and said to the procurator: Unless this man were an evil-doer, we should not have delivered him to thee. And Pilate said: Do you take him and judge him according to your law. The Jews said to Pilate: It is not lawful for us to put anyone to death. Pilate said: Has God said that you are not to put to death, but that I am?

And Pilate went again into the Pretorium and spoke to Jesus privately, and said to him: Art thou the king of the Jews? Jesus answered Pilate: Dost thou say this of thyself, or have others said it to thee of me? Pilate answered Jesus: Am I also a Jew? Thy nation and the chief priests have given thee up to me. What hast thou done? Jesus answered: My kingdom is not of this world; for if my kingdom were of this world, my servants would fight in order that I should not be given up to the Jews: but now my kingdom is not from thence. Pilate said to him: Art thou, then, a king? Jesus answered him: Thou sayest that I am king. Because for this have I been born, and I have come, in order that everyone who is of the truth might hear my voice. Pilate says to him: What is truth? Jesus says to him: Truth is from heaven. Pilate says: Is truth not upon earth? Jesus says to Pilate: Thou seest how those who speak the truth are judged by those that have the power upon earth.

CHAP. 4.—And leaving Jesus within the Pretorium, Pilate went out to the Jews and said to them: I find no fault in him. The Jews say to him: He said,

I can destroy this temple, and in three days build it. Pilate says: What temple? The Jews say: The one that Solomon built in forty-six years, and this man speaks of pulling it down and building it up in three days. Pilate says to them: I am innocent of the blood of this just man. See you to it. The Jews say: His blood be upon us and upon our children.

And Pilate, having summoned the elders and priests and Levites, said to them privately: Do not act thus, because no charge that you bring against him is worthy of death; for your charge is about curing and Sabbath profanation. The elders and the priests and the Levites say: If anyone speak evil against Cæsar, is he worthy of death or not? Pilate says: He is worthy of death. The Jews say to Pilate: If anyone speak evil against Cæsar, he is worthy of death; but this man has spoken evil against God.

And the procurator ordered the Jews to go outside of the Pretorium; and, summoning Jesus, he says to him: What shall I do to thee? Jesus says to Pilate: As it has been given to thee. Pilate says: How given? Jesus says: Moses and the prophets have proclaimed beforehand of my death and resurrection. And the Jews, noticing this and hearing it, say to Pilate: What more wilt thou hear of this blasphemy? Pilate says to the Jews: If these words be blasphemous, do you take him for the blasphemy, and lead him away to your synagogue and judge him according to your law. The Jews say to Pilate: Our law bears that a man who wrongs his fellow-men is worthy to receive forty save one: but he that blasphemeth God is to be stoned with stones.

Pilate says to them: Do you take him and punish him in whatever way you please. The Jews say to Pilate: We wish that he be crucified. Pilate says: He is not deserving of crucifixion.

And the procurator, looking round upon the crowds of the Jews standing by, sees many of the Jews weeping, and says: All the multitude do not wish him to die. The elders of the Jews say: For this reason all the multitude of us have come, that he should die. Pilate says to the Jews: Why should he die? The Jews say: Because he called himself the Son of God and King.

CHAP. 5.—And one Nicodemus, a Jew, stood before the procurator and said: I beseech your honor let me say a few words. Pilate says: Say on. Nicodemus says: I said to the elders and the priests and Levites, and to all the multitude of the Jews in the synagogue, What do you seek to do with this man? This man does many miracles and strange things, which no one has done or will do. Let him go and do not wish any evil against him. If the miracles which he does are of God, they will stand; but if of man, they will come to nothing. For assuredly Moses, being sent by God into Egypt, did many miracles, which the Lord commanded him to do before Pharaoh, king of Egypt. And there were Jannes and Jambres, servants of Pharaoh, and they also did not a few of the miracles which Moses did; and the Egyptians took them to be gods—this Jannes and Jambres. But, since the miracles which they did were not of God, both they and those who believed in them were destroyed. And now release this man, for he is not deserving of death.

The Jews say to Nicodemus: Thou hast become his disciple, and therefore thou defendest him. Nicodemus says to them: Perhaps, too, the procurator has become his disciple, because he defends him. Has the emperor not appointed him to this place of dignity? And the Jews were vehemently enraged, and gnashed their teeth against Nicodemus. Pilate says to them: Why do you gnash your teeth against him when you hear the truth? The Jews say to Nicodemus: Mayst thou receive his truth and his portion. Nicodemus says: Amen, amen; may I receive it, as you have said.

CHAP. 6.—One of the Jews, stepping up, asked leave of the procurator to say a word. The procurator says: If thou wishest to say anything, say on. And the Jew said: Thirty-eight years I lay in my bed in great agony. And when Jesus came, many demoniacs and many lying ill of various diseases were cured by him. And when Jesus saw me he had compassion on me, and said to me: Take up thy couch and walk. And I took up my couch and walked. The Jews say to Pilate: Ask him on what day it was when he was cured. He that had been cured says: On a Sabbath. The Jews say: Is not this the very thing we said, that on a Sabbath he cures and casts out demons?

And another Jew stepped up and said: I was born blind; I heard sounds, but saw not a face. And as Jesus passed by I cried out with a loud voice, Pity me, O son of David. And he pitied me and put his hands upon my eyes, and I instantly received my sight. And another Jew stepped up and said: I was crooked and he straightened me with a word. And another said: I was a leper, and be cured me with a word.

CHAP. 7.—And a woman cried out from a distance and said: I had an issue of blood, and I touched the hem of his garment, and the issue of blood, which I had had for twelve years, was stopped. The Jews say: We have a law that a woman's evidence is not received.

CHAP. 8.—And others, a multitude both of men and women, cried out, saying: This man is a prophet, and the demons are subject to him. Pilate says to them who said that the demons were subject to him: Why, then, were not your teachers also subject to him? They say to Pilate: We do not know. And others said: He raised Lazarus from the tomb after he had been dead four days. And the procurator trembled, and said to all the multitude of the Jews: Why do you wish to pour out innocent blood?

CHAP. 9.—And, having summoned Nicodemus and the twelve men that said he was not born of fornication, he says to them: What shall I do, because there is an insurrection among the people? They say to him: We know not; let them see to it. Again Pilate, having summoned all the multitude of the Jews, says: You know that it is customary, at the feast of unleavened bread, to release one prisoner to you. I have one condemned prisoner in the prison, a murderer named Bar Abbas, and this man standing in your presence, Jesus in whom I find no fault. Which of them do you wish me to release to you? And they cry out: Bar Abbas. Pilate says: What, then, shall we do to Jesus, who is called Christ? The Jews say: Let him be crucified. And others said: Thou art no friend of Cæsar's if thou release this man, because he called himself the Son of God and King. You wish this man, then, to be a king, and not Cæsar?

And Pilate, in a rage, says to the Jews: Always has your nation been rebellious, and you always speak against your benefactors. The Jews say: What benefactors? He says to them: Your God led you out of the land of Egypt from bitter slavery, and brought you safe through the sea as through dry land, and in the desert fed you with manna and gave you quails, and quenched your thirst with water from a rock, and gave you a law; and in all these things have you provoked your God to anger, and sought a molten calf. And you exasperated your God, and he sought to slay you. And Moses prayed for you, and you were not put to death. And now you charge me with hating the emperor.

And, rising up from the tribunal, he sought to go out. And the Jews cry out and say: We know that Cæsar is king, and not Jesus. For assuredly the magi brought gifts to him as to a king. And when Herod heard from the magi that a king had been born, he sought to slay him, and his father, Joseph, knowing this, took him and his mother, and they fled into Egypt. And Herod, hearing of it, destroyed the children of the Hebrews that had been born in Bethlehem.

And when Pilate heard these words he was afraid; and, ordering the crowd to keep silence, because they were crying out, he says to them: So this is he whom Herod sought? The Jews say: Yes, it is he. And, taking water, Pilate washed his hands in the face of the sun, saying: I am innocent of the blood of this just man: see you to it. Again the Jews cry out: His blood be upon us and upon our children.

Then Pilate ordered the curtain of the tribunal where he was sitting to be drawn, and says to Jesus: Thy nation has charged thee with being a king. On this account, I sentence thee first to be scourged, according to the enactment of venerable kings, and then to be fastened on the cross in the garden where thou was seized. And let Dysmas and Gestas, the two malefactors, be crucified with thee.

CHAP. 10.—And Jesus went forth out of the Pretorium, and the malefactors with him. And when they came to the place they stripped him of his clothes and girded him with a towel, and put a crown of thorns on him round his head. And they crucified him; and at the same time, also, they hung up the two malefactors along with him. And Jesus said: Father, forgive them, for they know not what they do. And the soldiers parted his clothes among them; and the people stood looking at him. And the chief priests and the rulers with them mocked him, saying: He saved others, let him save himself. If he be the Son of God, let him come down from the cross. And the soldiers made sport of him, coming near and offering him vinegar mixed with gall, and said: Thou art the king of the Jews; save thyself.

And Pilate, after the sentence, ordered the charge against him to be inscribed as a superscription in Greek and Latin and Hebrew, according to what the Jews had said: He is king of the Jews.

And one of the malefactors hanging up spoke to him, saying: If thou be the Christ, save thyself and us. And Dysmas answering reproved him, saying: Dost thou not fear God, because thou art in the same condemnation? And we, indeed, justly, for we receive the fit punishment of our deeds; but this man has done no evil. And he said to Jesus: Remember me, Lord, in thy kingdom. And Jesus said to him: Amen, amen; I say to thee, To-day shalt thou be with me in Paradise.

CHAP. 11.—And it was about the sixth hour, and there was darkness over the earth until the ninth hour, the sun being darkened; and the curtain of the temple was split in the middle. And, crying out with a loud voice, Jesus said: Father, *baddach ephkid ruel*, which is, interpreted, Into thy hands I commit my spirit. And, having said this, he gave up the ghost. And the centurion, seeing what had happened, glorified God and said: This was a just man. And all the crowds that were present at this spectacle, when they saw what had happened, beat their breasts and went away.

And the centurion reported what had happened to the procurator. And when the procurator and his wife heard it they were exceedingly grieved, and neither ate nor drank that day. And Pilate sent for the Jews and said to them:

Have you seen what has happened? And they say: There has been an eclipse of the sun in the usual way.

And his acquaintances were standing at a distance, and the women who came with him from Galilee, seeing these things. And a man named Joseph, a councillor from the city of Arimathea, who also waited for the kingdom of God, went to Pilate and begged the body of Jesus. And he took it down and wrapped it in a clean linen, and placed it in a tomb hewn out of the rock, in which no one had ever lain.

CHAP. 12.—And the Jews, hearing that Joseph had begged the body of Jesus, sought him, and the twelve who said that Jesus was not born of fornication, and Nicodemus and many others who had stepped up before Pilate and declared his good works. And of all these that were hid Nicodemus alone was seen by them, because he was a ruler of the Jews. And Nicodemus says to them: How have you come into the synagogue? The Jews say to him: How hast thou come into the synagogue? for thou art a confederate of his, and his portion is with thee in the world to come. Nicodemus says: Amen, amen. And likewise Joseph also stepped out and said to them: Why are you angry against me because I begged the body of Jesus? Behold, I have put him in my new tomb, wrapping him in clean linen; and I have rolled a stone to the door of the tomb. And you have acted not well against the just man, because you have not repented of crucifying him, but also have pierced him with a spear. And the Jews seized Joseph and ordered him to be secured until the first day of the week, and said to him: Know that the time does not allow us to do anything against thee, because the Sabbath is dawning: and know that thou shalt not be deemed worthy of burial, but we shall give thy flesh to the birds of the air. Joseph says to them: These are the words of the arrogant Goliath, who reproached the living God and holy David. For God has said by the prophet, Vengeance is mine, and I will repay, saith the Lord. And now that he is uncircumcised in flesh, but circumcised in heart, has taken water and washed his hands in the face of the sun, saying, I am innocent of the blood of this just man; see ye to it. And you answered and said to Pilate: His blood be upon us and upon our children. And now I am afraid, lest the wrath of God come upon you and upon your children, as you have said. And the Jews, hearing these words, were embittered in their souls, and seized Joseph and locked him into a room where there was no window; and guards were stationed at the door, and they sealed the door where Joseph was locked in.

And on the Sabbath the rulers of the synagogue and the priests and the Levites made a decree that all should be found in the synagogue on the first day of the week. And, rising up early, all the multitude in the synagogue consulted by what death they should slay him. And when the Sanhedrin was sitting, they ordered him to be brought with much indignity. And, having opened the door, they found him not. And all the people were surprised and struck with dismay, because they found the seals unbroken, and because Caiaphas had the key. And they no longer dared to lay hands upon those who had spoken before Pilate in Jesus' behalf.

CHAP. 13.—And while they were still sitting in the synagogue and wondering about Joseph, there came some of the guard whom the Jews had begged of Pilate to guard the tomb of Jesus, that his disciples might not come and steal him. And they reported to the rulers of the synagogue, and the priests and Levites, what had happened: how there had been an earthquake; and we saw an angel coming down from heaven, and he rolled away the stone from the mouth of the tomb and sat upon it; and he shone like snow and like lightning. And we were very much afraid, and lay like dead men; and we heard the voice of the angel, saying to the women who remained beside the tomb, Be not afraid, for I know that you seek Jesus, who was crucified. He is not here. He has risen, as he said. Come, see the place where the Lord lay; and go quickly and tell his disciples that he is risen from the dead, and is in Galilee.

The Jews say: To what women did he speak? The men of the guard say: We know not who they were. The Jews say: At what time was this? The men of the guard say: At midnight. The Jews say: And wherefore did you not lay hold of them? The men of the guard say: We were like dead men from fear, not expecting to see the light of day, and how could we lay hold of them? The Jews say: As the Lord liveth, we do not believe you. The men of the guard say to the Jews: You have seen so great miracles in the case of this man, and have not believed; and how can you believe us? And assuredly you have done well to swear that the Lord liveth, for indeed he does live. Again the men of the guard say: We have heard that you have locked up the man that begged the body of Jesus, and put a seal on the door; and that you have opened it and not found him. Do you, then, give us the man whom you were guarding, and we shall give you Jesus. The Jews say: Joseph has gone away to his own city. The men of the guard say to the Jews: And Jesus has risen, as we heard from the angel, and is in Galilee.

And when the Jews heard these words they were very much afraid, and said: We must take care lest this story be heard, and all incline to Jesus. And the Jews called a council, and paid down a considerable money and gave it to the soldiers, saying: Say, while he slept, his disciples came by night and stole him; and if this come to the ears of the procurator we shall persuade him and keep you out of trouble. And they took it, and said as they had been instructed.

CHAP. 14.—And Phinees, a priest, and Adas, a teacher, and Haggai, a Levite, came down from Galilee to Jerusalem, and said to the rulers of the synagogue, and the priests and the Levites: We saw Jesus and his disciples sitting on the mountain called Mamilch; and he said to his disciples, Go into all the world, and preach to every creature: he that believeth and is baptized shall be saved, and he that believeth not shall be condemned. And these signs shall attend those who have believed: in my name they shall cast out demons, speak new tongues, take up serpents; and if they drink any deadly thing it shall by no means hurt them, they shall lay hands on the sick, and they shall be well. And while Jesus was speaking to his disciples we saw him taken up into heaven.

The elders and priests and Levites say: Give glory to the God of Israel, and confess to him whether you have heard and seen those things, of which you have given us an account. And those who had given the account said: As the Lord liveth, the God of our fathers, Abraham, Isaac, and Jacob, we heard these things, and saw him taken up into heaven. The elders and the priests and the Levites say to them: Have you come to give us this announcement, or to offer prayer to God? And they say: To offer prayer to God. The elders and the chief priests and the Levites say to them: If you have come to offer prayer to God, why, then, have you told these idle tales in the presence of all the people? Says Phinees, the priest, and Adas, the teacher, and Haggai, the Levite, to the rulers of the synagogues, and the priests and the Levites: If what we have said and seen be sinful, behold, we are before you; do to us as seems good in your eyes. And they took the law and made them swear upon it not to give any more an account of these matters to anyone. And they gave them to eat and drink and sent them out of the city, having given them also money, and three men with them; and they sent them away to Galilee.

And these men, having gone into Galilee, the chief priests and the rulers of the synagogue, and the elders came together in the synagogue and locked the door, and lamented with great lamentation, saying: Is this a miracle that has happened in Israel? And Annas and Caiaphas said: Why are you so much moved? Why do you weep? Do you not know that his disciples have given a sum of gold to the guards of the tomb, and have instructed them to say that an angel came down and rolled away the stone from the door of the tomb? And the priests and elders said: Be it that his disciples have stolen his body; how is it that the life has come into his body, and that he is going about in Galilee? And they, being unable to give an answer to these things, said, after great hesitation: It is not lawful for us to believe the uncircumcised.

CHAP. 15.—And Nicodemus stood up, and stood before the Sanhedrin, saying: You say well; you are not ignorant, you people of the Lord, of these men that come down from Galilee, that they fear God, and are men of substance, haters of covetousness, men of peace; and they have declared with an oath, we saw Jesus upon the mountain Mamilch with his disciples, and he taught what we heard from him, and we saw him taken up into heaven. And no one asked them in what form he went up. For assuredly, as the book of the Holy Scriptures taught us, Helias also was taken up into heaven, and Elissæus cried out with a loud voice, and Helias threw his sheepskin upon Elissæus, and Elissæus threw his sheepskin upon the Jordan, and crossed and came into Jericho. And the children of the prophets met him and said, O Elissæus, where is thy master Helias? And he said, He has been taken up into heaven. And they said to Elissæus, Has not a spirit seized him, and thrown him upon one of the mountains? But let us take our servants with us and seek him. And they persuaded Elissæus, and he went away with them. And they sought him three days, and did not find him; and they knew that he had been taken up. And now listen to me, and let us send into every district of Israel and see, lest, perchance, Christ has been taken up by a spirit and thrown upon one of the mountains. And this proposal pleased all. And they sent into every district of Israel and sought Jesus, and did not find him; but they found Joseph in Arimathea, and no one dared to lay hands on him.

And they reported to the elders and the priests and the Levites: We have gone round to every district of Israel, and have not found Jesus; but Joseph we have found in Arimathea. And hearing about Joseph they were glad and gave glory to the God of Israel. And the rulers of the synagogue, and the priests and the Levites, having held a council as to the manner in which they should meet with Joseph, took a piece of paper and wrote to Joseph as follows:

Peace to thee! We know that we have sinned against God, and against thee; and we have prayed to the God of Israel that thou shouldst deign to come to thy fathers and to thy children, because we all have been grieved. For, having opened the door, we did not find thee. And we know that we have counseled evil counsel against thee; but the Lord has defended thee, and the Lord himself has scattered to the winds our counsel against thee, O honorable father Joseph.

And they chose from all Israel seven men, friends of Joseph, whom, also, Joseph himself was acquainted with; and the rulers of the synagogue, and the priests and the Levites say to them: Take notice; if, after receiving our letter he read it, know that he will come with you to us. But if he do not read it, know that he is ill-disposed towards us. And, having saluted him in peace, return to us. And having blest the men, they dismissed them. And the men came to Joseph and did reverence to him, and said to him: Peace to thee! And he said: Peace to you and to all the people of Israel! And they gave him the roll of the letter. And Joseph, having received it, read the letter and rolled it up, and blessed God and said: Blessed be the Lord God, who has delivered Israel, that they should not shed innocent blood, and blessed be the Lord, who sent out his angel and covered me under his wings. And he set a table for them: and they ate and drank and slept there.

And they rose up early and prayed. And Joseph saddled his ass and set out with the men: and they came to the holy city Jerusalem. And all the people met Joseph and cried out: Peace to thee in thy coming in! And be said to all the people: Peace to you! and he kissed them. And the people prayed with Joseph, and they were astonished at the sight of him. And Nicodemus received him into his house and made a great feast, and called Annas and Caiaphas and the elders and the priests and the Levites to his house. And they rejoiced, eating and drinking with Joseph; and, after singing hymns, each proceeded to his own house. But Joseph remained in the house of Nicodemus.

And on the following day, which was the preparation, the rulers of the synagogue and the priests and the Levites went early to the house of Nicodemus; and Nicodemus met them and said: Peace to you! And they said: Peace to thee and to Joseph, and to all thy house and to all the house of Joseph! And he brought them into his house. And all the Sanhedrin sat down, and Joseph sat down between Annas and Caiaphas; and no one dared to say a word to him. And Joseph said: Why have you called me? And they signaled to Nicodemus to speak to Joseph. And Nicodemus, opening his mouth, said to Joseph: Father, thou knowest that the honorable teachers and the priests and the Levites seek to learn a word from thee. And Joseph said: Ask. And Annas and Caiaphas, having taken the law, made Joseph swear, saying: Give glory to the God of Israel, and give him confession; for Achar, being made to swear by the prophet Jesus, did not forswear himself, but declared unto him all, and did not hide a word from him. Do thou also, accordingly, not hide from us to the extent of a word. And Joseph said: I shall not hide from you one word. And they said to him: With grief were we grieved because thou didst beg the body of Jesus and wrap it in clean linen and lay it in a tomb. And on account of this we secured thee in a room where there was no window; and we put locks and seals upon the doors, and guards kept watching where thou wast locked in. And on the first day of the week we opened and found thee not, and were grieved exceedingly; and astonishment fell upon all the people of the Lord until yesterday. And now relate to us what happened to thee.

And Joseph said: On the preparation, about the tenth hour, you locked me up, and I remained all the Sabbath. And at midnight, as I was standing and praying, the room where you locked me in was hung up by the four corners, and I saw a light like lightning into my eyes. And I was afraid and fell to the ground. And some one took me by the hand and removed me from the place where I had fallen; and moisture of water was poured from my head even to my feet, and a smell of perfumes came about my nostrils. And he wiped my face and kissed me, and said to me, Fear not, Joseph: open thine eyes and see who it is that speaks to thee. And, looking up, I saw Jesus. And I trembled and thought it was a phantom; and I said the commandments, and he said them with me. Even so you are not ignorant that a phantom, if it meet anybody and hear the commandments, takes to flight. And seeing that he said them with me, I said to him, Rabbi Helias. And he said to me, I am not Helias. And I said to him, Who art thou, my lord? And he said to me, I am Jesus, whose body thou didst beg from Pilate; and thou didst clothe me with clean linen, and didst put a napkin on my face, and didst lay me in thy new tomb, and didst roll a great stone to the door of the tomb. And I said to him that was speaking to me, Show me the place where I laid thee. And he carried me away and showed me the place where I laid him; and the linen cloth was lying in it, and the napkin for his face. And I knew that it was Jesus. And he took me by the hand and placed me, though the doors were locked, in the middle of my house, and led me away to my bed and said to me, Peace to thee! And he kissed me and said to me, For forty days go not forth out of thy house; for, behold, I go to my brethren in Galilee.

CHAP. 16.—And the rulers of the synagogue, and the priests and the Levites when they heard these words from Joseph, became as dead, and fell to the ground, and fasted until the ninth hour. And Nicodemus, along with Joseph, exhorted Annas and Caiaphas, the priests and the Levites, saying: Rise up and stand upon your feet, and taste bread and strengthen your souls, because to-morrow is the Sabbath of the Lord. And they rose up and prayed to God, and ate and drank, and departed every man to his own house.

And on the Sabbath our teachers and the priests and Levites sat questioning each other and saying: What is this wrath that has come upon us? for we know his father and mother. Levi, a teacher, says: I know that his parents fear God, and do not withdraw themselves from the prayers, and give the tithes thrice a year. And when Jesus was born his parents brought him to this place and gave sacrifices and burnt offerings to God. And when the great teacher, Symeon, took him into his arms, he said, Now thou sendest away thy servant, Lord, according to thy word, in peace; for mine eyes have seen thy salvation, which thou hast prepared before the face of all the peoples; a light for the revelation of the Gentiles, and the glory of thy people Israel. And Symeon blessed them, and said to Mary his mother, I give thee good news about this child. And Mary said, It is well, my lord. And Symeon said to her, It is well; behold, he lies for the fall and the rising again of many in

Israel, and for a sign spoken against; and of thee thyself a sword shall go through the soul, in order that the reasoning of many hearts may be revealed.

They say to the teacher Levi: How knowest thou these things? Levi says to them: Do you not know that from him I learned the law? The Sanhedrin say to him: We wish to see thy father. And they sent for his father. And they asked him, and he said to them: Why have you not believed my son? The blessed and just Symeon himself taught him the law. The Sanhedrin says to Rabbi Levi: Is the word that you have said true? And he said: It is true. And the rulers of the synagogue, and the priests and the Levites said to themselves: Come, let us send into Galilee to the three men that came and told about his teaching and his taking up, and let them tell us how they saw him taken up. And this saying pleased all. And they sent away the three men who had already gone away into Galilee with them; and they say to them: Say to Rabbi Adas and Rabbi Phinees and Rabbi Haggai, Peace to you and all who are with you! A great inquiry having taken place in the Sanhedrin, we have been sent to you to call you to this holy place, Jerusalem.

And the men set out into Galilee and found them sitting and considering the law: and they saluted them in peace. And the men who were in Galilee said to those who had come to them: Peace unto all Israel! And they said: Peace to you! And they again said to them: Why have you come? And those who had been sent said: The Sanhedrin call you to the holy city Jerusalem. And when the men heard that they were sought by the Sanhedrin they prayed to God, and reclined with the men and ate and drank, and rose up and set out in peace to Jerusalem.

And on the following day the Sanhedrin sat in the synagogue, and asked them, saying: Did you really see Jesus sitting on the mountain Mamilch teaching his eleven disciples, and did you see him taken up? And the men answered them and said: As we saw him taken up, so also we said.

Annas says: Take them away from one another and let us see whether their account agrees. And they took them away from one another. And first they call Adas and say to him: How didst thou see Jesus taken up? Adas says: While he was yet sitting on the mountain Mamilch and teaching his disciples, we saw a cloud overshadowing both him and his disciples. And the cloud took him up into heaven, and his disciples lay upon their faces upon the earth. And they call Phinees, the priest, and ask him also, saying: How didst thou see Jesus taken up? And he spoke in like manner. And they again asked Haggai, and he spoke in like manner. And the Sanhedrin said: The law of Moses holds: At the mouth of two or three every word shall be established. Buthem, a teacher, says: It is written in the law, And Enoch walked with God, and is not, because God took him. Jaïrus, a teacher, said: And the death of holy Moses we have heard of, and have not seen it; for it is written in the law of the Lord, and Moses died from the mouth of the Lord, and no man knoweth of his sepulchre unto this day. And Rabbi Levi said: Why did Rabbi Symeon say, when he saw Jesus, "Behold, he lies for the fall and rising again of many in Israel, and for a sign spoken against"? And Rabbi Isaac said: It is written in the law, Behold, I send my messenger before thy face, who shall go before thee to keep thee in every good way, because my name has been called upon him.

Then Annas and Caiaphas said: Rightly have you said what is written in the law of Moses, that no one saw the death of Enoch, and no one has named the death of Moses; but Jesus was tried before Pilate, and we saw him receiving blows and spittings on his face, and the soldiers put about him a crown of thorns, and he was scourged and received sentence from Pilate, and was crucified upon the Cranium, and two robbers with him; and they gave him to drink vinegar with gall, and Longinus, the soldier, pierced his side with a spear; and Joseph, our honorable father, begged his body, and he says he is risen; and as the three teachers say, We saw him taken up into heaven; and Rabbi Levi has given evidence of what was said by Rabbi Symeon, and that he said, Behold, he lies for the fall and rising again of many in Israel, and for a sign spoken against. And all the teachers said to all the people of the Lord: If this was from the Lord, and is wonderful in your eyes, knowing you shall know, O house of Jacob, that it is written, Cursed is every one that hangeth upon a tree. And another scripture teaches: The gods which have not made the heaven and the earth shall be destroyed. And the priests and the Levites said to each other: If this memorial be until the year that is called Jobel, know that it shall endure forever, and he hath raised for himself a new people. Then the rulers of the synagogue, and the priests and the Levites, announced to all Israel, saying: Cursed is that man who shall worship the work of man's hand, and cursed is the man who shall worship the creatures more than the Creator. And all the people said, Amen, amen.

And all the people praised the Lord, and said: Blessed is the Lord, who hath given rest to his people Israel, according to all that he hath spoken; there hath not fallen one word of every good word of his that he spoke to Moses, his servant. May the Lord our God be with us, as he was with our fathers; let him not destroy us. And let him not destroy us, that we may incline our hearts to him, that we may walk in all his ways, that we may keep his commandments and his judgments which he commanded to our fathers. And the Lord shall be for a king over all the earth in that day; and there shall be one Lord, and his name one. The Lord is our king; he shall save us. There is none like thee, O Lord. Great art thou, O Lord, and great is thy name. By thy power heal us, O Lord, and we shall be healed; save us, O Lord, and we shall be saved, because we are thy lot and heritage. And the Lord will not leave his people, for his great name's sake; for the Lord has begun to make us into his people.

And all, having sung praises, went away each man to his own house glorifying God; for his is the glory forever and ever. Amen.

FOOTNOTES:

[1] Mommsen, "Römisches Staatsrecht," III. I. p. 748.

[2] "The Jewish People in the Time of Jesus Christ," 2d Div., I. p. 185.

[3] "The Jewish People in the Time of Jesus Christ," 2d Div., I. p. 187.

[4] Josephus, "Wars of the Jews," II. 8, 1.

[5] Josephus, "Ant.," XX. 9, 1.

[6] John xix. 10.

[7] John xviii. 31.

[8] Acts xxv., xxvi.

[9] "The Trial of Jesus," p. 77.

[10] "The Jewish People in the Time of Jesus Christ," 1st Div., II. p. 74.

[11] "The Legal Procedure of Cicero's Time," p. 118.

[12] "The Legal Procedure of Cicero's Time," p. 118.

[13] "The Trial of Jesus," p. 293.

[14] "The Legal Procedure of Cicero's Time," p. 413.

[15] "Geschichte des römischen Criminalprocesses."

[16] "The Trial of Jesus," pp. 291-93.

[17] Dionysius II. 14.

[18] Liv. II. iv. 5.

[19] Heuzey, "Miss. archeol. de Maced.," p. 38.

[20] Accusatores multos esse in civitate utile est, ut metu contineatur audacia (pro Roscio Amer. 20).

[21] Persa V. 63 *seq*.

[22] Fiske, "Manual of Classical Literature," III. Sec. 264.

[23] Gibbon, "The Decline and Fall of the Roman Empire," Chap. XLIV.

[24] Const. crim. Theres., Art. 5, par. 2.

[25] Keim, "Jesus of Nazara," vol. vi. p. 250.

[26] Keim, "Jesus of Nazara," vol. vi. p. 250.

[27] John xix. 38-41.

[28] "History of Madagascar," vol. i. p. 371, 372.

[29] "Records of Travel in Turkey and Greece," vol. i. p. 447.

[30] "The Celtic Druids," p. 126; "Anacalypsis," vol. i. p. 317.

[31] "Anacalypsis," vol. i. p. 217.

[32] Colenso's "Pentateuch Examined," vol. vi. p. 115.

[33] Baring-Gould, "Curious Myths," p. 291.

[34] "Octavius," Chap. XXIX.

[35] "Ancient Art and Mythology," p. 30.

[36] Brinton, "The Myths of the New World," p. 95.

[37] Baring-Gould, "Curious Myths," p. 299.

[38] Vol. iii. Art., "Cross."

[39] Kingsborough, "Mexican Antiquities," vol. vi. 166. p.

[40] "Curious Myths," p. 311.

[41] "Digest," XLVIII. 4.

[42] "De Inventione," II. 17.

[43] Tacitus, "Annals," p. 215.

[44] Dio, Lib. LVIII.

[45] "Annals," B. VI. Chap. II.

[46] Döllinger, "The Gentile and the Jew," vol. ii. p. 33.

[47] Döllinger, "The Gentile and the Jew," vol. ii. p. 172.

[48] "Liberty, Equality, Fraternity," pp. 89, 90.

[49] De Legibus.

[50] Correspondence between Pliny and Trajan, Letters XCVII, XCVIII.

[51] Suet., "Cæsar Augustus," Chap. LXIV.

[52] Philo, "De Legatione ad Cajum," Sec. 38, ed. Mangey, II. 589 *sq*.

[53] Josephus, "Ant.," XVIII. 3, 1.

[54] Apol. c. 21 ("jam pro sua conscientia Cristianum").

[55] "Historical Lectures," 6th ed. p. 350.

[56] Josephus, "Ant.," XVIII. 3, 2.

[57] Scott, "Anne of Geierstein," Chap. I.

[58] Gessner, "Descript. Mont. Pilat," Zürich, 1555.

[59] Golbery, "Univers Pittoresque de la Suisse," p. 327.

[60] Matt. xxvii. 1, 2.

[61] Mark xv. 1.

[62] Keim, "Jesus of Nazara," vol. vi. p. 84.

[63] Josephus, "Wars of the Jews," II. 14, 8; II. 15, 1.

[64] Keim, "Jesus of Nazara," vol. vi. p. 87.

[65] Geikie, "The Life and Words of Christ," vol. ii. p. 533.

[66] Acts xxiv. 1.

[67] Acts xxv. 16.

[68] John xviii. 30.

[69] John xviii. 31.

[70] Act IV. Scene i.

[71] Luke xxiii. 2.

[72] Acts xviii. 14, 15.

[73] Matt. xxii. 21.

[74] Matt. xvii. 24, 25.

[75] Matt. xxvi. 18, 19.

[76] Josephus, "Ant.," XVII. 10, 5.

[77] Josephus, "Ant.," XVII. 10, 6.

[78] Josephus, "Ant.," XVII. 10, 7.

[79] John xviii. 33.

[80] Matt. xx. 25.

[81] Matt. xi. 8.

[82] John xviii. 34.

[83] John xviii. 36.

[84] John xviii. 37.

[85] John xviii. 38.

[86] Luke xxiii. 5.

[87] Luke xiii. 32.

[88] Luke xxiii. 8.

[89] Josephus, "Ant.," XVIII. 7, 1, 2.

[90] Luke xxiii. 9.

[91] Luke xxxii. 10.

[92] Luke xxiii. 11.

[93] Tacitus, "Hist.," II. 89.

[94] Luke xxiii. 12.

[95] Luke xxiii. 13-16.

[96] Luke xxiii. 17.

[97] Livy v. 13: "Vinctis quoque demptu vincula."

[98] Matt. xxvii. 16-18.

[99] Matt. xxvii. 20-22.

[100] Vie, par. 131.

[101] Luke xxvii. 19.

[102] John xix. 7.

[103] John xix. 9.

[104] John xix. 15.

[105] John xix. 15.

[106] John xix. 12.

[107] Matt. xxvii. 24.

[108] Matt. xxvii. 26-31.

[109] Keim, "Jesus of Nazara," vol. vi. p. 87.

[110] Geikie, "The Life and Words of Christ," vol. ii. p. 533.

[111] Geikie, "The Life and Words of Christ," vol. ii. p. 532.

[112] Acts xxiv.; xxv. II; xxvi. 32.

[113] Matt. xxvii. 11.

[114] Mark xv. 2.

[115] Luke xxiii. 3.

[116] John xviii. 37.

[117] Luke xxiii. 4-16.

[118] Luke xxiii. 23, 24.

[119] "Liberty, Equality, Fraternity," p. 87.

[120] "Liberty, Equality, Fraternity," pp. 93-95.

[121] L. 12, Cod. De pœnis, ix. 47: "Vanæ voces populi non sunt audiendæ, nec enim vocibus eorum credi oportet quando aut noxium crimine absolvi aut innocentem condemnari desiderant."

[122] John xix. 10.

[123] Dr. Smith's "History of Greece," Chap. XXXV. p. 418.

[124] 1 Tim. iii. 16.

[125] See Dict. Philos. Art. "Religion."

[126] "Emile."

[127] "Sartor Resartus," 137, 140.

[128] "Herzog's Encyc." vol. v. 751. Art. "Herder."

[129] "Vergängl. u. Bleibendes im Christenthum," 132.

[130] "Études d'Hist. Rel.," pp. 213, 214.

[131] "Jesus of Nazara," vol. vi. pp. 430, 431.

[132] Montholon, "Récit de la Captivité de l'Emp. Napoleon."

[133] Bertrand's "Memoirs," Paris, 1844.

[134] "Je meurs dans la religion catholique, apostolique et romaine, dans le sein de laquelle je suis né, il y a plus de cinquante ans."

[135] Döllinger, "The Gentile and the Jew," vol ii. p. 29.

[136] "Preparation of the World for Christ," pp. 380, 381.

[137] Suetonius, "Cæsar Augustus," Chap. XCV.

[138] Matt. i. 20.

[139] Matt. ii. 13.

[140] Suetonius, "Cæsar Augustus," Chap. XCIV.

[141] Suetonius, "Cæsar Augustus," Chap. XCII.

[142] Döllinger, "The Gentile and the Jew," vol. ii. p. 185.

[143] Liv. xl. 59.

[144] Ap. Aug. C.D. VI. 2.

[145] Döllinger, vol. ii. p. 183.

[146] Suetonius, "Caligula," Chap. V.

[147] Mabillon, "Iter. Ital." p. 77.

[148] Pausanias, ix. 17. 1.

[149] De Superst. 6.

[150] M. Dic, quæso, num te illa terrent? Triceps apud inferos Cerberus? Cocyti fremitus? travectio Acherontis?

"Mento summam aquam attingens enectus siti,Tantalus, tum illud quod,Sisiphus versatSaxum sudans nitendo neque proficit hilum,"

fortasse etiam inexorabiles judices Minor et Rhadamanthus? apud quos nec te L. Crassus defendet, nec M. Antonius; nec, quoniam apud Græcos judices res agetur, poteris adhibere Demosthenen; tibi ipsi pro te erit maxima corona causa dicenda. Hæc fortasse metuis, et idcirco mortem censes esse sempiternum malum. A. Adeone me delirare censes, ut ista esse credam? M. An tu hæc non credis? A. Minime vero. M. Male hercule narras. A. Cur, quæso. M. Quia disertus esse possem, si contra ista dicerem.

[151] Sallust, "Bellum Catilinarium, 50."

[152] Renan, "Les Apôtres."

[153] "Hamlet," Act III, Scene i.

[154] Döllinger, vol. ii. pp. 175-79.

[155] Dion. ii. 25.

[156] Döllinger, vol. ii. pp. 267-69.

[157] Suetonius, "Julius Cæsar," l-li.

[158] Xen. de Rep. Lac. i. 8.

[159] "Polyb. Fragm." in Scr. Vet. Nov. Coll. ed. Mav. ii. 384.

[160] Döllinger, vol. ii. p. 249.

[161] "Xen. Mem. Socr." iii. 13.

[162] Plutarch, "Life of Lucullus."

[163] Fisher, "The Beginnings of Christianity," p. 205.

[164] "Encyc. Brit." vol. iii. p. 436.

[165] Plutarch, "Life of Cato."

[166] Cicero, "Pro Cluent." 66.

[167] Tacitus, "Annals," 42-44.

[168] De Pressensé, "The Religions Before Christ," p. 158.

[169] Milman's "Gibbon's Rome," vol. i. p. 51.

[170] Suetonius, "Caligula," Chap. V.

[171] Fisher, "The Beginnings of Christianity," p. 213.

[172] Pliny, Ep. X. 38.

[173] Suetonius, "Julius Cæsar," Chap. XLIX.

[174] Döllinger, vol. ii. pp. 253, 254.

[175] Döllinger, vol. ii. pp. 205, 206.

[176] Döllinger, vol. ii. p. 207.

[177] Döllinger, vol. ii. p. 208.

[178] Livy, b. xxxix. Chaps. VII.-XX.

[179] "——non possum ferre, Quirites, Græcam urbem." (Sat. III.)

[180] Romans i. 29-31.

[181] Döllinger, vol ii. pp. 155, 156.

[182] Matthew Arnold's Poems—"Obermann Once More."

[183] Cicero, "De Fin." v. pp. 24, 69.

[184] Eclogue IV.

[185] Matt. ii. 4; xxi. 15; xxvi. 3, 47, 59; Mark xi. 18; xv. 11; Luke xix. 47; xx. 1; John xi. 47; xii. 20.

[186] Dérembourg, "Essai sur l'histoire et la géographie de la Palestine," p. 231, note 1.

[187] Josephus, "Ant.," Book XX. Chap. X. 1; XV. III. 1.

[188] Josephus, "Ant." Book XV. Chap. III. 1.

[189] Josephus, "Ant.," Book XVIII. Chap. II. 3; Book XX. Chap. IX, 1, 4.

[190] See "Talmud," "Yoma," or "the Day of Atonement," fol. 35, recto; also Dérembourg, work above quoted, p. 230, note 2.

[191] "Essai sur l'histoire et la géographie de la Palestine," p. 232.

[192] Jos., "Ant.," XX. VIII. 8.

[193] "Talmud," "Pesachim," or "of the Passover," fol. 57, verso.

[194] The high priests designated under the name of the descendants of Eli are those who, as sons of the high priest Eli, polluted the Temple by their immorality. (See 1 Kings iii. 22-25.)

[195] This Issachar was a priest of such a dainty nature that in order to touch the sacrifices he covered his hands with silk. ("Talmud," "Pesachim," or "of the Passover," fol. 57, verso.)

[196] Rabbi Nathan, son of Rabbi Yechiel, was the disciple of the celebrated Moses, the preacher and first rabbi of the synagogue at Rome in the ninth century. His work forms a large folio volume, and contains some minute explanations of the most difficult passages in the "Talmud."

[197] I. e., lord.

[198] "Talmud," Jerus., "Horayoth," or "Regulations of Justice," fol. 84. recto.

[199] "Talmud," Jerus., "Shevuoth," or "of Oaths," fol. 19, verso.

[200] "Tanchumah," or "Book of Consolation," fol. 68, recto.

[201] "Tanchumah," or "Book of Consolation," fol. 68, recto.

[202] "Tanchumah," or "Book of Consolation," fol. 68, recto, and "Sanhedrin," fol. 110, verso.

[203] "Talmud," "Shabbath," or "of the Sabbath," fol. 119, recto.

[204] Luke xx. 46; Matt. xxiii. 5-7; Mark xii. 38, 39.

[205] Some remarkable pages respecting the pride of the Jewish scribes and doctors may be found in Bossuet's "Meditations on the Gospel."

[206] Jos., "Ant.," XVIII. I. 4.

[207] Jos., "Ant.," XVIII. I. 4.

[208] Munk, "Palestine," p. 515.

[209] Psalms.

[210] Acts xxiii. 6.

[211] Matt. vi. 2, 5, 16; ix. 11, 14; xii. 2; xxiii. 5, 15, 23; Luke v. 30; vi. 2, 7; xi. 39, etc.; xviii. 12; John ix. 16; "Perkeh Avoth," or "Sentences of the Fathers," I. 16; Jos., "Ant.," XVII. II. 4; XVIII. I. 3; "Vita," 38; "Talmud," Bab., "Sotah," fol. 22, recto.

[212] "From that time forth began Jesus to show unto his disciples, how that he must go unto Jerusalem, and suffer many things of the elders and chief priests and scribes." (Matt. xvi. 21.)

[213] "The Credibility of the Gospel History," in the chapter on "Testimonies of Ancient Heathens," vol. vi. p. 605 *et seq*.

[214] "Origin of the Four Gospels," pp. 141-50.

BIBLIOGRAPHY

MAIN AUTHORITIES

THE BIBLE.	English Authorized Version of 1611.
THE TALMUD.	Babylonian Recension, translated into English by Michael L. Rodkinson. New Talmud Publishing Company, New York, 1896.
THE MISHNA.	Edition of Surenhusius. Amsterdam, 1698-1703. Consulted by the author in the Astor Library, New York City.

MINOR AUTHORITIES

ABBOTT.	Jesus of Nazareth, by Lyman Abbott. Harper Brothers, New York, 1882.
ANDREWS.	The Life of Our Lord, by Samuel J. Andrews. Charles Scribner's Sons, New York, 1906.
BARING-GOULD.	Curious Myths of the Middle Ages, by S. Baring-Gould. Roberts Brothers, Boston, 1880.
BAUR.	The Church History of the First Three Centuries, by F. C. Baur. Translated from German by A. Mendies. London, 1878.
BENNY.	The Criminal Code of the Jews, by Philip Berger Benny. Smith, Elder & Company, London, 1880.
BLACKSTONE.	Commentaries on the Laws of England, by Sir William Blackstone. Edited and annotated by Thomas M. Cooley. Callaghan & Company, Chicago, 1884.
CICERO.	M. Tullii Ciceronis orationes. Whittaker & Company, London, 1855.
DEUTSCH.	The Talmud, by Emanuel Deutsch. The Jewish Publication Society of America, Philadelphia, 1896.
DÖLLINGER.	The Gentile and the Jew, by John J. I. Döllinger. Two volumes. Gibbings & Company, London, 1906.

EDERSHEIM.	The Life and Times of Jesus the Messiah, by Alfred Edersheim. Two volumes. Longmans, Green & Company, New York, 1905.
FARRAR.	The Life of Christ, by Frederic W. Farrar. E. P. Dutton & Company, New York, 1883.
FISHER.	The Beginnings of Christianity, by George P. Fisher. Charles Scribner's Sons, New York, 1906.
GEIB.	Geschichte des römischen Criminalprocesses, von Dr. Gustav Geib. Weidmann'sche Buchhandlung. Leipzig, 1842.
GEIKIE.	The Life and Words of Christ, by Cunningham Geikie. Two volumes. Henry S. King & Company. London, 1877.
GIBBON.	The History of the Decline and Fall of the Roman Empire, by Edward Gibbon. With notes by Rev. H. H. Milman. Phillips, Sampson & Company, Boston, 1853.
GRAETZ.	History of the Jews, by Heinrich Graetz. Six volumes. The Jewish Publication Society of America, Philadelphia, 1891.
GREENLEAF.	The Testimony of the Evangelists, by Simon Greenleaf. Soney & Sage, Newark, N. J., 1903.
GREENIDGE.	The Legal Procedure of Cicero's Time, by A. H. J. Greenidge. Stevens & Sons, London, 1901.
HARNACK.	Reden und Aufsätze, von Adolf Harnack. J. Ricker'sche Verlagsbuchhandlung, Giessen, 1904.
HIGGINS.	Anacalypsis: An Enquiry into the Origin of Languages, Nations and Religions, by Godfrey Higgins. Longman, Brown & Longman, London, 1827.
HODGE.	Systematic Theology, by Charles Hodge. Charles Scribner's Sons, New York, 1892.
INNES.	The Trial of Jesus Christ, by A. Taylor Innes. T. & T. Clark, Edinburgh, 1905.

JOSEPHUS.	The Works of Flavius Josephus, Whiston's Translation.
JOST.	Geschichte des Judenthums, von I. M. Jost. Dörffling und Francke, Leipzig, 1857.
JUVENAL.	The Satires of Juvenal. George Bell & Sons, London, 1904.
KEIM.	Jesus of Nazara, by Theodor Keim. Six volumes. Williams & Norgate, London, 1883.
LARDNER.	Works of Nathaniel Lardner. Ten volumes. William Ball, London, 1838.
LÉMANN.	Valeur de l'assemblée qui prononça la peine de mort contre Jésus-Christ, par MM. Lémann. Translated from the French into English under the title "Jesus Before the Sanhedrin," by Prof. Julius Magath, of Oxford, Ga., in 1899.
LIVY.	The History of Rome, by Titus Livius. George Bell & Sons, London, 1906.
LOISY.	Les Évangiles Synoptiques, par Alfred Loisy. Librairie Fishbacher, Paris, 1907.
MENDELSOHN.	The Criminal Jurisprudence of the Ancient Hebrews, by S. Mendelsohn. M. Curlander, Baltimore, 1891.
MOMMSEN.	The Provinces of the Roman Empire, by Theodor Mommsen. Two volumes. Charles Scribner's Sons, New York, 1899.
MONTESQUIEU.	De l'Esprit Des Lois, par Montesquieu. Garnier Frères, Paris, 1905.
PALEY.	Evidences of Christianity, by William Paley. The Religious Tract Society, London, 1794.
RABBINOWICZ.	Législation Criminelle du Talmud, par I. J. M. Rabbinowicz. Chez l'auteur, Paris, 1876.
RENAN.	Histoire des origines du christianisme, par Joseph Ernest Renan. Paris, 1863. Livres 1-6: 1. Vie de Jésus. 2. Les apôtres. 3. Saint Paul. 4. L'Antichrist. 5. Les

	évangiles et la seconde génération chrétienne. 6. L'église chrétienne.
ROSADI.	The Trial of Jesus by Giovanni Rosadi. Dodd, Mead & Company, New York, 1905.
SALVADOR.	Histoire des Institutions de Moïse, par J. Salvador. Michel Lévy-Frères, Paris, 1862.
SCHÜRER.	The Jewish People in the Time of Jesus Christ, by Emil Schürer. Charles Scribner's Sons, New York, 1906.
STEPHEN.	Liberty, Equality, Fraternity, by James Fitzjames Stephen. Henry Holt & Company, New York, 1873.
SUETONIUS.	The Lives of the Twelve Cæsars, by C. Suetonius Tranquillus. George Bell & Sons, London, 1906.
TACITUS.	The Works of Tacitus. American Book Company, New York, 1904.
WISE.	The Martyrdom of Jesus, by Isaac M. Wise. The Bloch Publishing and Printing Company, Cincinnati & Chicago, 1888.

In addition to the above, many other authorities have been consulted in the preparation of the two volumes of this work. Quotations from them are frequently found in the text, and citations are given in the notes. The author, in closing the article, entitled "Bibliography," wishes to express his sense of great indebtedness and appreciation to the numerous very valuable encyclopedias that adorn the shelves of the various libraries of New York City; and especially to The Jewish Encyclopedia, published by Funk & Wagnalls, New York and London, 1901.

Milton Keynes UK
Ingram Content Group UK Ltd.
UKHW030740071024
449371UK00006B/707